PHL

D1388064

THE
PAUL HAMLYN
LIBRARY

DONATED BY
THE PAUL HAMLYN
FOUNDATION
TO THE
BRITISH MUSEUM

opened December 2000

WITHDRAWN

271.10457194 HOD

Light in the Dark Ages

Light in the Dark Ages

THE RISE AND FALL OF
SAN VINCENZO
AL VOLTURNO

Richard Hodges

Duckworth

First published in 1997 by
Gerald Duckworth & Co. Ltd.
The Old Piano Factory
48 Hoxton Square, London N1 6PB
Tel: 0171 729 5986
Fax: 0171 729 0015

© 1997 by Richard Hodges

All rights reserved. No part of this publication
may be reproduced, stored in a retrieval system, or
transmitted, in any form or by any means, electronic,
mechanical, photocopying, recording or otherwise,
without the prior permission of the publisher.

A catalogue record for this book is available
from the British Library.

ISBN 0 7156 2370 2

Typeset by Ray Davies
Printed in Great Britain by
Redwood Books Ltd, Trowbridge

THE BRITISH MUSEUM WITHDRAWN
THE PAUL HAMLYN LIBRARY

Contents

To Riccardo

Archaeology is a kind of surgery, a selective operation into the extensive humus of ancient life. But its best reward is not its scientific result or a single object in a museum or any fulfilment of ambition. It is the sense of place, I think. It is the rhythm and form of villages that have survived, imposed on the unexhausted soil. It is the olive trees and the mountain-sides and the traces of the dead.

Peter Levi, *The Hill of Kronos*, 1980, 125.

By examining the abundant objects dug up by archaeologists, which for the first time reveal the atmosphere of the interior of a peasant's hut, the plan of a village, the organisation of an estate, or the tools to be found in a craftsman's workshop, it is possible to uncover economic reality and to lay bare, with the help of some quantitative data, the mechanics of growth and decline.

Georges Duby, *The Chivalrous Society*, 1977, 11.

Preface

To bless this region, its vendanges, and those
    Who call it home: though one cannot always
Remember exactly why one has been happy,
    There is no forgetting that one was.
            W.H. Auden, 'Good-bye to the Mezzogiorno'.

1 July 1994. Franco, in appearance a pirate worthy of the Mezzogiorno, looked hard at me: 'You're certain that there is a crypt under here?', he asked shyly. He had never doubted my interpretation of San Vincenzo before, but a great deal was now at stake. The ploughed field had been turned into an excavation area measuring 50 by 20 metres after a month of heroic effort, but as yet there was no trace of the crypt that I believed to be here. The future of San Vincenzo rested on its discovery. Franco Valente had persuaded the Abbot of Monte Cassino and San Vincenzo al Volturno that these excavations provided the key to creating an archaeological park. But if there was no crypt, even Franco's legendary ability to sell dreams might falter. Six weeks later, on 10 August, with an army of sixty archaeologists we removed the last earth in the relic chamber of the crypt. I shall never forget Bill walloping his way through the demolition layers, egged on by Sally, half his height, with Lucy beside her, both intoxicated by the discovery of the succession of brightly painted panels coming to light as they dug onwards. And then there was Chris Marshall's shriek of ecstasy as she exposed one of the niches in the relic chamber. Franco was present, of course; so was the Abbot, the President of the *regione*, the Prefect, countless officials and two television crews. In the twilight of that ferociously hot day, as if by magic, Chris exposed the portrait of a bearded ninth-century abbot – a painting as rich as any great renaissance work. In those extraordinary moments San Vincenzo's future was guaranteed.

It had all started so differently. In 1979 the Soprintendente of Antiquities at Campobasso had commended me to visit 'the' crypt at San Vincenzo. I found a toothless old man who gave me a huge bunch of keys but failed to tell me where the crypt was. We entered the present abbey church. Sparrows were flying around the nave; it was a sad place. After lunch my companions and I visited the nearest village, Castel San Vincenzo, to see if the crypt was there. The village was deserted. With a great

ix

key we managed to enter the main church, a monument to the Neapolitan baroque, but it was completely ruined. Outside I was surrounded by children and then, quite suddenly, a *carabiniero* arrived in a jeep. He commanded me to get in with him, and whisked me off to the *caserma*. The *maresciallo* interrogated me fiercely in German, believing, because I had fair hair and drove a Volkswagen, that I was a German terrorist. I replied patiently that I was there to visit the crypt. He laughed; no one visited Molise! Eventually I compelled him to read my permit, and crestfallen he gave me directions to the crypt. Like the abbey church and the village church, the crypt was suffering. Mountainous brambles covered the path to the door. Inside, the flickering light induced a small army of jumping spiders to pounce, quitting their perches on the faintly green mould covering the great cycle of ninth-century paintings.

At that time I was searching Europe for a Dark Age monastery to excavate. I pondered whether this could be the place. Various walls protruded from the brambles on the south side of the crypt. It had promise, just as it had a great history, the *Chronicon Vulturnense*. Above all, on that September day, despite the encounter with the irascible *maresciallo*, it seemed an idyllic part of Italy. It puzzled me that this oasis in the foothills of the Mainarde was not better known. So began our project, which is still far from finished.

This book is about the project. Its first aim is to summarize the large scientific reports on the excavations and survey carried out at San Vincenzo al Volturno by the Universities of East Anglia and Sheffield together with the British School at Rome over the past fifteen years. The second aim is to illustrate how modern archaeology can help to rewrite the history of western Europe, shedding light on undocumented episodes and compelling us to reconsider long-held interpretations of the past.

Acknowledgments

Archaeology today is a team enterprise. The story told here is the sum of the labours of hundreds of people and the financial support of many research bodies. They are too many to list, so necessarily I must select a few who have made a special contribution to the success of the project. First, I am indebted to Dott.ssa Gabriella D'Henry, Soprintendente for Beni Culturali for Molise between 1981 and 1993 and Arch. Constantino Centroni, her successor, for their vital collaboration over many seasons. Secondly, I owe a great debt to his eminence Don Bernardo d'Onorio, Abbot of Monte Cassino and San Vincenzo al Volturno, who has been instrumental in the purchase of the site of the monastery, its large-scale exploration and its conservation. Thirdly, I am indebted to the following for material and financial support: the British School at Rome (my particular thanks to Maria-Pia Malvezzi and Tommaso Astolfi), the British Academy, the Craven Fund, the Istituto Regionale Storico di Molise, the Getty Grant

Program, the Leverhulme Trust, the Provincia di Isernia (my special thanks to its President, Dott. Domenico Pellegrino), the region of Molise, the Society of Antiquaries, the Economic and Social Science Research Council, the University of East Anglia, and especially the University of Sheffield.

In the field and subsequently while compiling the detailed reports describing the results my debts are legion. I cannot quantify my enormous debt to Federico Marazzi, the energetic assistant director of the San Vincenzo Project between 1989 and 1995. His humour and wisdom have proved a priceless asset for the project, but I should also like to record my esteem for his friendship and spirited academic curiousity. My warm thanks too to Cathy Coutts, my research assistant in 1983-84, and archaeological field officer at the British School at Rome from 1990-95, who has played a key part in more than a dozen seasons of excavations.

Picking out a few names from the hundreds who have dug at San Vincenzo I think of Nigel Baker, Will Bowden, Jane Bromley, Adam Brossler, Antonia Castellani, John Clipson, Stefano Coccia, Francesca del Acqua, Linden Elmhirst, Patrick Foster, Karen Francis, Oliver Gilkes, Andrew Hanasz, Inge Hansen, Tom Loader, Seema Mann, Chris Marshall, Sally Martin, Steven Mithen, Cameron Moffett, Matthew Moran, John Moreland, James Murdoch, Bill Murphy, Andrew Nelson, Jacqueline Nowakowski, Pippa Pearce, Barbara Polci, Simon Probert, Ian Riddler, Alessia Rovelli, Richard Sabin, Antonio Sennis, Corrado Sigismondo, Ken Smith, Judy Stevenson, Jim Symonds, Keith Wade, Lucy Watson, and David Wilkinson. I am especially indebted to Amanda Claridge, Ian Freestone, Sheila Gibson, Peter Hayes, Helen Patterson, John Patterson and Chris Wickham who have patiently made a story from the bits and pieces we found, and above all have educated me. I could not have completed this work without their support. I should also like to thank the people to whom I have turned for advice: Beat Brenk, Gian-Pietro Brogiolo, Andrea Carandini, Paolo Delogu, Karin Einaudi, Richard Gem, Pier-Luigi Guzzo, the late Richard Krautheimer, Klavs Randsborg, Colin Renfrew and Ian Wood.

All archaeologists remember the circumstances of their investigations with great feeling. I am no exception. I recall several different images of San Vincenzo. First, there was the pleasure and privilege of knowing and working with the late Don Angelo Pantoni, the historian of Monte Cassino and San Vincenzo (see p. 5). He was an inspiration. His torch is carried onwards by Don Faustino Avagliano, the archivist of Monte Cassino, and the remarkable Benedictine nuns of San Vincenzo (especially Mothers Agnes, Benedict, Miriam and Philip Kline). Secondly, I think of the people of the villages of the upper Volturno valley, and in particular of the people of Castel San Vincenzo: summer after summer they have accommodated us, helped us and encouraged us. Franco Colantonio and Lucio Carracillo, to name our two greatest counsellors, have shown us boundless generosity.

Thirdly, I should also like to convey my heartfelt thanks to Architect Franco Valente, a brilliant and tireless crusader on our behalf. Single-handedly, he has transformed our opportunity at San Vincenzo, making it a project consonant with its great historical promise. To these people we entrust the future of San Vincenzo.

Finally, I should like to thank three people who have made it possible for me to undertake and conclude this research in the happiest circumstances. My wife Debbie persuaded me to excavate at San Vincenzo, and thereafter worked with equal conviction on the excavations and on this manuscript. Along with our children, William and Charlotte, we have spent great tracts of our lives in Molise. Secondly, on 1 September 1981 John Mitchell joined us at San Vincenzo al Volturno. Within days the scope of our investigations had been enlarged exponentially. John brought great intellectual vitality to the project as well as priceless humour. I should add that I have benefited enormously from his invaluable knowledge of early medieval cultural history. His friendship has made San Vincenzo special for me, and in many respects I regard him as a co-author of this book, because much of it is distilled from our shared experiences. Thirdly, by a stroke of great fortune I met Riccardo Francovich a matter of days after the conclusion of the first campaign of excavations in 1980. Instantly, we formed a collaboration that has persisted ever since. His friendship, generosity and wise counsel have proved of inestimable value as I embarked upon and developed the San Vincenzo Project. I recall with particular affection my three years as visiting professor at Siena University where, thanks to Riccardo, I studied Italian medieval archaeology. As a small token of my regard, I dedicate this book to him.

Illustrations

Illustrations

Chronology

The Abbots of San Vincenzo al Volturno, 703-1154
(from the *Chronicon Vulturnense*)

703?-720	Paldo
720-721?	Taso
721?-729	Tato
729-739	Taso (again)
739-760	Ato
760-763	Hermepertus
763-777	John I
777-778	Autpert
778-780	Hayrirad
780-783	Poto
783-792	Paul I
792-817	Joshua
817-823	Talaricus
	vacancy 4 October 823 – 5 October 824
824-842	Epyphanius
842-844	Toto
844-853	Jacob
853-856	Teuto
856-863	John II
863-872	Artefusus
872-901	Maio
901-920	Godelpertus
920-944	Rambald
944-957	Leo
957-981	Paul II
981-984	John III
984-998	Roffrid
998-1007	John IV
1007-1011	Marald
1011-1045	Ilarius
1045-1053	Liutfrid
1053-1076	John V
1076-1109	Gerard
1109-1117	Benedict
1117-1139	Amicus
1139-1144	John VI (author of the *Chronicon Vulturnense*)
1153-1154	Elia

1

Rewriting History

San Vincenzo al Volturno is located on the Rocchetta plain, a small plateau perched like a hanging garden on the sides of the Abruzzo mountains at the head of valleys descending to Italy's Tyrrhenian coast (Fig. 1.1). The river Volturno rises on the plateau, 2 km from San Vincenzo. The present abbey overlooks the Volturno's deep gorge as it flows down to the sea at Naples via the ancient town of Venafro. The administrative status of the abbey is anomalous as its grounds straddle three communes in the far north-west of the little-known region of Molise. Except in the month of August, when numerous Molisani emigrés return to their family homes from Chicago, Glasgow, Toronto and the metropolitan cities of Italy, this is a picturesque but forgotten corner of the Mezzogiorno.

Fig. 1.1. View of Colle della Torre, site of early medieval San Vincenzo al Volturno, and the Mainarde mountains beyond. Bottom left: the late medieval portico in front of the present monastery; far right: the village of Castel San Vincenzo on an exposed hilltop. (Photo: Ray Manley)

In the early Middle Ages, however, San Vincenzo was one of the great monasteries of western Europe. Its story, told in the *Chronicon Vulturnense* compiled by a twelfth-century monk called John, shows that it was at the forefront of European affairs as the Middle Ages took shape between *c.* 700 and 1100. Its history, like that of numerous abbeys, has many landmarks. Its founders, three Lombard monks called Paldo, Tato and Taso, were charged with the task of creating a new monastery in the land of their birth. They chose an old Roman site associated with the fourth-century Christian Emperor, Constantine, in a wild, sylvan place. Seventy years later, its monks became embroiled in a controversy about the monastery's relations with Charlemagne, the Carolingian king. According to the chronicler, it was Frankish patronage that enabled Abbot Joshua (792-817) in the early ninth century to expand the monastery and construct a great abbey church. San Vincenzo's fame and wealth, in common with so many monasteries, attracted Saracen raiders who sacked it on 10 October 881. During the tenth century San Vincenzo experienced a phase of abject poverty before its monks set about developing its property after the 960s. Not until the eleventh century did the monastic community amass the means to restore the abbey church and other buildings destroyed in 881. This epic story is not exceptional. In many ways, the *Chronicon Vulturnense* could be the history of any major abbey in north Italy, southern France or Germany.

But San Vincenzo failed to sustain its wealth and standing. Its star began to wane in the twelfth century. By the fifteenth century it was a forgotten abbey belonging to another age. On 5 January 1699 the abbey and its remaining lands were acquired by Monte Cassino – its powerful neighbour and sometime rival. (Monte Cassino, it should be noted, had been refounded with the assistance of monks from San Vincenzo in the early eighth century.) The last monk to reside here permanently departed in 1821. With the suppression of the monasteries, San Vincenzo's lands and buildings were acquired in 1865 by Duke Catemario di Quadri. In 1942 the ducal family returned the property to Monte Cassino, but the abbey was damaged the following year during the bitter conflict here as the Allies attempted to break through the German Gustav Line which stretched from Cassino past San Vincenzo and down the Sangro valley. Since the war much has altered.

The abbey church was rebuilt in the 1960s, and today elegantly dominates the landscape as it did in the early twelfth century when John was writing his chronicle. Since 1990 a community of Benedictine nuns has given it renewed purpose and spirit. Of course, as it is only 200 km from Rome and little over 100 km from Naples, the abbey and its mountain territory are no longer remote. A major road, constructed at great cost across the deep gorges and mountains of the Abruzzo, passes through the upper Volturno valley carrying winter ski traffic and summer walkers to the mountains.

The geographical position of San Vincenzo (Fig. 1.2) explains a good deal, as we shall see. This point was lucidly made by the Hon. Keppel Craven, a Victorian traveller, whose wanderings through the kingdom of Naples led him from the high Abruzzo to Campobasso by way of San Vincenzo. As he descended from the Abruzzo, he tells us, his attention 'was suddenly arrested by the sight of the Volturno some way below ... whose winding course nearly described a circle in a small plain surrounded by a belt of high mountains'. Of San Vincenzo's location Craven writes: 'It is difficult to combine in one landscape features more favourable to its general impact than those exhibited by the various objects with which it is surrounded.'

But Keppel Craven was not visiting San Vincenzo to see its historic abbey. He had come to visit the sheep-fair held in the meadows beside the river Volturno and to see the inscriptions associated, he was told, with the lost city of Samnium. Craven paid scant attention to the abbey church and was unaware that a painted crypt depicting one of San Vincenzo's great

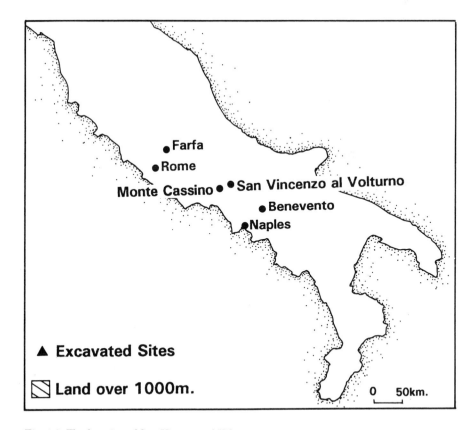

Fig. 1.2. The location of San Vincenzo al Volturno.

Fig. 1.3. The barn above the crypt discovered in 1832. The farm and accompanying barn were destroyed in the 1960s. (Photo: courtesy of ICCD (Rome), negative N9671)

early medieval abbots, Epyphanius (824-42), had been discovered here only five years before in 1832.

Don Ottavio Fraia-Frangipane, archivist at Monte Cassino from about 1780 until 1843, was the first to mention this crypt. Fraia-Frangipane lived through the end of the *ancien régime*, the Napoleonic suppression of the monastery, and the subsequent restoration of Monte Cassino and renewed interest in its history. In an entry in his journal kept in the archive of Monte Cassino, Fraia-Frangipane records how Nicola Padula, the parish priest of Castel San Vincenzo, had discovered a crypt at San Vincenzo. (In fact, the crypt was discovered on 10 March 1832 by a certain Domenico Notardonato, who immediately informed his local priest. Padula then wrote a lengthy letter to the Abbot of Monte Cassino.) The priest described to Fraia-Frangipane a room with inscriptions on its walls which he believed to have formed part of the celebrated monastery of San Vincenzo. After consulting the Chronicle of San Vincenzo, Fraia-Frangi-pane identified the structure as the chapel of St Laurence, built by Abbot Epyphanius in the ninth century. At that time the original entrance to the crypt was blocked and the only access was through the rectangular north window. The interior may have been partially filled with earth, to judge from the early graffiti scratched high on the vaulted ceiling (Fig. 1.3).

Sixty years later, the prior of Monte Cassino, Don Oderisio Piscicelli Taeggi, describes how he ventured into the crypt and recorded its cycle of paintings. Piscicelli Taeggi was the first to identify the picture of Abbot Epyphanius, and his late nineteenth-century publication attracted great

4

interest. Since then the cycle of frescoes has been studied by scholars from many different countries. The fact that Abbot Epyphanius was almost certainly alive when his portrait was painted – as is indicated by the square nimbus above his head – makes it possible to date the cycle accurately, using the *Chronicon Vulturnense*, to between 824 and 842.

Despite these discoveries, before 1980 it was always believed that the present abbey occupied the same site as its early medieval predecessor. This is true for most European abbeys, monasteries and cathedrals. Monte Cassino, for example, occupies more or less the same position today as St Benedict's fifth-century oratory. The same is true for the great abbeys of Farfa, Lorsch and St Denys. In each case the present church was built upon the demolished remains of its predecessor. Up until 1980, when the excavations began at San Vincenzo, there was every reason to believe that the present abbey church concealed the remains of earlier ages beneath its floors. As for the crypt by the Ponte della Zingara, this was assumed to be part of another church some distance from the precinct of the great ninth-century monastery. Only the local farmers contested this informed opinion. The church with the crypt, according to local oral tradition, belonged to a city sacked by the Saracens.

The first, rather haphazard excavations at San Vincenzo were directed by Don Angelo Pantoni. His investigations were made when the old, bombed abbey was entirely rebuilt during the 1960s (Fig. 1.4). (The

Fig. 1.4. The present abbey before renovation. This photograph, taken in the late nineteenth century, shows the baroque abbey church and the remains of a fourteenth-century portico in front of the perimeter gate. (Photo: courtesy of ICCD (Rome), negative E34952)

Fig. 1.5. Don Angelo Pantoni on a visit to the excavations in 1983. (Photo: author)

present abbey was completed and consecrated in 1965.) Pantoni is a special figure in the study of San Vincenzo. His book on the excavations (*Le Chiese e gli Edifici del Monastero di San Vincenzo al Volturno*, 1980) and his many essays have earned him a distinguished place in its history. Born in Florence in 1905, Pantoni studied engineering at the University of Padova before taking holy orders in 1929. In 1935 he became assistant to Monte Cassino's eminent archivist, Don Tommaso Leccisotti. For almost half a century they worked together on aspects of Cassino's history. During the infamous bombardment of Monte Cassino in February 1944 Pantoni was in Rome and Perugia, continuing to write for the journal *Benedictina*. After the war he returned to Monte Cassino where he conducted excavations in the shelled ruins before the reconstruction of the monastery got underway. These excavations have been the subject of numerous essays and books. It was with this experience behind him that Pantoni became involved in the rebuilding of San Vincenzo (Fig. 1.5).

Unlike Monte Cassino, San Vincenzo's abbey church was an unprepossessing building with a plain baroque façade before the Second World War. Late nineteenth-century photographs show that it was a typical eighteenth-century church of modest proportions. Pantoni conceived of his new church on altogether different lines, harking back to San Vincenzo's epic past. His intention was to emulate the Romanesque abbey of the age of the chronicler.

Pantoni's excavations showed that the previous baroque church had occupied only a small part of the ground covered by the twelfth-century abbey. The earlier church had had a spacious nave flanked by side aisles with associated rooms. The church was floored with cosmatesque pavements typical of the Norman age. The pavements, however, conjured up San Vincenzo's rich history. Several fragments of ninth-century inscriptions were set into the floor; some of these captured Pantoni's imagination. Some of the fragments had formed part of a monumental marble inscription which, according to the *Chronicon*, had featured prominently on the façade of the ninth-century abbey church, San Vincenzo Maggiore, which had been consecrated in 808. It was sufficient to affirm Pantoni's belief that the abbey church had always stood on the same site.

Outside the ensemble of monastic buildings Pantoni drew attention to the existence of inscriptions and pottery dating back to the Roman Republic. The painted crypt in which Abbot Epyphanius is depicted is also featured in Pantoni's book. The crypt and the associated ruins are described without any attempt to explain why they were situated at some distance from the monastery. As in his books about Monte Cassino, Pantoni, the consummate antiquarian, posed as many questions about San Vincenzo as he gave answers.

The San Vincenzo Project

By pure coincidence, within months of the publication of Pantoni's book in 1980 the San Vincenzo Project was launched. From the beginning our work had two important aims. The first was to identify and investigate the early medieval monastery and some of its lost villages, described in the *Chronicon*. The other was to develop this splendidly situated site for sustainable tourism – to use it as a resource that might bring extra income to this long neglected area. In formulating these aims at the outset, we accepted Pantoni's interpretation of his findings (Fig. 1.6).

Our first aim was to contribute to a long-running debate about the European Dark Ages. This debate concerns the character and economy of European society between the seventh and eleventh centuries. Some historians believe the Roman Empire survived the problems of the fifth and sixth centuries, maintaining many classical institutions and traditions intact. Other scholars argue that the classical world and its institutions and traditions were catastrophically overwhelmed and virtu-

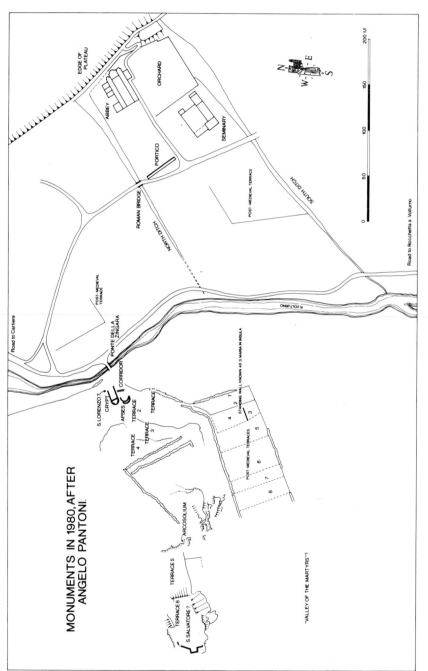

MONUMENTS IN 1980, AFTER ANGELO PANTONI.

Fig. 1.6. San Vincenzo al Volturno showing the monuments known in 1980, based upon research by Don Angelo Pantoni.

ally perished. The latter contend that great depopulation accompanied the decline of the ancient world, that the apparatus of the state disappeared to be replaced by largely kin-based (family) political arrangements reminiscent of later prehistory, and that commerce was no longer transacted in market places, but by personal mechanisms such as gift exchange and simple barter.

This polarisation of the arguments for and against continuity of Roman institutions depends on the interpretation of the historical sources. Few written records have survived. Most of those that have were written by monks, who formed a small literate minority. These authors carried the torch of classical knowledge after the eclipse of the Roman Empire, and their terminology was largely derived from the world of antiquity. For example, when an eighth-century monk describes a town he invariably uses the same Latin word, *urbs*, as a first-century author, but the word describes an altogether different reality. Archaeological remains have made us well aware of the scale and complexity of a first-century town; likewise, the archaeology of eighth-century towns as diverse as Cologne, London, Milan or Rome shows that these were tiny communities offering only a fraction of the facilities or services available in their first- to fourth-century predecessors. It is essential to take account of the physical remains of early medieval society, or the classical language of the written sources will be misleading. Above all, these sources project an ethos of continuity.

Added to this, we tend to interpret history as progress from one civilization to the next. Considerable effort is required to grasp the discontinuities of history, and most of all the virtual collapse of civilization in the case of the demise of the Roman Empire. Beyond this, it is extremely difficult to grasp the medieval imagination and propensity for creation from a late twentieth-century standpoint.

Archaeology is a major source of evidence for the history of the first millennium AD. Too often, however, it has been treated as a supermarket for historians to shop in selectively, taking odd items off the shelves to illustrate their narratives. Its primary importance is that it gives a sense of the scale of the past, providing measurements not only of the élite who made history, but also the peasantry who were effectively denied any direct access to history.

The archaeological record emphasizes the discontinuities of the past. The separated, sequential nature of the different layers forming the stratigraphic record is a telling counterpoint to the ethos of continuity in the written sources. Seventh- to tenth-century archaeological remains, however, are extraordinarily elusive. Commonly, they have been destroyed by later medieval activity. Most often when such levels occur in European towns, the sense of discontinuity is conspicuous: for example, typically, a layer of brown or black humic loam, the accumulation of centuries of vegetation and perhaps animals, separates classical levels from those that can be dated to the eleventh century. Dark Age activity is invariably no more than vestigial by any classical standard.

Archaeologists of the early Middle Ages have had their greatest success in discovering trading places in north-west Europe. The large mercantile settlements at Dorestad in the Rhine delta, Southampton (Hamwic) in the English kingdom of Wessex and Hedeby at the base of what was then Denmark offer profoundly new insights into this enigmatic period. Similar trading places probably existed in Italy, participating in the slow revival of post-classical trade in the Mediterranean, but the written sources make only oblique references to such places, and the archaeological evidence remains tantalisingly elusive. Places like Venice and Ravenna in the north, and Amalfi, Gaeta, Naples and Salerno in the south may well have been Mediterranean versions of Dorestad, but in the absence of archaeological evidence it is difficult to judge.

The North Sea trading sites and their rich material remains bear witness to a world of social and economic configurations constructed on different principles to those of the Roman *imperium*. Instead of a constellation of large, medium-sized and small towns, it appears that each trading town monopolised the urban activity of the kingdom it served. The archaeology of these places shows us that we must take an entirely different approach to economic matters in this period.

Trading sites figure only marginally in the literary sources of the time, which, written almost exclusively by monks, naturally focus on religious and monastic matters. The monks described the personalities of their world, their own views on life, and, to a lesser extent, the handling of administrative matters which affected them. Monastic histories such as the *Chronicon Vulturnense* – the twelfth-century author drew upon at least two other sources for the eighth and ninth centuries respectively – are a prominent part of the written record of this age. Land charters provide another documentary source. These spell out property rights and, often, local taxation. Families are named and their lands are described. Such documents furnish rare written descriptions of the world of the peasantry, though they tell us almost nothing about the lives of the peasants themselves. Together these documents give us an elliptical view of daily life in monasteries, their lay-out and broad architectural history, their estate-histories, the pattern of rents and, to some extent, their agricultural practices.

Monasteries are, then, the best documented places of the early Middle Ages. These were not only religious centres, but also ideological nodes – centres of civilization – fundamental to the transformation of Europe. A small army of historians has constructed a picture of western Europe on the basis of this monastic evidence. One of the most eminent of these historians, Henri Pirenne, characterized early medieval monasteries as centres of economic self-sufficiency. Pirenne and his disciples argued that the diversification of production on monastic domaines made it unnecessary to foster mercantilism. Pirenne's thesis, published in the 1930s, has not passed uncontested. Recently, a number of Belgian and French historians have painted a different picture of these great Dark Age centres. Monasteries are defined as powerful centres which stimulated not only the movement of goods within the territory, but also the spirit of mercantile enterprise. By Carolingian times, this wealth was deployed to create a terrestrial version of 'the celestial city', inhabited by men dedicated to the praise of God. The wealth helped to sustain the community, which at the same time served as limb, or vital part, of the Carolingian Empire itself (*membrum regni*). The historical debate, however, has been limited by the scope of the written sources. As we have already noted, economic affairs are rarely described. Apart from the improbable discovery of literary sources written by secular authors, the surest prospect for evaluating the present models rests with making more sense of the material culture.

Few monasteries have been investigated by archaeologists, and little attempt has been made to relate the archaeology of their territories to the written sources. At best, we have full-scale excavations of early Christian Irish monasteries such as Church Island (Co. Kerry), clearance excavations at places such as Herzfeld and Lorsch (Germany) (made before modern archaeological techniques had been devised), and small-scale modern excavations of monasteries such as Corvey (Germany), Müstair (Switzerland) and Whithorn (Scotland). Historians have relied on contemporary descriptions of monasteries such as Abbot Anglibert's for Centula (St Riquier) and Abbot Hugo's vivid picture of Farfa. Early medieval sites are difficult to locate or, in the case of most monasteries, as we have seen, obliterated by later building on the same spot. Yet neither the significance of the trading sites described above nor their part in the resurgence of the European economy will be understood until we can reconstruct the life of their hinterlands. Nor shall we fully grasp the transformation of the Roman world into the Middle Ages until we can witness its material diversity and the breadth of its iconography.

1979 was a landmark in the history of medieval monasteries. In that year a three-volume study of the St Gall plan was published by Walter Horn, professor of art history at the University of California, and magnificently illustrated by Ernest Born. This book investigates every aspect of the hypothetical plan of a ninth-century monastery kept in the library of the former monastery of St Gall in Switzerland. Horn describes the manuscript as follows: a large sheet of vellum (77 x 112 cm) sewn together from five separate pieces, it exhibits on the smooth side the outlines, drawn in red ink at a scale of 1:192, of all the buildings required for the life and work of an exemplary Carolingian monastery (Fig. 1.7). The drawings are annotated by a wealth of explanatory titles written in brown ink which define the purpose of each structure, the functions of its individual rooms, and the nature of its furnishings.

Horn deduced from the style of the script that the plan was drawn up

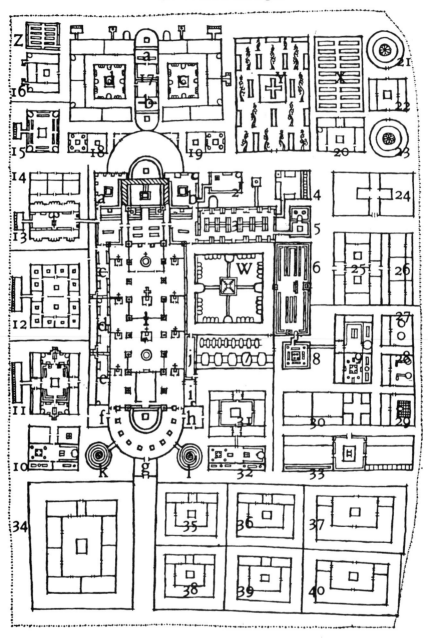

Fig. 1.7. The St Gall plan (*c*. 820).

at the monastery of Reichenau (on an island in Lake Constance). A dedicatory note or letter explains the circumstances surrounding its creation. Horn believed that it was made under the direction of Abbot Gozbert who presided over the monastery of St Gall from 816 to 836 and that its author was of higher rank than Abbot Gozbert. By a process of deduction, he ascribed it to Bishop Haito of Basel, who was abbot of Reichenau until 823. The scheme was drawn up, in Horn's opinion, after the momentous synods at Aachen in 816 and 817 which discussed wide-ranging reform of monastic life. Greater attention was henceforth to be paid to religious rituals and their public promotion, while lay servants were to be engaged to undertake a variety of routine tasks. Following the resolutions taken at the synod, monasteries were no longer to be retreats, but centres of civilization. The plan reflects this programme by laying down guidelines for the architectural lay-out of a monastic settlement.

In Horn's opinion, the plan was a blueprint for monasteries all over the Carolingian Empire and those Christian territories beyond which were affected by this monastic reform. Not everyone has been persuaded by these arguments. Paul Meyvaert, for example, in common with a number of critics, disputes the reading of the critical inscription on the manuscript. He believes that the plan can only be considered a private communication and not as a paradigmatic document. To illustrate his point Meyvaert focuses upon the dedication of the plan. Horn and Born translate the dedication as 'For thee, my sweetest son Gozbertus, have I drawn out this briefly elaborated copy of the layout of the monastic buildings ...'. Meyvaert argues that the neuter plural *haec exemplata* cannot mean 'this copy'. Instead, the ninth-century author of the inscription should be understood to mean that it is the particulars of the plan that he has worked out. Added to this Meyvaert claims that there is no indication from the dedication that the recipient was to regard the plans as officially prescribed. First, he is to exercise his ingenuity with them (*'quibus sollertiam exerceas tua'*) and secondly, the plans are intended for his eyes only (*'tibi soli perscrutinanda'*). More recently, in a detailed re-examination of the plan, Werner Jacobsen has shown that it is a palimpsest of complex drafting. Its author changed his mind many times. Horn's critics have an indisputable point: the St Gall plan is not a blueprint prepared for all monasteries following the reforms of Aachen but a rendering of the lay-out of a particular Carolingian monastery. Nevertheless, until the discovery of San Vincenzo al Volturno, the plan of St Gall provided an unique insight into the form and topography of a major ninth-century settlement.

The plan depicts a monastery covering an area of about a hectare. The ensemble of forty buildings is dominated by a large abbey and its associated cloisters, around which are gathered a number of separate buildings in which monastic services and industries were carried on. In many respects the settlement had a modular composition reminiscent of a Roman legionary fortress. Horn estimates that it could accommodate

13

about 120 monks and a similar number of lay servants. By ninth-century standards this was the size of a small town.

The St Gall plan clarifies and complements the verbal descriptions of monasteries dating from this period. It is the first known example of the concept of an integrated monastery, a medieval ideal familiar to us from the eleventh-century study of Cluny or the many twelfth-century Romanesque remains dotted throughout Europe. But the plan raises as many questions as it answers. Moreover, monasteries cannot be examined in isolation. Dark Age monasteries were as dependent on their hinterlands as towns were. At least, this is the substance of the debate which has fascinated historians since Henri Pirenne advanced his model. Another view of their economic bases has been advanced by the eminent French historian Georges Duby. In several important studies Duby characterizes ninth-century monastic estates as 'overpopulated islands where biological increase stimulated by agrarian prosperity pushed men to the verge of scarcity, contrasted with ocean-like stretches of country where farming was virtually impossible'. The rebuilding of the monastery of St Gall, if we adhere to the these studies in economic history, would be reflected in a concurrent increase in agricultural activity. As it happens, the estate records of St Gall show this was the case. At the same time, according to Rosamond McKitterick, as St Gall's influence and wealth increased, its tenants enjoyed increased standards of literacy. St Gall enlarged the size of its territory and concurrently sought to administer its lands more efficiently. But is this rational approach to management a model for all monastic development in the early Middle Ages? San Vincenzo, for example, greatly enlarged its property during this period, as did Monte Cassino. But was the land actively farmed to produce a surplus? If so, what happened to this surplus?

As we planned the San Vincenzo project we hoped to illuminate the origins of the Middle Ages from a new standpoint. In 1980 we therefore set out to chart the broad outlines of a leading monastery through this crucial period, and to compare these with the data from its dependent villages. It seemed an ideal place in which to examine the evolution of a Dark Age centre and its territory, for San Vincenzo's early history has not been obliterated by later activity of any note. Being off the beaten track is, as far as the archaeology is concerned, an advantage.

We anticipated, following Pantoni's studies, that the remains of the monastery itself would be slight. At most we expected thin archaeological levels in the fields around the present abbey church that were once covered with Romanesque and post-medieval buildings. The paucity of material brought to light in Pantoni's excavations in the abbey church itself implied that only wall footings and the holes and slots left by the posts of timber buildings might be discovered. Our greatest concern was to identify the elusive ninth-century levels which until 1980 had largely defied detection in the Mediterranean countries. To do this our strategy was to try to understand the archaeology associated with the church in which the painted crypt was located. Finds from levels related stratigraphically to the precisely dated crypt, we surmised, might make it possible to identify the location of villages of this period in the upper Volturno valley. Excavations concentrated around the crypt with its celebrated cycle of paintings might also fulfil our second aim of helping to make the site more attractive to tourists.

Excavations are expensive, so it is essential to have a strategy before beginning. Small armies of diggers and specialists are involved, necessitating complex logistical arrangements. Accommodation, eating arrangements, transport and day-to-day contingencies demand constant attention when a dig is in progress. Conservation, restoration, permits and, of course, the weather invariably complicate matters. If a clearly defined strategy is not in place the minutiae of living all too easily divert the excavation from its purpose.

The strategy at San Vincenzo was largely based upon Don Angelo Pantoni's work. The first task was to define the extent of the early medieval monastery. In 1980 we believed that only vestigial remains from the eighth to eleventh century survived in the precinct of the present abbey. In other words, we expected shallow archaeological layers and features (post-holes and pits), sealed and possibly partially destroyed by the subsequent Romanesque rebuilding. We also expected to find remains of structures outside the monastic precinct. Recent research at St Riquier (Centula) in northern France, for example, shows that this important Carolingian abbey possessed several churches outside its precinct. We had no expectations of encountering deeply buried remains.

The second task was to identify the remains of early medieval villages in the territory of San Vincenzo. The only means of pinpointing these places was with the aid of potsherds and other refuse which could be correlated with the precisely dated early medieval archaeological layers associated with the crypt (in which Abbot Epyphanius is depicted).

Field survey has become very fashionable in recent years largely because it is an inexpensive means of acquiring a good deal of archaeological information. It involves systematically walking a defined territory and mapping the ancient rubbish scattered across the landscape. This may be rubbish pertaining to a demolished building or homestead, or simply kitchen waste thrown on the fields, as likely as not in the form of manure. The rubbish of our past covers the European landscape, much of which, unfortunately, is in danger of being ploughed away. These modest remains are often the only surviving historical record of the peasantry through the millennia.

Interpreting scatters of archaeological debris, however, is not entirely straightforward. As a rule only a few pieces of flint, worked stone, or potsherds survive. For the most part this kind of refuse is unhelpful. The objects are often badly damaged or abraded by ploughing and difficult to identify. So how can these sites be related to a people without history? Put more colourfully, paraphrasing Sir Mortimer Wheeler, how are we to avoid these dots (ploughsoil scatters) on archaeological maps becoming the driest dust that blows? The simple answer is to relate the scatters of ancient rubbish to excavated and dated sites. Ploughsoil scatters need a historical context. The archaeology of the many minor sites – those without history – depends upon our comprehension of the archaeology of the few major ones which do have a history. In addition, some unprepossessing surface scatters must also be excavated and investigated more thoroughly.

The painted crypt in which Abbot Epyphanius is depicted provides a historical reference point *par excellence*. As we have seen, the square halo or nimbus indicated that Epyphanius was probably alive when his portrait was painted. According to the *Chronicon*, this was between 824 and 842. A fundamental part of the San Vincenzo strategy was therefore to find layers containing material which could be directly related to the crypt. The pottery and other refuse around the crypt might then be compared with the misshapen, battered fragments found in the ploughed fields and exposed terrace edges of San Vincenzo's territory. This was fine in theory. But our sunny optimism in 1980 was to be dented by the problems on the ground.

The excavations: a summary

In 1980 we launched a pilot project. First, at the behest of the Soprintendenza Archeologica, we excavated the area around the painted crypt. Here, as we have seen, we hoped to find layers of material with crucial data for the field survey. At the same time we surveyed the present abbey and its precinct. Finally, we began the field survey of San Vincenzo's territory, walking the greater part of the Rocchetta plain (in other words, the immediate vicinity of the monastery) and a tract of the Volturno valley.

The initial discoveries were confusing. The excavations immediately south of the crypt revealed a complicated sequence of apsidal buildings. Located on a dais in one of these apses was a brilliantly painted altar which at first sight seemed to belong to the eighth century. Despite this, late Roman pottery occurred in abundance and early medieval debris was scarce. The survey around the present abbey revealed that it was situated within a great scatter of classical refuse covering more than ten hectares. To add to our confusion, three small trial pits within the precinct of the present monastery showed no traces whatsoever of the early medieval monastery. A puzzling contrast existed around the sides of Colle della Torre. A hundred metres to the south of the crypt were the remains of a massive building, described by the mayor of Castel San Vincenzo as the church of Santa Maria *in insula*. These discoveries made us question Pantoni's thesis about the location of the early medieval monastery of San Vincenzo. The field survey of the Rocchetta plain and Volturno valley was no less puzzling. Many classical sites came to light, but none from late Roman times; nor was there any trace of early medieval settlements.

In the second season, in 1981, we continued by extending the excavations to the south of the crypt, making a cutting into the lowest terrace on the side of Colle della Torre. We also opened up three trenches in the orchard beside the present abbey. At the same time our surveyor began to map the densely overgrown hillside known as Colle della Torre directly behind the crypt. After two weeks we had obtained an intimation of what was in store.

The three trenches in the orchard south of the present abbey revealed nothing substantial. The baked earth contained only twelfth- to fifteenth-century material. The barest traces of post-built structures were cut into the ground surface, obliterated by ploughing in the 1950s. But in the excavations to the south of the apses by the crypt deep layers full of early medieval material made up the bulk of what we now call terrace 1. Late in August 1981 the last of these layers was removed to reveal painted walls, against which were badly scorched, painted benches. These buildings were paved with inscribed tiles. Handfuls of coloured window glass, pottery and metalwork beside boxes of ninth-century painted plaster fragments showed beyond doubt that we had found some substantial part of the lost Carolingian-period monastery. This was our first glimpse of the age of Abbot Joshua.

Our surveyor, battling with the dense vegetation covering Colle della Torre behind the crypt, showed that it was littered with monuments. To the locals this came as no surprise. They had always said that there had once been a small town here. A toothless old lady, Rosalinda Iannotta, even showed us where, in her opinion, the monks had perished in the pitched battle with the Arabs in 881 (the Valley of the Martyrs), and where they had gathered before their flight to Capua. Several small trial excavations provided corroboration that this was a large ancient site. Quite clearly, Pantoni's interpretation of San Vincenzo needed to be radically revised.

The field survey team continued to investigate further parts of San Vincenzo's *terra*. The results were similar to those obtained in 1980. Many classical sites were identified; most had been deserted in the third or fourth centuries. One thing was crystal clear: none of the classical villas or farms discovered during the survey had been occupied in medieval times. It was a vivid illustration of the collapse of the Roman Empire on the one hand, and clear evidence that the great abbey had recourse to peasants living in other places. A new strategy was called for to take account of these discoveries if we were to pinpoint San Vincenzo's elusive early medieval villages. This will be described in Chapter 9.

One aim of the third season was to make sense of the discoveries just south of the apses. A great effort was made to uncover a large area, first by hand and then with machinery. The results were almost beyond belief. Splendidly decorated rooms were unearthed. A catastrophic fire had

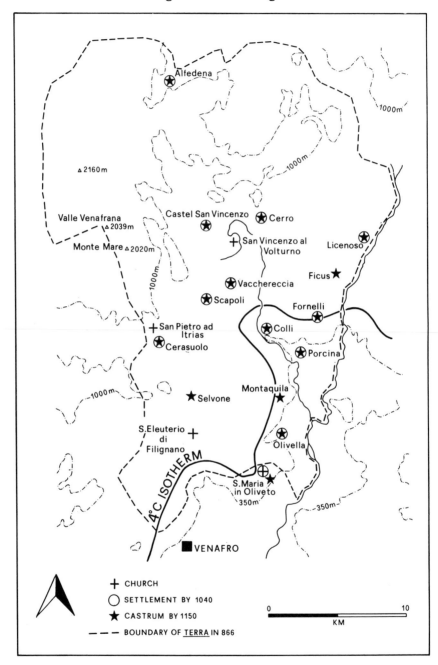

Fig. 1.8. The location of the 4°C isotherm, separating continental and Mediterranean climates, in the upper Volturno valley.

sealed large amounts of their painted decorations. Careful sifting of the scorched and burnt debris made it possible to reconstruct a large tract of paintings on one wall. These discoveries demonstrated that the great ninth-century monastery had been sited next to the Ponte della Zingara by the river Volturno, and that the painted crypt belonged to this grand complex.

Over the following decade the complicated story of this lost site has begun to unfold. As more and more of it was uncovered, the grandeur of the monastery in the ninth century could be measured against what preceded and followed it. Having once identified one part of the jigsaw we could begin to predict the approximate lay-out of the place using the St Gall plan (see above) as a rough guide. We are fairly convinced (though only further excavations can prove the point beyond doubt) that the ruins cover more than five hectares and themselves overlie the remains of settlements of earlier periods. Just as the local peasants repeatedly told us, it was a small town.

These discoveries far exceeded our expectations, and badly stretched our slender budget. But the implications of the archaeology were far richer than might have been imagined in 1980. Perhaps most sensationally, San Vincenzo Maggiore, Abbot Joshua's ninth-century abbey church, as we shall see, ranked alongside the very largest churches in Latin Christendom. At first we assumed it to be a church of 40-50 metres in length. Large-scale excavations in 1989-93, however, showed that it had a massive eastwork, worthy of a great Carolingian abbey or, indeed, of St Peter's. On 25 August 1992 we excavated a line of test pits westwards from the eastwork in an attempt to establish its precise length. That afternoon, in a field which hitherto had produced not a trace of anything archaeological, despite regular ploughing, we discovered the south apse of the great basilica. Abbot Joshua's basilica had been more than 100 metres long. The following spring we carried out a geophysical survey to establish the main characteristics of the complex, then in August 1993 we made three trial trenches in order to pinpoint its principal features. The second trench showed beyond doubt that a crypt lay buried beneath the ploughed field. This amazing discovery proved the final incentive for the *regione* of Molise, which approved a plan to make San Vincenzo into an archaeological park. Hence, in 1994, with funds from the *regione*, we uncovered the entire apsidal end of San Vincenzo Maggiore. On 10 August 1994, in the presence of the abbot of Monte Cassino and San Vincenzo al Volturno and the president of the *regione*, we removed the last of the soil filling the relic chamber of the ninth-century crypt. There, in a niche, was a portrait of a monk whom we believe to be Abbot Joshua, the architect of this enterprise.

Angelo Pantoni visited the ruins regularly until his death in 1988. On one occasion, in great excitement, he christened the site 'a monastic Pompeii'. The parallel is not entirely farfetched. Pompeii, of course, is far grander, far larger and far more complete. But it was a rich, small town of

19

Fig. 1.9. View from Colle della Torre across the site of the monastery to the present abbey. Note (left) the excavations in progress in 1983. (Photo: author)

Campania – no more. San Vincenzo was rather more: it was one of the great places of ninth-century Europe, and today a unique illustration of a monument from the time of transition from antiquity to the Middle Ages.

San Vincenzo's past and future

Archaeology is concerned not just with famous names of history, but with the remains of those whom the chroniclers have ignored. These remains give a context in which to place the makers of history and a valuable means of measuring their achievements. The urban and rural developments occurring in the time of the second-century Emperor Hadrian, for example, in provinces as remote as Britain, tell us as much about the man as his palatial villa outside Rome. Charlemagne's contribution to history should be assessed not just by his palace at Aachen, but by what was happening in manors, monasteries and villages throughout Germany, France and Italy as he imposed his will on an Empire. In Molise – a backwater of the Mezzogiorno – as in many less affluent regions of the world, the ability of archaeology to reveal the imprint of those ignored by written history should not be underestimated.

Molise is part of what Carlo Levi, the painter exiled by the Fascists to southern Italy in the 1930s, has called 'the other Italy'. In a memorable passage in his book *Christ Stopped at Eboli* (1947), Levi writes: '[the peasants] have led exactly the same life since the beginning of time, and History has swept over them without effect. Of the two Italys that share the land between them, the peasant Italy is by far the older; so old that no one knows whence it came, and it may have been here forever.'

Ask anyone who knows the area about Molise and almost all will agree with Carlo Levi's sentiments. Yet in Neolithic, Bronze Age, Iron Age, classical and early medieval times this part of Italy sustained some of the most advanced cultural institutions in western Europe. Its Iron Age Samnite culture, for instance, clashed with Rome on equal terms. Its classical cities were as affluent as those of Tuscany. Its classical farms were as numerous as in Emilia. An ancient Roman would have been shocked by Molise's twentieth-century poverty and lack of self-esteem. Abbot Epyphanius, portrayed in the ninth-century frescoes of the crypt, master of one of Europe's greatest monasteries in the ninth century, would have been no less perplexed to learn the fate of his patrimony a millennium later.

In our work at San Vincenzo we set out to endow the place with a renewed sense of identity. Roman and early medieval San Vincenzo was emphatically not part of the 'other Italy'. The monastery's ninth-century abbots, in particular, performed on a European stage. With the coming of the Normans this changed abruptly. In the subsequent millennium Molise has suffered, not least in the past century, from some of the greatest emigration of any region in western Europe. But times can change again.

The archaeological remains of the past can prove a catalyst for future development. Past glories can contribute to future prosperity. This was the substance of the 1992 meeting on Malta concerned with a 'European Convention on the Protection of the Archaeological Heritage'. Monuments and their settings are great resources for a Europe that is no longer concerned with farming or with manufacturing, but with service industries such as tourism. At San Vincenzo this is the purpose of the project mounted in 1994 by the *regione* of Molise in collaboration with the Abbey of Monte Cassino. The archaeological site has been purchased and fenced. A programme of conservation has commenced alongside the continuing excavations. A small museum has been opened. Above all there is the promise of a significant educational attraction bringing a steady stream of tourists to the site, who in turn will provide a flow of revenue sufficient to create new opportunities for employment. With time San Vincenzo al Volturno will become a symbol of the first post-classical renaissance, a place which has an identity that is as enduring as Burgundian or Loire valley churches are for the Romanesque renaissance, or the Uffizi Gallery in Florence for the late medieval renaissance.

The dangers are most apparent. Will this new entity complete the growing alienation of the land and its history from the people of this corner of Molise? Will late twentieth-century tourism make San Vincenzo into a foreign country for the citizens of the villages located around it? No one can deny that it is certain to transform the locality, its sense of purpose and its understanding of its history. Yet if the results of the excavations are presented in a comprehensible way, then this symbol will relegate Levi's sentiment in this part of the Mezzogiorno to history. San Vincenzo will once more be on the beaten track for European pilgrims and travellers.

2

The San Vincenzo Chronicles

San Vincenzo's early history is recounted in the twelfth-century *Chronicon Vulturnense*. The author of this manuscript, a monk called John, was abbot of San Vincenzo between 1139 and 1144. The illuminated book was kept at the monastery until the sixteenth century when it was taken first to Naples, then to Rome.

In 1601 the book was in the possession of Costantino Gaetano, a monk from Monte Cassino who founded the Aniciana Library in Rome. By 1685 it had found its way to the celebrated library of the Barbarini family where it was to remain for two centuries. During this time several great scholars worked on transcriptions of the manuscript. L.A. Muratori published a version in 1725; Ludwig Bethmann and G. Waitz made edited versions which were published in the late nineteenth century. In 1902 the Barbarini Library was given to the Vatican, and there the manuscript remains. In 1914 Vincenzo Federici, professor of history at the University of Rome, began work on a new edition of the *Chronicon*. The results were published in three volumes between 1925 and 1939. Federici's volumes have been widely studied by historians, making San Vincenzo one of the best known monasteries of the early Middle Ages.

Other copies of the chronicle are known to have existed. A fragment of one version was discovered as recently as 1925 among other texts in the library of Gaetano Sabatini at Pescocostanzo (in the Abruzzo, 30 km from San Vincenzo). Sabatini generously donated the fragment to the Istituto Storico Italiano at Rome in 1940. Unfortunately, after the war it was found to be missing. The fragment is likely to be in Germany or Russia, but an extensive search has failed to locate it. The so-called Sabatini fragment pre-dates John's chronicle, and was probably written at the end of the eleventh century. Illustrated with miniatures, it recounts the legendary journey made by Charlemagne to San Vincenzo and describes the lives of the monastery's abbots between Ambrosius Autpert (777-8) and Maio (872-901).

John's history was written a generation later. It followed an established format, being in a sense a great muniment book, a type of medieval scrap-book. It begins with a long, dedicatory prologue and then describes San Vincenzo's history from its earliest days up to the twelfth century. Beautifully painted miniatures illustrate each stage of the story. At one

Fig. 2.1. Italy in the early eighth century (the hatched areas were under Lombard control).

point, a planctus – a gregorian chant, accented with neums – adds another dimension to the tale. But while much of the style is vivid, even melodramatic, there are also detailed descriptions of the abbey's landholdings. The pages devoted to the tenth century include the foundation charters granted to many villages created within San Vincenzo's territory at this time (see Chapter 9).

John's book, in common with many books of his age, has an archaeological character. Like an excavation, the book comprises a palimpsest of earlier sources, providing a wide-ranging sweep of San Vincenzo's history. In common with an excavation, the author embarked on the project with a particular objective in mind. At present, in advance of a detailed textual 'excavation', only the main lines of the palimpsest are known to us. For example: the Provençal monk Ambrosius Autpert (abbot of San Vincenzo in 777-8) almost certainly wrote a short book on the early history of the monastery which John incorporated in his work. Other histories of San Vincenzo in the ninth century almost certainly existed. Unfortunately, only five manuscripts ascribed to the monastery's scriptorium, including the *Chronicon*, have survived. This is likely to represent a fraction of the monastery's literary output. The wealth of archaeological evidence for writing at San Vincenzo, as we shall see, strongly suggests that in the ninth century the monastery possessed a great library which perished in the sack of 881.

Paldo, Tato, Taso and their legacy

The chronicler tells us that three young Beneventans, Paldo, Tato and Taso, fled their native territory in the early years of the eighth century (Fig. 2.2). Destiny took them to Farfa, a newly-founded Benedictine abbey in the Sabine Hills, close to Rome, whose abbot, Thomas of Maurienne, instructed them to be monks. Following the intervention of their families, they returned to their homeland, and with the blessing of Abbot Thomas founded their own monastery. The biblical overtone of the exile, education and repatriation of the three Beneventans conforms to a typical medieval foundation myth. Yet its underlying theme is the connection between Farfa, a major frontier monastery in the Lombard duchy of Spoleto, and San Vincenzo, a frontier monastery in the Lombard duchy of Benevento (Fig. 2.3).

Duke Gisulf I of Benevento donated the land to these monks before his death in 706. The description of the grant in the *Chronicon* is a forgery, so we can only speculate on the initial arrangement between the duke and San Vincenzo's founding fathers. Some details, however, are clear. The monastery and its lands formed a block on the northern frontier of the duchy, close to the Via Numicia which ran down the dorsal spine of Italy, connecting the Lombard duchies of Spoleto and Benevento to the great Lombard kingdom in northern Italy. The site of the monastery itself was in *silva densissima* (dense woodland), the haunt of thieves and wild beasts. Yet the chosen place was also the site of an ancient settlement. According to the chronicler, three centuries earlier the Emperor Constantine, resting in the cool Appennines, fell asleep here after a large meal. While asleep he saw a vision of three saints which persuaded him to found a primitive oratory on this spot. (The origins of San Stefano at Capua and Santa

Fig. 2.2. Illustration from the *Chronicon Vulturnense* showing Paldo, Tato and Taso leaving Benevento for their journey to Rome and Farfa. (Photo: courtesy of Biblioteca Apostolica Vaticana)

Restituta at Naples were also attributed to Constantine, who seems to have been well-regarded during the tenth century with the revival of Byzantine power in southern Italy.) This Constantinian oratory was discovered by Paldo, Tato and Taso, who made it into their abbey. The dedication was to Saint Vincent, though whether this was the well-known Spanish martyr of Saragossa or a local saint is not known.

The foundation story is not exceptional. The wild, dangerous place, for example, is a common theme, which historians believe was intended to draw parallels with biblical references to deserts. These were interpreted as places of solitude, and yet a corner of paradise-on-earth. Similarly, Constantine, a favourite among medieval authors, as a father of Christianity, was frequently identified as the founder of an original church. From these humble beginnings the story unfolds.

Paldo became the first abbot, an office he held until October 720. Duke Gisulf endowed San Vincenzo with a modest array of lands including the church of Santa Maria in Canneto in the Trigno valley, about 100 km to the east. (Santa Maria exists today as a small abbey where remains of the early medieval phases have come to light within the ruins of the Roman villa upon which the present monastery was constructed.) Taso succeeded him for a year, and then Tato was abbot from about 721 until 729. Abbots

Fig. 2.3. Illustration from the *Chronicon Vulturnense* showing Thomas of Maurienne, abbot of Farfa, instructing Paldo, Tato and Taso to found a monastery at the oratory of San Vincenzo. (Photo: courtesy of Biblioteca Apostolica Vaticana)

Taso II (729-39), Ato (739-60), Hermepertus (760-63) and John I (763-77) preceded the Provençal philosopher Ambrosius Autpert (777-8). The monastery expanded modestly in these years. Taso II built the church of Santa Maria Minore; Abbot Ato built San Pietro. The Beneventan Duke Godescalc (738-42) gave Santa Maria in Isernia to the monastery, but his successor, Gisulf II (742-50) abruptly took it back. At the same time, Lupus, Duke of Spoleto (745-51) donated several minor estates in mountain-valleys close to the Via Numicia in the Abruzzo, and doubtless San Vincenzo profited from the occasions when the northern Lombard kings Aistulf and Desiderius stayed at the abbey.

The overall impression given by the narrative is of a monastery of unexceptional proportions and wealth, seeking to expand within the eastern foothills of the Abruzzo. Nonetheless, San Vincenzo had attained some political standing. In about October 752 Abbot Ato, accompanied by the abbot of Monte Cassino, was sent by Pope Stephen on an abortive diplomatic mission to seek peace with Aistulf, king of the Lombards. The one outstanding object attributed to San Vincenzo at this time is the subject of academic debate. The *Codex Beneventanus* is a sumptuously ornamented eighth-century manuscript now kept in the British Museum. Much of it is undoubtedly the work of a Beneventan scribe, but many aspects of it are also strikingly late Roman in style. Its elegantly painted canon tables have

27

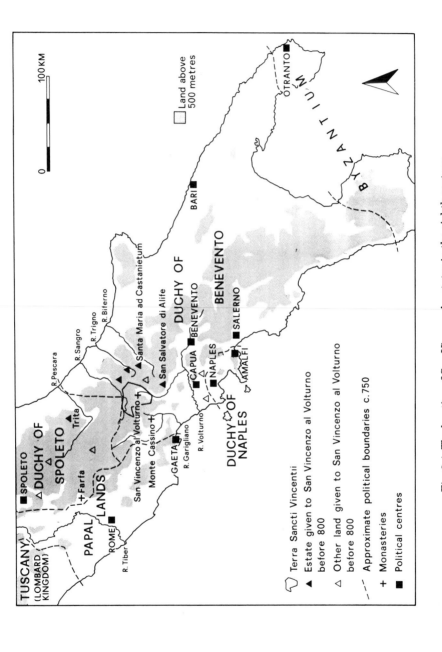

Fig. 2.4. The location of San Vincenzo's estates in the eighth century.

been ascribed to San Vincenzo because the author, a monk named Lupus, dedicates it to his abbot, Ato. In a verse on folio 76 of the *Codex* a reference is made to the monastery of San Pietro at Benevento, a dependency of San Vincenzo. Several historians believe the book may have been made in the scriptorium at San Vincenzo when Ato was abbot between 739 and 760. If so, it reflects a rich classical tradition of book illumination. Caution must prevail at present. We need to know much more about San Vincenzo in the mid-eighth century before we can attribute this grand work of art with certainty to what, at this time, was an apparently minor monastery.

The Frankish connection

In 773 Charlemagne launched his campaign against Desiderius, the powerful king of the Lombards. Desiderius stoutly resisted the invader throughout the winter of 773-4 before Charlemagne forced a passage into Pavia, the Lombard capital, and, to quote the Royal Frankish Annals, 'all the Lombards came from every city of Italy and submitted to the rule of the glorious Lord King Charles'. With the Lombard defeat, the balance of power in Italy was fundamentally altered. Soon afterwards Charlemagne marched south to menace the Beneventans. Although he halted his advance at Capua, he nevertheless compelled the southern Lombards to acknowledge his hegemony. The Franks took hostages and imposed a price for their victory on the Beneventan dukes. Over the next fifty years Beneventan leaders alternated between policies of enthusiasm, support and opposition to their Frankish overlord.

The Frankish invasion made a great impact upon San Vincenzo, as it did upon other Italian monasteries. The impact owed everything to the spirit of the Carolingian movement. Frankish stormtroopers did not occupy the Italian peninsula; nor was there an attempt to overturn the existing Lombard social structure. Indeed, the converse was the case. The Carolingians generally fostered and supported the Lombard social system, and were seduced by its rich artistic culture as well as its antique traditions. The invaders, however, introduced a great range of technical skills that imposed greater efficiency upon the underdeveloped post-classical communities of Italy. The rule of the written law as opposed to custom was encouraged. Literacy was promoted. The exercise of cultural values at all levels of Lombard society was introduced, which meant that the new imperial ideology reached all sections of society. The Church, being a key political as well as a religious force in Italy, was necessarily the instrument of Charlemagne's renaissance movement. The leading abbeys of Novolesa, Amiata, Farfa, Monte Cassino and San Vincenzo, occupying the great swathes of land beyond the bounds of urban centres such as Ravenna and Rome, received conspicuous patronage, to the extent that the historian

Karl Schmid has described Charlemagne's military success in Italy as a monastic conquest.

San Vincenzo was becoming a strategically important and influential community. Pope Hadrian I described it in *c.* 783 to Charlemagne as *'tam magnam congregationem'* ('so large a community'). As if to illustrate its growing status, San Vincenzo appeared in the pope's correspondence with Charlemagne in a letter remarking on its monks' bitter division in their attitude towards the Franks. In the late 770s and the 780s a strong Frankish faction emerged within the community, led by the distinguished Frankish theologian Ambrosius Autpert. Elected abbot in 777, Ambrosius sadly remains an elusive character in the pantheon of San Vincenzo's abbots. Born in Provence, he is said by one account to have been a member of the Carolingian court before joining San Vincenzo. Once there, he set about writing a number of major works on the apocalypse, of which his most notable, the *Expositio in Apocalypsin*, was completed in 772. Ambrosius remained abbot for little more than a year, before being deposed by the Lombard, Poto. Five years later, in 783, Poto was accused by one of the Frankish faction of refusing to join the monks in praying for the safety and health of the Carolingian king, as had become customary. Poto, it was said, went even further. This was the news that reached Charlemagne by way of the Pope; Charlemagne commanded that Poto be arraigned before a papal court in Rome. Abbot Poto, Ambrosius, and Poto's accuser, a monk called Rodicasus, set out for Rome that January. On the journey Ambrosius Autpert died. Poto and Rodicasus alone presented themselves at the papal court. In the ensuing hearings it was claimed that Rodicasus had been caught *in flagrante* with his niece. His evidence, as a result, was deemed untrustworthy. Poto was acquitted and reinstated as abbot, but died shortly afterwards, some say on the return journey to San Vincenzo.

This convoluted story leaves much to our imagination, but it illustrates San Vincenzo's increasing status as well as, apparently, Charlemagne's concern for his own standing in this farflung corner of Italy. Ambrosius Autpert may be one factor in this story. Some art historians interpret the ninth-century cycle of paintings in the crypt of Epyphanius, with its emphasis upon the apocalypse, as a memorial to him. Was he one of those Dark Age holy men like Bede, Benedict of Aniane or Boniface whose education and philosophy lent their spheres European status which long outlived their lifetimes?

In Poto's place the monastery elected a Frankish abbot called Paul (783-92). In 787, shortly after Charlemagne's brief military campaign in the duchy of Benevento, Paul won from him a confirmation of the abbey's titles to its property, immunity from any kind of lay interference and the right of the abbey to elect its own abbot. As a royal (and later, imperial) abbey, as opposed to a ducal one, it benefited from gifts made over to it by the aristocracy. As a result its wealth was transformed. This plainly influenced the chronicler (and the author of the Sabatini fragment) to ascribe San Vincenzo's great rise under Abbot Joshua directly to the Carolingians. Charlemagne has an almost mythic status in the mind of the chronicler.

During Paul's rulè, the Lombardic dukes to the north and south made gifts of land to the monastery. Duke Arichis II of Benevento gave San Vincenzo lands near Capua, while Duke Hildebrand of Spoleto donated several estates in the Abruzzo. Nevertheless, the *Chronicon* records that only one church, Santa Maria Minore *iuxta flumen*, was built during this period. Paul the Deacon, the celebrated historian of the Lombards, records in *c.* 790 that San Vincenzo was 'now celebrated for its great community of monks'.

The *Chronicon* is not so reticent about the achievements of Abbot Paul's successor. The chronicler singles out Abbot Joshua (792-817) for special praise. According to the chronicler, Joshua was a Frank of royal blood who had been educated at the Carolingian court. Joshua's sister, Ermengard, so we are informed, was the first wife of Charlemagne's son, Louis the Pious. John would have us believe that Louis lavished gifts on the monastery and visited it a number of times, taking a real interest in the rebuilding of the abbey church – San Vincenzo Maggiore – and presented his kinsman with 32 columns and other building materials from an ancient Roman temple in Capua to be used in this great monument. Most of this was almost certainly an invention. Joshua's relationship to Louis is unknown. Moreover, it is doubtful that Louis ever visited San Vincenzo. Joshua might have met the German Emperor if, in his last year, he took part in the great synod at Aachen in 816, but no record of his attendence exists. On one point, however, the chronicler leaves us in no doubt. Under Joshua, and possibly under his short-lived successor Talaricus (817-23), San Vincenzo obtained gifts of at least sixty estates, mostly in the

Fig. 2.5. Illustration from the *Chronicon Vulturnense* showing Abbot Joshua being received by Pope Pascal I. (Photo: courtesy of Biblioteca Apostolica Vaticana)

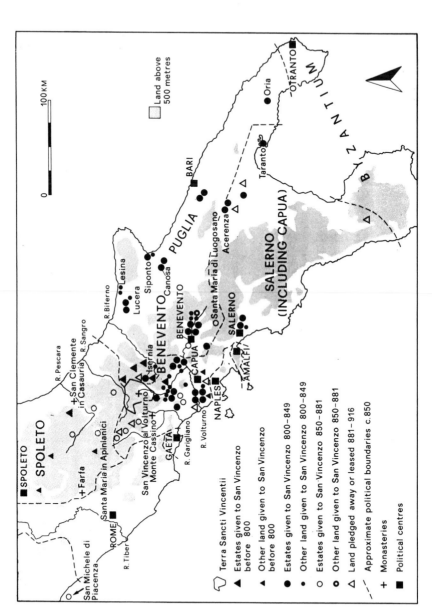

Fig. 2.6. The location of San Vincenzo's estates in the ninth century.

SPOLETO

Santa Maria in Apinianici

ROME

R. Tiber

San Michele di Piacenza

+Farfa

R. Pescara

+San Clemente in Casauria

R. Sangro

R. Biferno

San Vincenzo al Volturno
Monte Cassino+

GAETA

R. Garigliano

R. Volturno

NAPLES

CAPUA

AMALFI

Isernia

BENEVENTO

BENEVENTO

Lucera

Lesina

Siponto

Canosa

PUGLIA

BARI

oSanta Maria di Luogosano

SALERNO

SALERNO
(INCLUDING CAPUA)

Acerenza

Taranto

Oria

OTRANTO

BYZANTIUM

100 KM

0

Land above
500 metres

Terra Sancti Vincentii

▲ Estates given to San Vincenzo before 800

▲ Other land given to San Vincenzo before 800

● Estates given to San Vincenzo 800–849

• Other land given to San Vincenzo 800–849

○ Estates given to San Vincenzo 850–881

◉ Other land given to San Vincenzo 850–881

△ Land pledged away or leased 881–916

--- Approximate political boundaries c. 850

+ Monasteries

■ Political centres

Beneventan heartlands and on the Apulian coast (Fig. 2.6). There is an underlying pattern to these estates, according to Federico Marazzi. The Via Numicia, running down the Appennine spine of Italy from Spoleto to Benevento, remained a fundamental axis around which the new estates formed. This was a Lombard route, avoiding papal Rome. Now, however, estates were acquired in the valleys leading to the Adriatic as well as on the Adriatic littoral itself. San Vincenzo maintained important estates at Lesina and Siponto near the Gargano peninsula. These gave access to maritime trade at coastal landing-places and were also important sources of supply for fish and salt. A smaller number of estates were held on the Tyrrhenian coast, beyond the territorial influence of Gaeta and Naples. These donations made the monastery one of the major landowners of Italy with access to a wide range of resources. Its abbot assumed the status of a great landlord.

Joshua's territorial acquisitions in many parts of Central Italy were matched by comparable achievements within the monastery's precincts. The tradition of San Vincenzo's wealth and status was still a source of pride for the twelfth-century chronicler. How far this tradition is reflected in reality is an issue which is examined in later chapters.

Abbot Talaricus (817-23), Joshua's successor, built two churches at San Vincenzo. One of these was San Salvatore, a prominent church in the tenth century; the other was San Michele. The next abbot, Epyphanius, built two churches: Santa Maria *in insula* and San Lorenzo *in alia insula*. Epyphanius, as we saw in Chapter 1, is San Vincenzo's best-known abbot. His portrait in the cycle of paintings in the crypt found in the nineteenth century has assured his historical reputation. Indeed many historians have thought that the importance accorded to St Laurence in the crypt paintings identifies the building with San Lorenzo *in alia insula*. This is discussed in more detail in Chapter 6.

After 820, gifts of land to San Vincenzo were fewer in number, although there was a brief flurry of donations in the early 830s. By this time the Carolingian aristocracy was in conflict and its troubles affected all parts of its farflung polity. By 840 civil war had engulfed the principate of Benevento. Two years later a band of Beneventan nobles robbed Monte Cassino of its great treasury amassed by Abbot Gisulf, Joshua's contemporary. Abbot Epyphanius and his successors had to come to terms with a new age. Greater problems were in store: in common with most of central Italy, San Vincenzo suffered a terrible earthquake in 848 when many of its buildings were damaged (Fig. 2.7). Despite these calamities the Carolingian Emperor Lothar and his successor Louis II confirmed the monastery's privileges, and from time to time Beneventan aristocrats still made over gifts of new estates to San Vincenzo. The programme of church-building proceeded, though on a reduced scale. Abbot Toto (842-4) built a church, San Pietro, by the marble bridge leading to the monastery. Another San Pietro was built by Abbot Jacob (844-53) some kilometres away near the

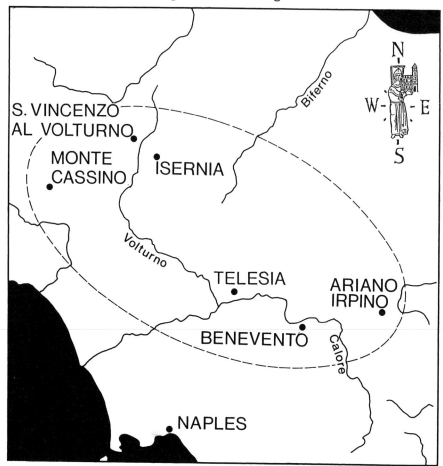

Fig. 2.7. The extent of the earthquake in June 848.

village of Cerasuolo. Jacob's successor, Abbot Teuto (853-6), constructed the church of San Eleuterio at Filignano close to the boundary with Monte Cassino's *terra*. Then in 861 a premonition of the catastrophe to come appeared before the gates of San Vincenzo.

The Arab sack of San Vincenzo

The Arabs arrived decisively on the Italian scene when in August 846 their army invested Rome and devastated the basilica of St Peter. The Emperor Lothar rushed to the aid of Pope Leo IV, who organized the building of a mighty brick-built wall around the Vatican, the so-called Leonine wall, tracts of which survive to this day. The sack of Rome in 846 was a watershed. Hitherto Arab corsairs had repeatedly attacked ships in the Tyrrhenian Sea as well as ports from Provence to Campania. But assailing the urban centres of Latin Christendom had seemed beyond the capability of these Mediterranean Vikings.

At this time the Arabs operated from a base, initially at Bari in Apulia (847-71), and later (883-915) from the Gargano peninsula where the modern region of Molise borders Apulia. A great swathe of territory now lay open to their depredations.

The chronicler Erchempertus, historian of Monte Cassino, tells us that Emir Sawdan occupied *Castrum Benafranum*, modern Venafro, in 861. Soon afterwards Sawdan, 'with the speed of a rapacious bird', arrived at the abbey of San Vincenzo. The emir threatened to demolish the place unless a ransom was paid. In the end Abbot John II handed over several thousand pieces of gold and the Arabs departed. For the time being, at least, San Vincenzo was spared. But the Arab menace continued to threaten the community. In 870 Teodemund, a monk from San Vincenzo, was journeying to the Holy Land with two companions when all three were captured and enslaved by Sawdan. Along with a shipload of other Beneventan Christians, these three pilgrims were taken to Tripoli in Syria, then to Alexandria, before they eventually gained their freedom.

San Vincenzo's fate was decided on 10 October 881. The chronicler tells us that the war-band was led by Emir Sawdan, but this is unlikely, as we shall see in Chapter 7. Abbot Maio realized that this time the raiders had to be met with force. His monks bravely defended the marble bridge leading to the monastery but were eventually overwhelmed. The chronicler conveys some sense of the ferocity of the battle. Hundreds perished before the monks retreated. As the community faced disaster, many of the servants of the monastery treacherously changed sides. The remaining monks sought refuge in a nearby *castrum* before fleeing to Capua. Here, the citizens, 'afflicted by grief for the destruction of the monastery', gave the monks a piece of land just outside the old Roman town, beside the river Volturno, on which to build a new community. Over subsequent generations the monastery of San Vincenzo at Capua grew to be an important church.

The Arab army desecrated the abbey, fired the scriptorium and threw the monastery's stores into the river Volturno. According to the chronicler, the revelling lasted for several days. The chronicler leaves us in no doubt about the scale of the calamity. San Vincenzo, he reminds us, 'surpassed all the outstanding monasteries of Italy'. The sack, he leads us to believe, was an outrage changing the course of history. The poignant passage describing these events in the *Chronicon Vulturnense* is illustrated with a *planctus* written for gregorian chant. San Vincenzo's martyrs, in the chronicler's version, were symbols of the monastery's eclipse. With the hindsight of history, writing two centuries later, John was right that this marked the end of one age and the beginning of another at San Vincenzo.

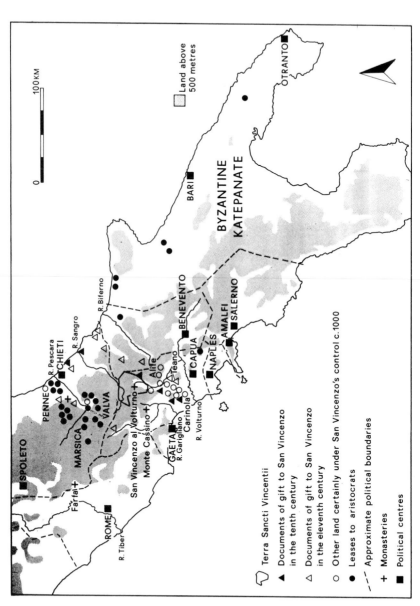

Fig. 2.8. The location of San Vincenzo's estates in the tenth and eleventh centuries.

The following labels appear on the map:

100KM

Land above 500 metres

BYZANTINE KATEPANATE

OTRANTO

BARI

R. Biferno

R. Sangro

R. Pescara

CHIETI

PENNE

Teano

Alife

SPOLETO

MARSICA

VALVA

Farfa

R. Tiber

ROME

San Vincenzo al Volturno

Monte Cassino

GAETA

R. Garigliano

Carinola

R. Volturno

CAPUA

BENEVENTO

NAPLES

AMALFI

SALERNO

Terra Sancti Vincentii

Documents of gift to San Vincenzo in the tenth century

Documents of gift to San Vincenzo in the eleventh century

Other land certainly under San Vincenzo's control c.1000

Leases to aristocrats

Approximate political boundaries

Monasteries

Political centres

But San Vincenzo did not face this future alone. Two years later, in 883, Monte Cassino was sacked, and in 898 the monastery at Farfa shared the same fate. In reality, while the golden age of monasteries ended violently, their influence and prosperity had been waning long before the 880s.

The age of *incastellamento*

In 916, when the monks of San Vincenzo returned from exile to the monastery, a pitiful scene evidently awaited them. They appealed for help and support, but, if the chronicler's silence is to be correctly interpreted, received little. Monasteries throughout western Europe shared the same fate. The Arabs in the South and Vikings in the North had undermined monastic credibility, destroying the power of abbots who had been petty princes in all but name. The secular reconstruction of post-classical Europe was under way. New kingdoms were being formed in the aftermath of the collapse of the Carolingian Empire. Byzantium was actively reasserting its political and economic authority in the western Mediterranean. For the first time in three hundred years regular shipping was crisscrossing the Mediterranean from west to east. Although San Vincenzo was far from the new ports and capitals, the winds of change were bound to affect it.

San Vincenzo Maggiore remained in ruins throughout the tenth century – a conspicuous symbol of the monks' plight. Abbot Godelpert (902-20) and his successor, Rambaldus (920-44) opted instead to repair San Salvatore, a church built when Talaricus was abbot. Rambaldus also built a church, Santa Maria, in front of the monastery gates. It is likely, however, that these were markers for the future rather than signs of the revival of the monastery. Successive abbots throughout the century seem to have retained a considerable presence at Capua, allowing much of San Vincenzo to remain in ruins.

The abbey had lost much of its property. Abbot Maio had leased off substantial tracts of land while in exile at Capua. By 930 San Vincenzo held only nine estates outside its *terra* (in the upper Volturno valley). Over the next two centuries successive abbots actively repaired this position (Fig. 2.8). The process of *incastellamento* – the founding of villages and the clearance of landscapes abandoned since classical times – mostly postdates 970. It owed much to Pandulfus Capodiferro, prince of Capua and Benevento, who in a diploma of 27 July 967 recognized the rights of Monte Cassino and San Vincenzo to embark on *ius incastellandi*. By 983 San Vincenzo owned 38 estates; this had risen to 41 in 1038, and at least 54 are mentioned in a papal bull of Nicholas II dating to 1059. Initially, the nucleus of these holdings was, not surprisingly, in the plain of Capua, not far from the surrogate monastery in Capua itself. By 1000, however, San Vincenzo had founded or formally confirmed the existence of villages throughout its *terra* in the upper Volturno valley. The uplands were steadily repopulated; the woodlands were cut back and colonized; and agricultural production was increased.

With the monastery's estates being actively developed, at the end of the millennium Abbot John IV (998-1007) undertook the restoration of Joshua's great basilica. From this moment San Vincenzo's abbots sought to reinstate the abbey's status as a frontier monastery, while retaining a base in the renascent urban centre of Capua. After John IV, Abbot Ilarius (1011-45) decorated the basilica and added a bell-tower to the abbey church. Ilarius also renovated Santa Maria Maggiore, San Pietro and San Michele. In the 1040s Pope Nicholas visited San Vincenzo and, we are told, was greatly impressed by the place. 'Indeed, this is a holy place, and it has been appointed by God,' he allegedly commented. The reconstruction continued under Abbot John V (1053-76) with further new works, including a new cloister. Abbot John must have been impressed, if not influenced by Abbot Desiderius' celebrated rebuilding of Monte Cassino.

But the reconstruction did not end here. After his election in 1076, Abbot Gerard, formerly a monk at Monte Cassino, embarked upon a programme of building works that emulated Abbot Joshua's achievements at the beginning of the ninth century. The programme of works outlasted Gerard and even his successor Benedict, and may have been completed towards the middle of the twelfth century when John the chronicler was almost certainly elected abbot. The *Chronicon*, however, is not entirely clear about Gerard's works. It records no more than a 'transmigration' – a shift of the monastery during this period. This is strange because Abbot Gerard, without doubt, built a new abbey church '*a fundamentis*' which was consecrated by Pope Pasqual II in 1117, as well as making a complete monastic plan.

What were Abbot Gerard's motives for leaving the old site and starting afresh? Several reasons are discussed in Chapter 8, but undoubtedly peer-pressure was not insignificant. With the turn of the millennium monasteries all over Europe were being redesigned, enlarged and aggrandized. This was the beginning of the Romanesque movement, which reached its climax in the twelfth-century renaissance. From the late tenth century onwards the achievements of the Carolingians were recast in a grander form. The abbey of Cluny in Burgundy was one model for this movement. Its grand church, like the abbey church on the St Gall plan of *c.* 820, was surrounded by a great variety of service buildings and workshops. But unlike the Carolingian movement, which had embodied images of antiquity, the Romanesque explicitly espoused new art and architectural forms. The most famous building programme of this age was at Monte Cassino. Between 1066 and 1072 Abbot Desiderius completely rebuilt the Carolingian church, creating the imposing complex that in outline survives today. Over the following years, Desiderius' monastery was planned and built on a similarly huge scale; the most public areas were sumptuously decorated with polychrome marble pavements and wall mosaics made of glass tesserae, some covered with gold foil, as well as with paintings. Much of this survived encased in the later fabric until the monastery was obliterated in the bombardment of 1944. Today only fragments remain to hint at the splendour that impressed medieval visitors.

We are left in no doubt about the impact made by Desiderius' new buildings at Monte Cassino on the secular and ecclesiastical world of central Italy. Robert Guiscard, the bellicose Norman conqueror of southern Italy, was awe-struck by the achievement. So too, we may suspect, were abbots throughout Europe. It may be no coincidence that Abbot Berardo II of Farfa set about building a new monastery, San Martino, in 1097 on the nearby summit of Monte Acuziano, one of the highest points of the Sabine Hills overlooking the old (and present) site where Paldo, Tato and Taso had taken instruction. Berardo's death, however, brought an end to this ambitious project. San Martino, had it been finished, given its commanding position overlooking the Tiber valley, would have emulated Monte Cassino as a truly imposing monument.

Other factors also menaced the monastery and may have influenced Gerard's action. With the development of its lands, it might seem, the abbey had regained its ninth-century status. However, this was an illusion. First, it faced increasing difficulty in administering its estates. Parvenu Norman counts ruthlessly robbed its rents and then seized many of these lands. Local counts forcibly stole large blocks of San Vincenzo's *terra*. Between 1045 and 1053 the Borrelli family, based in the Sangro valley to the east of San Vincenzo, took possession of many of San Vincenzo's eastern territories. In these years they even sacked the abbey itself. By 1050 all the immediate villages on the south side of San Vincenzo were lost to the Borrelli (see Chapter 9). As early as *c.* 1020 the counts of Venafro had occupied Cerasuolo and Filignano in the western zone of the *terra*. Finally, in the mid-eleventh century the monks were forced to fortify S. Maria Oliveto on the southern bounds of their territory in the face of increasing threats from the Normans. It proved a pointless exercise. By 1100 the political geography of central Italy had changed radically. The age-old frontier running along the Mainarde mountains was relocated to the northern fringes of the Abruzzo. At a stroke much of the political rationale for the existence of San Vincenzo was removed. The monastery soon suffered the impact of its dwindling status. The *Catalogus Baronum*, the Normans' Domesday survey of their south Italian lands, shows that S. Maria and its southern territories had been seized by 1150. When the chronicler was at work on his history the formerly vast estates of San Vincenzo had been whittled down to a rump around the monastery.

This history of decline contrasts with the increasing stature of Monte Cassino, which opted to challenge the secular threats to its patrimony. Its villages were fortified and became strategic military centres. Monte Cassino, especially under Abbot Desiderius, was prepared to be bellicose, as on the occasion in 1045 when the Normans were hunted out of the Cam-

Fig. 2.9. The Ponte della Zingara: a nineteenth-century view of the late Roman bridge in front of the early medieval monastery. (Photo: courtesy of ICCD (Rome), negative C405)

panian village of Sant' Angelo. To meet this menace, Monte Cassino maintained a small militia: in 1150, for example, it had sixty knights. San Vincenzo, by contrast, appears to have been impotent to contest its fate. Its charters suggest that either by design or by accident it generally eschewed such a policy. Monte Cassino also actively engaged in the mercantile activity of the age through its suburb on the Via Casilina, at S. Germano. At San Vincenzo, with the fixing of new frontiers, the opportunity to develop a comparable vicus was diminished. Its most attractive prospects for investment lay at Capua, where it might participate in the thriving Campanian economy. Given these configurations, Gerard's new monastery was destined to be a folly.

The chronicler's reticence about the rebuilding with which he was associated may betray his own misgivings about the project. The history of San Vincenzo was written as the monastery began its inexorable slide into obscurity. The grandiosity of the text belies its motives. The illuminated miniatures are exquisitely painted in the Cassinese style. They reveal the presence of great artists in San Vincenzo's scriptorium, all working to recall the monastery's imperial heritage. The humble beginnings, the bitter controversy aroused by Charlemagne, the depredations by pagan Saracens, the poverty of the tenth century, the inception of estate management and the Romanesque revival are all typical of many other monasteries. The thread of the story is straightforward: this place grew to be worthy of the mythic champion of early medieval Europe – Charlemagne. The sub-text for the twelfth-century reader was: is no one willing to re-establish the monastery's power and purpose?

Until around 1050 San Vincenzo's story runs parallel with Monte Cassino, Farfa, Monte Amiata (Tuscany), Novolesa (at the foot of the Mount Cenis pass), and many other Benedictine houses. The historical problem is that we have been dependent on the hyperbole of chroniclers such as John, far removed from the times they described, for our knowledge of these places. Many Romanesque abbeys survive, so we have a fair impression of what they looked like in the twelfth century. But what of their earlier phases? What was so special about Abbot Joshua's basilica that the chronicler associated its construction with the Frankish Emperor? And how were the ups and downs of monastic history affected by territorial, regional and national events? Our project embarked on the writing of a new chronicle, constructed by no less laborious means from an analysis of the buried remains, in order to cross-examine John.

3

Samnium? San Vincenzo Before the Monastery

This is a landscape with a long history. Mousterian flint implements of the Middle Palaeolithic occur on the tiny islets within the relic marshes on the Rocchetta plain. Fine examples have also come to light in the excavations, evidently collected by the monks. The flint itself comes from outcrops immediately to the north-east of San Vincenzo on Monte Santa Croce. Survey on this *altopiano* in 1993 revealed a rich assemblage of debris from working the tools (Fig. 3.1). These date to about 50,000 BP during the first

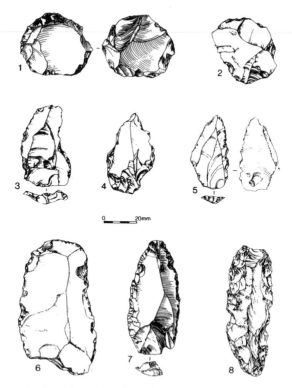

Fig. 3.1. Mousterian flints from Monte Santa Croce.

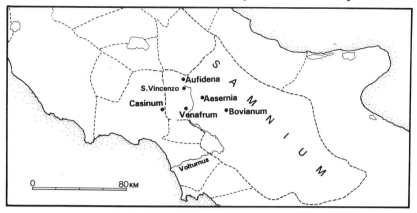

Fig. 3.2. The location of San Vincenzo in the Samnite period.

Wurm interstadial when the snowlines were higher. In those times the Neanderthals would have moved down in wintertime to the marshes around the Volturno.

The first major occupation at San Vincenzo dates to the sixth century BC (Fig. 3.2). In the grounds of the modern abbey a Samnite cemetery has been found. Its discovery utterly surprised us, for before 1995 no trace of a Samnite tomb had ever been recorded in these parts (Fig. 3.3). The region of Molise, which boasts fewer than 300,000 inhabitants, traces its roots to the Samnites, the confederation of tribes that vigorously resisted the Roman advance into Central Italy. The origin myth, as far as the Samnites are concerned, is a powerful constant in today's Molise. Nowhere is this more apparent than at San Vincenzo, a place associated with the capital of Samnium for nearly two millennia. The Samnites, like the Etruscans and Oscans, were Iron Age tribes who lay within the greater social and economic sphere of Greece. Like their counterparts in Tuscany and Lazio, these tribesmen had a rich material culture. They built numerous fortresses with great cyclopean enclosures as well as modestly proportioned sanctuaries. The majority of these peoples, however, to judge from the farmstead excavated at Matrice in the Biferno Valley, lived in modest drystone or timber dwellings.

Around the fourth century BC a Samnite village was created at this end of the Rocchetta plain. How this related to the surrounding fortifications occupying hilltops is not yet known. The greatest Samnite hillfort of all was Monte San Paolo, situated 6 km south of San Vincenzo al Volturno overlooking the village of Colli a Volturno. Around the crown of this now densely wooded hill run about 20 km of cyclopean walling. Not surprisingly, in its vicinity were numerous satellite settlements: smaller forts and sanctuaries. The closest of these to San Vincenzo was Monte S. Croce, the highest hill overlooking the plateau. The northern flank of this pinnacle is

43

Fig. 3.3. Samnite grave of the sixth century BC from the new abbey cemetery. (Photo: Will Bowden)

44

defended by a stretch of massive cyclopean walling. The Monte S. Croce fortress was perhaps a refuge, or an outpost controlling the route from Monte S. Paolo to the mountains.

The substantial scatter of pottery of this period at San Vincenzo shows that this was a village of some size and affluence. This, it might be said, was the first San Vincenzo. Its exact size, topography and history are difficult to estimate. Before it was abandoned in the age of the Emperor Augustus, or thereabouts, it occupied an area of at least ten hectares either side of the river. Was this the lost city of Samnium? Several ancient sources refer to Samnium – the capital of the warlike Samnites. The association with San Vincenzo is most clearly described by the twelfth-century chronicler, John, in the *Chronicon Vulturnense*. Moreover, in a charter granting land at Benevento to San Vincenzo, Charlemagne refers to the monastery as occupying the *partibus Samnie*. A little later, Castel San Vincenzo was called *Castro Samnie* in its foundation charter of 982 (see Chapter 9). In the opinion of John Patterson, Samnium was a region rather than a town. For him 'the most striking aspect of the whole question … was the way in which the tradition of Samnite glory survived centuries of Roman and Lombard domination. Even today, the tradition remains.' Whatever the truth of this matter, and Patterson's remarks have attracted a good deal of controversy, the early classical nucleus at San Vincenzo was not insignificant. Indeed, it was the only urban site discovered during the San Vincenzo survey of the upper Volturno valley.

As yet we possess only a sketchy idea of the topography of San Vincenzo in ancient times. Significantly, it was bisected by the river Volturno. On the east side of the river the settlement spread from the steep travertine cliffs marking the northern edge of the Rocchetta plain, for a distance of some 400 m to a deep ditch which marked its southern edge. This ditch was shallow at its river end, but 20 m deep at the other end. It served not only as a boundary defining the southern limits of the settlement, but also as a vital diversion for winter flood waters, taking them away from the vulnerable, low-lying parts of the settlement. Trenches and holes fortuitously made for planting olive trees have enabled us to form some impression of what this part of the site was like. A large, roughly paved area, perhaps a piazza, stood on a natural shelf close to the river in the centre of the settlement. Around this have been found traces of monumental buildings, and timber structures. The most complete relic of this age is a fine hump-back bridge over the deep ditch. This was constructed in the later Republican period, possibly on a road connecting the settlement with the towns of Isernia and Alfedena.

The nucleus of the early classical settlement nestled around the lower flanks of Colle della Torre on the west bank of the river. At its northern end were the remains of a major building, possibly a sanctuary or temple into which the later crypt was cut. An inscription re-used in the tenth-century monastery records a votive offering by Afinia Phieris, a *sacerdos*,

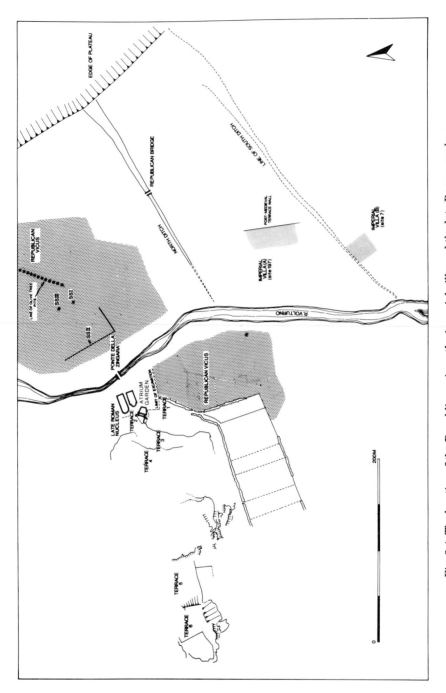

Fig. 3.4. The location of the Republican *vicus*, the imperial villa and the late Roman nucleus.

while another found before the present excavations seems to provide regulations for a sanctuary (Fig. 3.5). Immediately to the south of this sanctuary or temple was another monumental building which in turn overlooked a garden or yard. (This area remained in use as a garden until the eleventh century.) On the slope of the hill overlooking this garden, traces of yet another monumental building were discovered. Much further to the south, in the area of the ninth-century monastic workshops, traces of other buildings were found. These had been razed to their footings in medieval times.

In the late first century BC this settlement must have had a population numbering at least a thousand. In many ways it resembled the celebrated Samnite centre at Pietrabondante and the Samnite and later Republican settlement of *Iuvanum*, located high up in the Abruzzo. Beyond doubt it was a place of some substance graced with temples and perhaps a market place, linking the world of Mediterranean polyculture to the pastoralists of the Appennines.

The age of the Emperor Augustus brought great changes to all parts of Italy. New investment was made in old towns; new land was cultivated; the scale of maritime commerce was appreciably enlarged; and the empire was managed more efficiently. San Vincenzo experienced these changes as profoundly as any other part of the peninsula. A fine inscription tells us that an aqueduct was built (possibly following an earlier line) to channel the fresh mountain water from the source of the Volturno, 2 km from San Vincenzo, to Venafro. Stretches of this remarkable engineering feat still survive in the valley. At the same time the small Samnite nucleus at Venafro was systematically enlarged as a colony for veteran soldiers, while ancient Isernia was also enlarged. Why no comparable investment was made at San Vincenzo remains puzzling. Instead, the population appears to have deserted the sprawling settlement either in favour of these richer urban centres or in order to occupy new, smaller homesteads which suddenly appear in prolific numbers in the locality.

Pre-eminent among the new sites of the Augustan age was a villa built on the east side of the river, just beyond the ditch at the southern edge of the old settlement. It seems that as the old vicus decayed, a new country house was erected just beyond it. (The pattern is not uncommon in the villages of Molise today.) The scatter of debris in the soil leaves us in no doubt that the villa's owner enjoyed a high level of prosperity. Its gardens and yards must have run down to the river's edge, while from its windows there would have been splendid panoramic views of the Mainarde mountains. Several inscriptions, some of which drew Keppel Craven here in 1836, as well as some found in the excavations, shed a little light on this new community. One inscription is on the tombstone of Cn. Afranius Cn. f. Vol. Priscus Sabinianus, erected by his father Cn. Afranius Sabinus. This family is mentioned in inscriptions at Isernia, a major Roman town at this time, and suggests the villa at San Vincenzo lay within its administrative

Fig. 3.5. Inscription recording a *sacerdos* called Afinia Phieris (re-used in a tenth-century AD context). (Photo: author)

sphere, as it does today. This is confirmed by the existence of another tombstone at San Vincenzo which records one C. Herius Sabinus, who is said to have been a *sevir* at Isernia.

This villa at San Vincenzo was one of several found during the field survey of the Rocchetta plain. Small pottery scatters dotted about the plateau reveal the existence of numerous cottages close by. The transformation of the settlement pattern owed a good deal to the new policies of the imperial government, as it attempted to maximize the agricultural potential of each of its many regions – not only in Italy but scattered all over the western world. Here at San Vincenzo the impact of the aqueduct cannot be underestimated. For the first time it was now possible to drain the ancient marshes on the Rocchetta plain, thus extending the area available for cultivation.

Favoured with elements of both continental and Mediterranean climates, San Vincenzo's farmers could profitably engage in a diversity of agrarian activities. Transhumance was one element in this economy. Two types of transhumants existed hereabouts until recently: pastoralists who drove flocks over great distances to use the high pastures in summertime; and local villagers who shared the rich grass, ascending to the *altopiano* on the mountains most days. One aspect of these activities came to light when a first-century transhumance cabin for shepherds was discovered high in the Mainarde mountains (at 2,000 m), overlooking the plateau (see Chapter 9). San Vincenzo may well have profited from the long-distance movement of sheep from Apulia to the Abruzzo which began to figure prominently in the agrarian history of Italy at this date. The Rocchetta plain was admirably situated: Apulian flocks could graze here immediately before and after visiting the high Mainarde pastures, thereby lengthening the transhumance season by a month or more. The community probably maintained its own flocks of sheep in the Mainarde as well.

The inscriptions associated with the villa show that its heyday was in the first century AD. Occupation of the villa, judging from the surface pottery, continued until the fourth century. By then, though, it may have been only a modest establishment. Like all the other farms on the Rocchetta plain, the villa was abandoned by about 400, but unlike the other farms a community continued to exist here, occupying a defensive niche on the west bank of the river.

The next phase in the history of San Vincenzo was to play a formative part in the future monastery. It is not known why the move to the other side of the river was made. Possibly the first-century aqueduct taking water from the source of the Volturno no longer functioned properly and the old villa was periodically flooded. Alternatively, a more defensive location might have been desirable. The Hunnic attack on Rome, and the deterioration of law and order on the peninsula may have affected even a rural area such as this.

The first phase of the new villa was comparatively modest (Fig. 3.6).

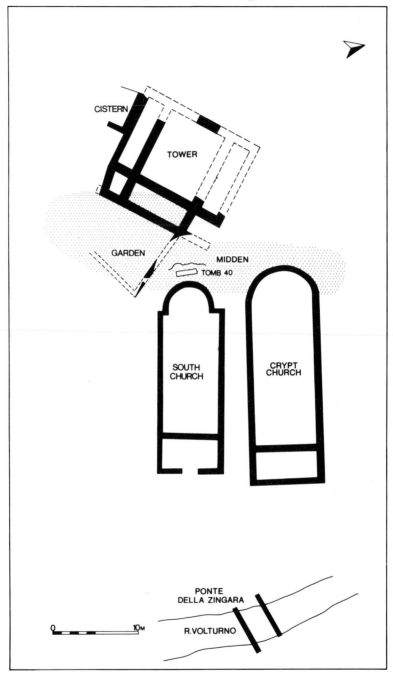

Fig. 3.6. Simplified plan of the late Roman settlement.

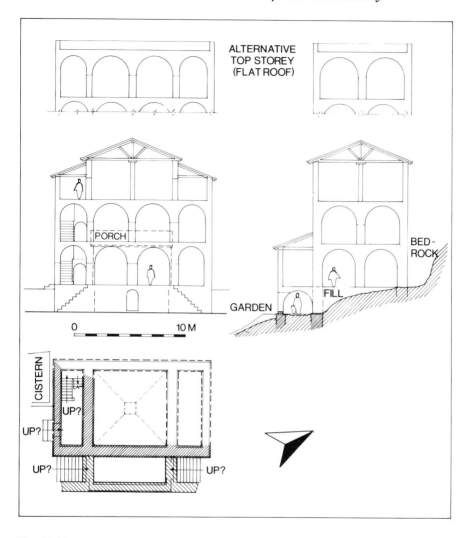

Fig. 3.7. Reconstruction of the late Roman tower, by Sheila Gibson.

The Ponte della Zingara was probably constructed at this time, mostly from re-used Republican masonry. Its low, rather primitive profile is strikingly different from the elegant hump-back bridge of Republican date across the ditch nearby. The Ponte della Zingara led towards the garden that had existed in Republican times. Overlooking this, on the slope of the hill, was a substantial building. Only its massive footings survive, but these suggest that it was a tower of a kind that became quite common in late antiquity. The original building measured 15 x 9 m and was almost certainly between two and four storeys high (Fig. 3.7). It would have commanded a view up through the valley to the east, as well as across much of the Rocchetta plain.

One notable feature of this building is the refuse midden spilling down the slope in front. Black and high in organic content, it must have smelled revolting to anyone approaching the building in summertime. (The excavators of the fifth-century villa at San Giovanni di Ruoti in Basilicata found a similar attitude to rubbish. Kitchen waste and other refuse were dumped in corridors, empty rooms and immediately outside entrances.) The valuable collection of pottery and bronze coins (*nummi*) contained in these middens fixes the tower to the first half of the fifth century. In all likelihood other buildings formed part of this complex, but none has yet been identified.

In the second half of the century the settlement underwent great changes. Directly west of the bridge, to the north of the garden, a funerary church was built. To the north, next to this, a large apsidal building was erected. Was this a basilica serving the settlement? At this time the tower was altered too: an east-facing portico was added to the front, built out over the earlier rubbish middens. Below this a small walled garden was made with fresh soil to bury the early fifth-century midden level. The garden separated the tower from the apsidal end of the new cemetery church. Rubbish was no longer disposed of down the slope of the hill. The emphasis was upon organizing a succession of spaces entered one from another, lending a hierarchical arrangement to the later fifth-century complex.

Only the foundations of the northern basilica in the complex have survived (the first crypt church). The building was 25 m long and 9 m wide. The bottom half of its rounded apse was used in the earliest medieval building. Apart from this, its only distinctive feature was a sunken entrance hall or narthex through which one passed into a slightly raised nave. Nothing proves that it was a church except for its proximity to the funerary church.

The funerary church was 18 m long and 8 m wide and closely resembles the remains of the fifth-century church found by Pantoni at Monte Cassino (which was a little larger at 21 x 9 m) (Fig. 3.8). The east wall of this building (its façade) retained part of an earlier Republican building; elsewhere, though, the construction was poor. One door was set in the east end (beyond which was a marble threshold slab) and another in the north wall. It was packed with graves, as was a small walled but open annexe to the south. About 40 per cent of this cemetery was fully excavated (23 tombs out of an estimated 60), so we have a fairly detailed impression of the mortuary history of the place. The tombs were made of tiles. Some tombs took a tent-like form known as 'cappuccino', while others were rectangular coffins (Fig. 3.9). Most contained the skeletal remains of several bodies. Almost all the skeletons had been disturbed in antiquity. Some tombs, for

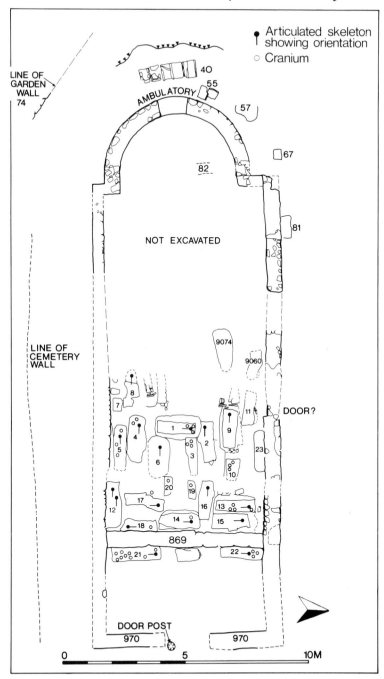

Fig. 3.8. Plan of the late Roman funerary church.

Fig. 3.9. *Cappuccino* grave from the late Roman funerary church. (Photo: author)

example, contained several skulls and comparatively few bones. Others contained body after body piled one on top of another. An analysis of the skeletons indicates approximately 25 males, 28 females, 2 unidentifiable adults and 41 children. A closer inspection reveals high mortality at the age of two to three years and again for women in the teens. The majority, however, lived until their 30s or 40s with few of the dead being conspicuously old. On balance this appears to have been a fairly normal peasant community. In such societies children were vulnerable soon after weaning, and teenage girls during their first pregnancies.

Unlike medieval and modern graveyards, this one shows no signs of one tomb cutting another. Instead the tile tombs were either set in their own 'plot' or, in some cases, a late one was positioned directly on top of an earlier one. Grave markers may have been used, indicating to individual families (or groups) the location of their own simple mausolea. Few of the graves contained any objects. Silver marriage rings, however, were found on two women. Several small bronze coins (*nummi*), fragments of pottery and glass vessels occurred not only in the tombs but in the graveyard soil as well. These objects relate to the funeral feasts and subsequent votive offerings made to the dead. The glassware is particularly informative. Painstaking reconstruction by Judy Stevenson shows that numerous smashed vessels were lamps and tiny phials – the waste of funerary feasts

and rites. The number of vessels is itself a modest tribute to the comparative affluence of the dead.

One important feature of the cemetery is the ambulatory beyond the
apse at the west end. This ambulatory was a simple passage left between
the apse and the craggy, travertine rock face. A number of tombs were
placed here. One tomb, in fact, lay just beyond the apex of the apse,
critically placed so that it might be viewed through a window in the apse.

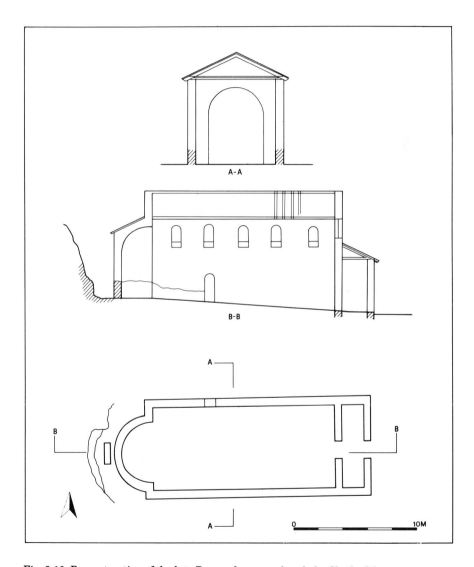

Fig. 3.10. Reconstruction of the late Roman funerary church, by Sheila Gibson.

A tile-lined box contained a few fragments of bone, several crudely worked pieces of bone and the broken handle of an elegantly carved ivory asperge with which holy water was sprayed on the congregation. The other two tombs were similar to those inside the building.

Ambulatories are normally associated with the main urban churches of the late Roman and early medieval periods where pilgrims visited relics. Was the strategically placed tomb the grave of someone special? Was the tile box a reliquary of sorts? Was the broken asperge a relic? Late Roman relics came in many forms, as Gregory of Tours reminds us. He attests examples as diverse as flasks of blood, manna with the appearance of flour, splinters of a plank miraculously extended by St Laurence, and even a handkerchief associated with St Stephen that had been dipped in sea-water. The critical issue was not the object but that a living martyr was present with the dead, articulating a progressive breakdown of the physi-cal and symbolic barriers between the living and dead. The common dead under the protection of saints might hope for resurrection in Christ and salvation in the life hereafter.

These features raise intriguing questions about the purpose of the cemetery. Did it serve the villa at San Vincenzo alone or several commu-nities in the upper Volturno? To answer this we must estimate the approximate size of the cemetery population. By multiplying the esti-mated 40 per cent sample of adult skeletons (73) by the average life span (35) and dividing this figure by the number of years over which the cemetery was used (maximum 100-130), we can arrive at an approximate calculation. The result is an estimated population of 60+. The figure must be treated with caution, but it tallies with the expected population of a medium-sized villa estate of the imperial Roman period. If the calculation is correct it seems the cemetery contains the dead of one community only. Added to this, there is evidence from the field survey of the territory (see Chapter 9). Local farmers described the existence of similar cemeteries in the upper Volturno valley. These cemeteries, we assume, belonged to villas similar to the one uncovered at San Vincenzo.

Funerary churches were commonly attached to villas during the fifth century. The high-ranking Lady Magetia set up chapels in the diocese of Sora, in the mountains to the west of San Vincenzo. Trigentius, possibly a senator, founded an estate church in the diocese of Potenza. At about the same time two court officials from Ravenna founded a similar church near Larino in the neighbouring Biferno valley. In addition, it should be noted that A. Pompeiacus of Agen, the head of an aristocratic family, erected a church of this kind in memory of his ancestors and dedicated it to San Vincenzo. However, after 500 successive popes attempted to control and license estate churches. In particular, they tried to ensure that no ordinary church could be used for burials. They also opposed the holding of public services and insisted on approving the relics at these churches. The motives of the popes are easily explained. They and their diocesan repre-

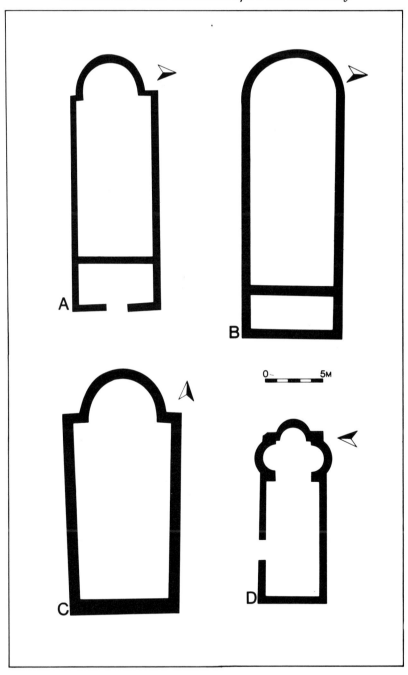

Fig. 3.11. Comparative plan of (A) south church; (B) crypt church; (C) St John, Monte Cassino; (D) San Martino di Copanello.

sentatives were trying to monopolize control over Christian services under the guise of preventing the growth of irregular cults around graves and relics. Meanwhile, landlords suffering high taxation saw an opportunity of making an income from church services: fees and offerings were potentially lucrative.

San Vincenzo fits this pattern well. Did an aspiring landlord build the churches for his tenants? The coins, glassware and evidence of feasts attest to conspicuous mortuary rites held within the funerary church. Yet the number and arrangement of the tombs suggest that the cemetery was used for two to three generations at most. Significantly, too, the tombs indicate that these people had roughly the same social standing. There is little distinction between the cemetery plots. Perhaps the farm was run by a cooperative of tenant farmers after *c.* 450, or more probably, the landlord's family was interred in a more propitious and as yet unlocated place, while the cemetery was used by his tenants and servants.

One other possibility exists: was this the seat of a bishop? The Council of Pope Symmachus on 6 November 502 lists a bishop *Marcus Samninus* between *Vulturnum* (*Paschesius Vulturnensis*) and *Nuceria* (*Aprilis Nucerinus*), indicating that his diocese lay in central Italy. This brings us back to this enigmatic place called Samnium. The only compelling argument against this is the absence of a baptistry which would have been a normal feature of a bishop's seat. Perhaps it is wisest to conclude simply that this was a villa rustica – an estate centre – the home of a member of the élite and his entourage, the last in the thousand-year line of classical communities at San Vincenzo.

The coming of the Lombards

The paucity of later sixth- and seventh-century coins supports the view that the villa was occupied for a comparatively short period. Like the contemporary villa recently excavated at San Giovanni di Ruoti in Basilicata, San Vincenzo appears to have been deserted in the early to mid-sixth century. The abandonment of both these inland villas coincides with the collapse of central government in Italy and the onset of the Gothic wars. Such estates, it appears, were no longer viable in remoter mountain areas. The Dark Ages had begun.

Late Roman San Vincenzo, however, was not completely abandoned. A tile grave in the funerary church containing a woman attired with silver openwork ear-rings can be ascribed to the later sixth or even the seventh century. Similarly, a grave cut into the ground floor of the tower containing a badly disturbed body attired with a necklace of pear-shaped beads probably belongs to the same phase. Roman villas were commonly turned into graveyards. Graves were found in the Posto villa, near Capua; and inside the senatorial villa at Settefenestre near Cosa in Etruria; and the practice occurs commonly in provinces as far away as Holland and Britain.

The deserted buildings evidently retained a special aura, almost certainly reinforced by oral tradition. The funerary church remained an old grave-yard, respected perhaps for some minor cult. The tower was seen, perhaps, as a monument to an age of grandeur. Some Christians doubtless wished to be associated with this past. It is not difficult to imagine why this was so. By the later sixth and seventh centuries, the descendants of the fifth-century tenant farmers were settled in modest homesteads occupying ecological niches on hillslopes. These places will be described in Chapter 9.

Tradition emphasizes the escalation of hostilities in this region after the early sixth century as the Lombards swept in to create Longobardia Minor – the duchy and later principate of Benevento. Since Paul the Deacon wrote the history of the Lombards in the late eighth century, their conquest of Samnium has been regarded as synonymous with the extinction of classical civilization. The reality is rather different. The villa at San Vincenzo, like many more throughout the province, had probably ceased to exist long before the Lombards began their piecemeal conquest of Samnium in the 560s. The demise of classical life and the ensuing hostilities were two manifestations of the 'most awful scene known to man' (to quote Edward Gibbon), the collapse of the Roman state.

Little is known of the Lombard conquerors of Benevento and its territory. They appeared in Samnium, as they did in northern Italy and the region of Spoleto, during the late 560s. Taking advantage of the political chaos, they usurped the disorganized political machinery to fashion their own territories. The Byzantine guardians of classical tradition in southern Italy fought in vain to oust them. Political turmoil followed, accelerating the transition from antiquity to a Dark Age. Valley after valley was conquered in a long war of attrition, as Andrea Staffa has shown. By the end of the seventh century the Lombard dukes of Benevento commanded a territory with a northern border that ran along the peaks of the Mainarde.

No trace of the conquerors has been found at San Vincenzo. Indeed, the archaeology of the Lombards in Beneventum is strikingly meagre. A newly-discovered seventh-century cemetery found at Vicenne, near the old Roman town of Boiano, 60 km south of San Vincenzo, throws a little light on this age. Over a hundred graves were found in excavations between 1987 and 1990, of which, remarkably, ten were warriors accompanied by horses (Fig. 3.12). Several of the inhumations were accompanied by high-value objects such as Byzantine gold coins and decorated Byzantine metalwork. But normal mass-produced commodities such as pottery are rare, and it is illustrative of the circumstances that crude hand-made vessels accompanied some of the dead. The cemetery is believed to be that of a Bulgar community which, according to the later eighth-century chronicler Paul the Deacon, settled near Boiano, Saepinum and Isernia in the 660s. This interpretation merits further consideration. Nevertheless,

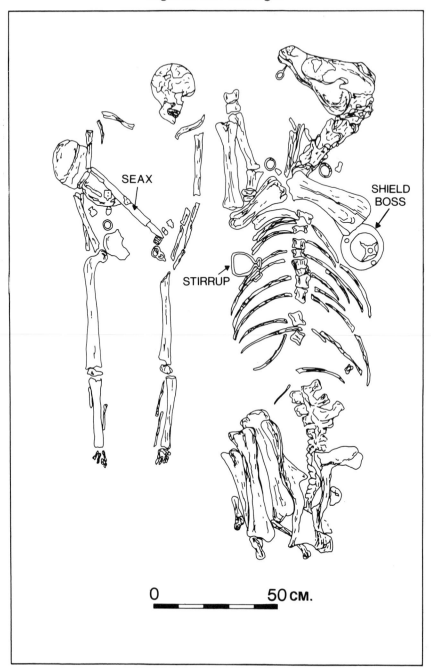

Fig. 3.12. Warrior grave from the later seventh-century cemetery at Vicenne: a man with a seax accompanied by a horse.

the Vicenne assemblage reveals the unpromising inheritance of the aristocracy at this time. Benevento itself was almost certainly a depopulated shadow of its former self. Towns such as Isernia, Larino, Saepinum and Venafro no longer existed. San Vincenzo, like many villas in Molise known from recent surveys, lay in ruins. But then, as the chronicler informs us, shortly after 700 three young Beneventans arrived at San Vincenzo and set about restoring its status. In giving these young men a large tract of border country, Duke Gisulf, the Lombard leader, must have trusted that they would bring new prospects to his run-down territory.

4

The Makings of a Medieval
Monastery

Paldo, Tato and Taso's monastery, like other monasteries in eighth-century Christendom, was a retreat, deliberately remote from the main axes of civilization. The *Chronicon Vulturnense* tells us only that the three founders set about refurbishing a Constantinian oratory (see Chapter 2). As the grand ninth-century basilica is described in the *Chronicon* as San Vincenzo (*Maiore*) Maggiore (see p. 83), the first abbey church, in the mind of John the chronicler at least, was presumably San Vincenzo Minore. The rest of the monastery remains unknown. Only towards the end of the century are we independently informed by Pope Hadrian I and the Cassinese historian, Paul the Deacon, that San Vincenzo was a large community (see Chapter 2).

The remains of the earliest monastery are modest, but quite consistent with the epoch. It is a period which, because of its architectural, artistic and archaeological poverty, tends to defy the late twentieth-century imagination. For this reason it needs to be put in perspective before we examine the archaeology of eighth-century San Vincenzo.

At this time Rome, in common with most ancient cities, was largely unoccupied. Only niches were inhabited within the staggering ruins. These were islands of conspicuous material wealth and comparative grandeur. One such niche was discovered in excavations of signal importance made by Daniele Manacorda and Lucia Saguì in the Cripta Balbi, part of the Campus Martius. In these excavations the rubbish deposits of an adjacent monastery, San Salvatore in Pensilis, were encountered, containing vast amounts of industrial and kitchen waste. Amongst the many objects were lead moulds for bronze crosses and plaques, clearly used not only by the monastery's community and visiting pilgrims, but also by some of the Lombards buried in the seventh-century cemetery at Nocera Umbra in Umbria, 150 km north of Rome. Liturgical objects were thus being manufactured by the monastery's craftsmen for restricted exchange purposes. Evidently, by the late seventh century, with the dramatic reduction in commodity production, an economic incentive existed for trade between this Roman community and the Lombards of the newly formed duchy of Spoleto. The conspicuous presence of small numbers of Sicilian transport amphorae and simply-made Sicilian oil lamps also shows that the monastery maintained active trade links with Byzantine production centres on Sicilian estates. But the poverty of the economic system is most tellingly illustrated by the coins in circulation at the time. Large numbers of illegible fifth-century coins, a few bronze coins of the early seventh century and over a hundred wafer-thin bronze and silver square *nummi* were found in the rubbish mounds. Only the latter coins were minted at the time. These crude objects seem to have been a low value coinage used by Rome's impoverished aristocracy for exchange purposes within the ruined metropolis.

Another notable niche from this era is the church of S. Maria Antiqua in the forum. The early eighth-century frescoes decorating the nave and atrium of church are ascribed to the short papacy of Pope John VII. These bear the hallmark of Byzantine influence, and show the survival of major artists working within a Mediterranean-wide idiom. The excavations of the Temple of Saturn, however, make a telling contrast. The great classical monument which once dominated the flank of the Capitoline Hill was being looted at this time for its stone. Close by, the recent excavation of the Via Argileto, once one of the great streets of ancient Rome, is equally revealing. The paved road had become a track surfaced with broken tile and rubble; in every sense it was an index of degenerate conditions.

At the other end of Italy, the fine stuccos decorating the regal chapel of Santa Maria in Valle, Cividale, almost certainly inspired by Byzantine work in Justinian's Ravenna, provide a glimpse of the cultural aspirations of the emerging Lombard court. The artist's mastery of his art is no less impressive than the evocative paintings from S. Maria Antiqua. The two sides of eighth-century Italy, however, are to be seen in the Tempietto di Clitunno, a wayside shrine – perhaps a regal chapel – near Spoleto. This pocket-sized classical temple is constructed on a podium, with columns supporting an elegant inscription, above which is an ornamented pediment carved by a supreme artist. Inside, the shrine situated in the apse is framed within elegantly carved stonework, around which are paintings evoking Byzantine connections. The eye is attracted to the details, and in particular the classicizing features. In fact much of the masonry is rubble, gathered together in the crudest style.

Yet, despite these isolated beacons of cultural continuity between antiquity and the Middle Ages, the world of towns and villas had disappeared, and that of villages was as yet unknown. For the most part it was an aboriginal age of wooden dwellings such as the simple timber roundhouse on the hilltop above Poggibonsi (Tuscany).

Further afield, early eighth-century monasteries were relatively small places. Echternach (Luxembourg) and the first, mid-eighth-century monastery at Lorsch (Germany) covered the area of a small *villa rustica* of Roman times. The Northumbrian monasteries of Jarrow, Monkwearmouth and Whithorn, the motors of Northumbrian culture, were a little larger as settlements, but scarcely the cities that contemporary authors would have us believe.

We had no expectations of identifying any remains of this enigmatic period at San Vincenzo. However, by the standards of the time, the founders made a conspicuous investment in their new monastery. First and foremost, the late Roman funerary church was rebuilt; this building lay immediately beyond the bridge over the river Volturno, the Ponte della Zingara. This, it seems likely, was San Vincenzo Minore, the abbey church (Fig. 4.1). The architect was expedient in making the transformation of the earlier cemetery (see p. 52) into an abbey church. The line of the late Roman north nave wall and apse was retained, but the south wall of the nave was moved half a metre southwards. The old Roman south nave wall was chopped down to serve as a bench inside the new church. The façade was also rebuilt, and again the Roman façade wall was made into a bench, though this time it was situated on the outside of the wall, either side of the main door. The spirit of the Roman past was conspicuous to all visitors in a cornice prised from a Republican monumental building which was employed as the base for the north corner of the new front of the church. The façade may have incorporated other fragments of Roman *spolia*, much as at the Tempietto di Clitunno.

Inside the church a friable, uneven white mortar floor was laid over the top of the earlier graves, and a dais with a painted mortar floor was constructed in the small apse at the west end. The effect was rudimentary. The walls of the church itself were brightly decorated, though the exact date of the paintings is difficult to pinpoint and may belong to the later eighth century. From the evidence of fallen plaster various aspects of the decoration of the apse can be described. There are bold bands of grey-blue, deep brick-red, ochre, dark brown and bright orange with borders defined by white lines, carrying inscriptions in large white letters. Other fragments of plaster suggest the presence of drapery in the scheme of decoration.

Around San Vincenzo Minore a monastic complex slowly evolved. To its north the basilica of late Roman date was refurbished as a small chapel. On its south side, the late Roman garden served as a natural cloister yard. The late Roman buildings gathered around the west and south sides of this garden may have provided accommodation and other facilities for the new community. The later Roman tower on the terrace overlooking the churches, now in ruins, was used as the monastery's graveyard. On the one hand, the simplicity of these remains tell us much about the community founded by Paldo, Tato and Taso. On the other, we should not underestimate the founders' capabilities: they dismantled the fifth-century funerary church and built a new basilica on the same spot.

The subsequent history of San Vincenzo Minore is the only measure we have, in the absence of material finds, of the monastery's growing status. First, beyond its west end, the late Roman ambulatory was brought back

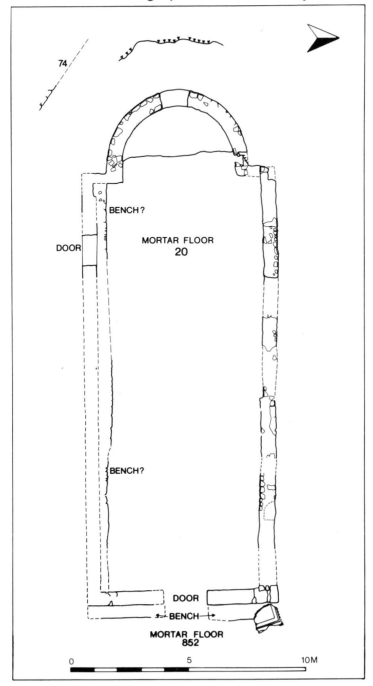

Fig. 4.1. Plan of San Vincenzo Minore in the early eighth century.

65

into use. The new ambulatory was entered by squeezing through doors inserted either side of the chancel arch. The makeshift arrangement is reminiscent of the Lombard church of Santa Maria Annunziata at Prata near Benevento. At San Vincenzo the south side of the ambulatory was blocked off by a crudely made rubble wall, its stones bonded together with clay. This pisé construction is of a type associated with the poorest peasant dwellings in later times. Any traces of a similar wall on the north side were removed by later rebuilding. The addition of an ambulatory, even a simple one like this, has to be associated with the public veneration of relics – as we have seen, a common feature in late antiquity (see p. 56). Within a generation or two of its foundation, pilgrims and visitors were evidently beginning to participate in the life of the monastery. This simple alteration is a harbinger of the far-reaching changes which were to come.

We have attributed the crypt church, built immediately to the north of the abbey church, to the first addition of an ambulatory. The new church, as was noted above, replaced the late Roman basilica that had stood here (p. 52). Like the primitive ambulatory of San Vincenzo Minore, the walls of this church were made of rubble bonded together with a clay-based mortar. In later Roman times the crypt church basilica had been 25 m long with a simple rounded apse. Clearly, this large building did not suit the needs of the eighth-century monastery. The new medieval church was only 18.2 m long and 9 m wide. By any standards it was no more than a chapel, an annexe to San Vincenzo Minore on its north side. The solidly built late Roman apse was retained, and the old and new were rudely fused together. The angle-quoins of the front wall were supported on re-used cornices from a Republican monumental building. Nothing much survives to indicate the appearance of the church inside, but fragments of painted plaster show that parts of it were brightly painted.

The next episode in the sequence of monastic building is grander than anything that preceded it. A coherent rebuilding of the monastery seems to have taken place involving not only San Vincenzo Minore and the crypt church, but also associated buildings to the south (Fig. 4.2). For the first time the monks were trying to break out of the straitjacket imposed by the arrangement of pre-existing late Roman buildings. The boldest innovation was a new ambulatory replacing the rudimentary one at the apsidal end of the basilica. This consisted of a second, splendidly built outer apse added beyond and enclosing the existing apse of San Vincenzo Minore. A hard lime-mortar, with ample rendering over the jointing of the stones, distinguishes this phase of construction. The quality of the construction reveals the hand of a *sapiens architectus*, a master architect. Presumably the number of existing or potential visitors justified these alterations. A well-known example of this type of crypt, possibly built as early as the 770s, survives at the abbey of Farfa in the Sabine Hills.

Pilgrims and visitors now entered the new ambulatory from the south side of the church. The doors inserted beside the chancel arch were

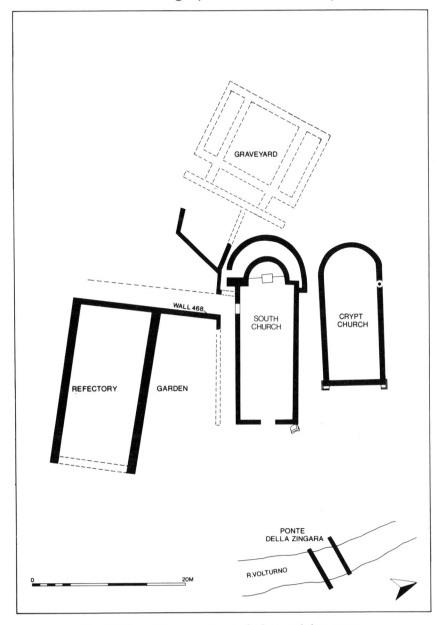

Fig. 4.2. Plan of the monastery in the later eighth century.

Fig. 4.3. The apsidal end of San Vincenzo Minore showing the remains of the painted altar on a raised dais. (Photo: author)

blocked. From the ambulatory passage visitors could look through the window placed at the apex of the old apse onto a brightly painted altar, which was probably made at this time. The altar was discovered in a broken state in the first week of the San Vincenzo Project in 1980 (Fig. 4.3). Spread around its painted base were the shattered parts of the superstructure of the altar. In the ninth century the whole structure had been broken apart by levering a crowbar through the central tunnel in which the relics had been kept. It was the rudest violation of its sacred nature, but the shattered fragments enabled us to piece together its original appearance.

The altar rose from a low base to about one metre high. Its front was pierced by a vaulted tunnel which ran through it to within 25 cm of its rear. Like many other early medieval altars, this one may have incorporated a *confessio*, a central tunnel. This, we believe, would have been the repository of the relics of St Vincent himself. (Whether this was the celebrated Spanish saint or a local martryr of the late Roman age is unknown (see p. 26). Each of the four sides of the altar bore a bold design. Small jewelled crosses and brightly coloured rosettes were set either side of the tunnel on the front. The two sides were each decorated with a large blue disc, divided into eight equal converging sectors. On the back was a large grey panelled cross. The form of this altar is revealing about San Vincenzo in the later

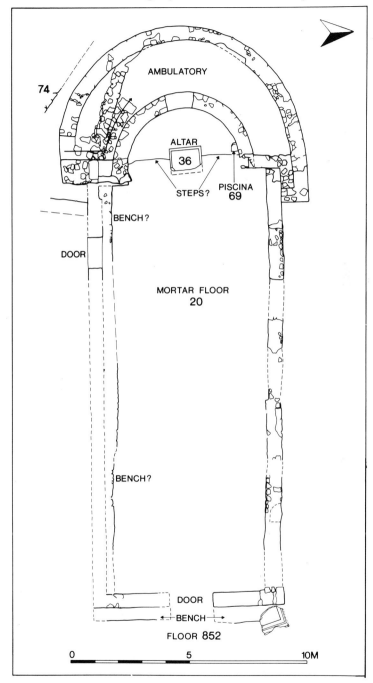

Fig. 4.4. Plan of San Vincenzo Minore in the late eighth century.

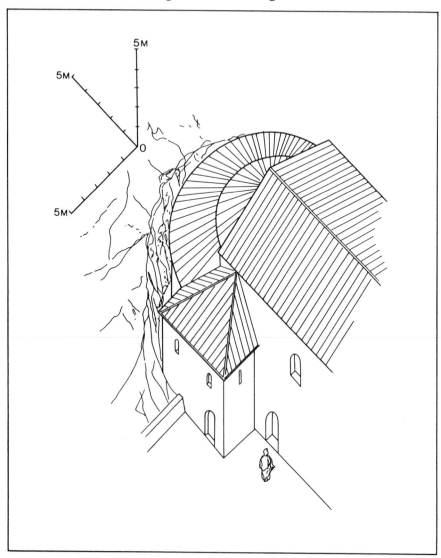

Fig. 4.5. Reconstruction of the ambulatory of San Vincenzo Minore in the late eighth century, by Sheila Gibson.

eighth century. Striking though it was, it was rustic by comparison with the elegantly carved stone altar of this date from the Lombard regal chapel at Cividale in North Italy, and the magnificent gilded example in San Ambrogio, Milan. The formal design and the precise quality of the painting are in a classical tradition. The rubble core of the altar further reflects the rudimentary nature of the workmanship involved.

As the apsidal end of the south church was aggrandized, the architect saw fit to take in hand the apse of the crypt church. The irregular Roman apse was demolished and replaced by a new apse distinguished by the same lime mortar rendering found in the new ambulatory of San Vincenzo Minore. A fragmentary scheme of painting survives in the new apse from this time, involving pinkish orange linear configurations and areas of pinkish yellow wash against a black background. From the nave of the crypt church are traces of figurative painting, though no individual can be made out.

The architect was also responsible for new monastic buildings immediately south of the abbey church. It is impossible to form any sense of the spirit of these alterations to the monastery because the short lengths of walls lie deeply buried below later ninth-century ones. Yet with a little detective work we have formed some idea of the size of the later eighth-century settlement. A wide corridor ran from the south door of San Vincenzo Minore, forming the west side of the old garden, to a large building. Only the outline of this building is known, revealed in a twentieth-century pipe-trench as well as by the tell-tale undulations in the ninth-century tiled floor of the (later) refectory. The building, situated on the south side of the garden, measured about 21 m long and about 11.6 m wide. As the subsequent early ninth-century building on this spot was a refectory, there is reason to assume that this ghost of a structure served the same purpose a generation earlier in the last twenty years or so of the eighth century.

This ensemble of buildings reveals San Vincenzo's changing fortunes. Most importantly, the late eighth-century refectory provides us with a measure by which to estimate the monastery's population. Using the plan of St Gall as an approximate yardstick we might reckon that this space would have accommodated at least two rows of tables in the room and four lines of wooden benches amounting to 60 m in length. A space would have remained in the centre of the room for moving around between the tables. Given that each monk needed a minimum of 60 cm of benching, the hypothetical length of benching indicates that about 100 monks might have been accommodated at a sitting. This figure may be a little on the high side, but it shows that the number of monks in the monastery had expanded swiftly since Paldo, Tato and Taso took over the Roman ruins.

Hypothetical though much of our reconstruction is, the evidence suggests the formation of a cloister square with the abbey church situated on the north side of the pre-existing Roman garden, and the monastic refectory directly opposite on the south side. Other buildings were presumably situated on the east and west sides of the garden. The reconstruction gives the impression of a classic monastery, albeit on a small scale. It may be no coincidence that Walter Horn ascribes the origins of the cloister square to the eighth century. He proposes that the form of the cloister owes much to the Roman sites on which many monasteries were built. The cloister

71

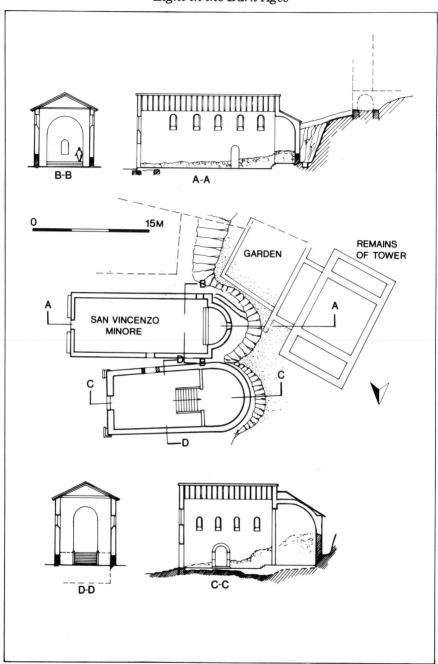

Fig. 4.6. Reconstruction of San Vincenzo Minore and the crypt church to the north in the late eighth century, by Sheila Gibson.

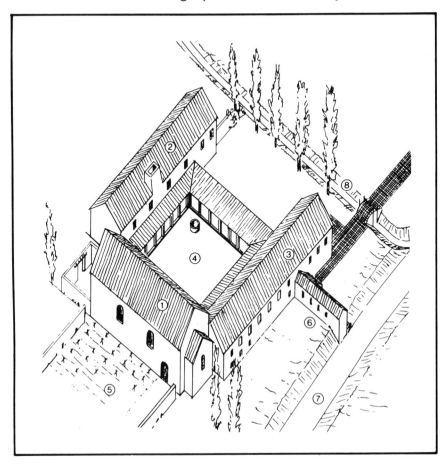

Fig. 4.7. Reconstruction of the eighth-century monastery of St Peter's at Altenmünster, Lorsch, Germany.

seems to have been absent on earlier eighth-century sites such as the Anglo-Saxon monasteries of Monkwearmouth and Jarrow, within Irish monasteries, and even in later Merovingian monasteries such as Echternach and Fulda. The earliest example of the cloister square occurs at the German monasteries of Lorsch and Reichenau. The monastery of Saint Peter's at Altenmünster, Lorsch, was built by Bishop Chrodegang, its first abbot, between 760 and 774 (Fig. 4.7). According to the excavator of this site, Friedrich Behn, the lay-out was determined by a pre-existing *villa rustica*. Recent excavations at Mittelzell, Reichenau, have identified part of the cloister attached to the abbey church. A similar relationship has been demonstrated in excavations beside Rouen cathedral. The early

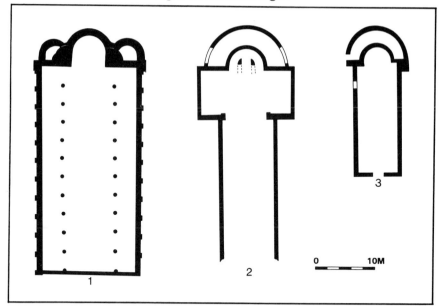

Fig. 4.8. Comparative plans of (1) San Salvatore at Brescia; (2) Santa Maria at Farfa; and (3) San Vincenzo Minore.

medieval cloister plan was determined in this case by a preceding Gallo-Roman *domus*. At San Salvatore at Brescia, the eighth-century cloister, dating from the age of King Desiderius, was built on top of the ranges of a ruinous Roman town house located around a courtyard. At the Sabine abbey of Farfa the circumstances are similar. The abbey occupied a large, pre-existing villa, and it is likely that the high medieval cloister followed the lay-out of the eighth- to ninth-century one, which in turn made use of pre-existing Roman ranges. In sum, the later eighth-century lay-out of San Vincenzo belongs to an architectural and spatial arrangement which evolved in the central decades of the century.

In 783 Pope Hadrian I described San Vincenzo as a large monastery. A few years later the Lombard historian, Paul the Deacon, then at Monte Cassino, confidently echoed this observation: 'The monastery ... of the blessed martyr Vincent which is situated near the source of the river Volturno and is now celebrated for its great community of monks ....' Their descriptions throw light upon the archaeological remains. Both the pope and the chronicler were presumably referring to the enlarged monastery with its fine new annular crypt and large refectory. It seems safe to postulate, therefore, that the character of San Vincenzo al Volturno began to change in the 780s when the monastery was granted privileges by Charlemagne. The new west end of the abbey church as well as the refectory bear witness to increased numbers of visitors and the growing

74

ADELGII · DOMNA AD
ELPERGA
XPIANIS
SIMA BE
NEUENTI
DOCTRI
CE CON
IUS DOM
NI ARGIS
SAPIEN
TIS SIMIEI
CATHOLICI
PRINCIPIS.
DEINCEPS
QUAESECUNTUR IDEM PAULUS EXDIUER

Fig. 4.9. Paul the Deacon (*Historia Romana*, Ms. Plut. 63. 35, c.4r). (Photo: courtesy of the Biblioteca Medicea Laurenziana, Florence)

community of monks. Both were features of the Carolingian movement, when monasteries became centres of civilization, renouncing their traditional roles as retreats. San Vincenzo, in short, though off the beaten track, had kept pace with architectural developments, and was evidently participating in the fermenting liturgical changes within the Benedictine world that were now generating immense controversy.

Nevertheless, San Vincenzo was by no means exceptional. The monastery effectively occupied the space taken up by the earlier *villa rustica*. The abbey church itself was modest by comparison with the eighth-century abbey church at Farfa. Its architecture was simple by comparison with San Salvatore at Spoleto or the nearby Tempietto di Clitunno. Its internal decoration was undistinguished by the standards of the Lombard regal chapel at Santa Maria in Valle at Cividale. Even San Vincenzo's altar was a rustic affair scarcely comparable with the bejewelled example made for San Ambrogio, Milan. Finally, the complex was probably modest in size by comparison with monasteries such as Farfa and San Salvatore at Brescia.

But we are making comparisons with monasteries and churches in other Lombard kingdoms. How are we to interpret eighth-century San Vincenzo within its Beneventan context? The pertinent comparison is with Santa Sophia at Benevento, Duke Arichis' great church. Santa Sophia was built as the national sanctuary of the southern Lombards, a long day's journey from San Vincenzo. This architecturally ambitious endeavour with its rich and highly original artistic decor illustrates the growing creativity and internationalism of the Lombards. It reveals the breadth of their imagination. Above all, it shows a lingering attachment to the culture of Constantinople, whose own Santa Sophia served as a model for the Beneventan church. The architecture, art and archaeology of eighth-century San Vincenzo manifest neither this internationalism, nor such overt creativity. Instead, they illustrate a Lombard norm that was regional in its cultural display, and, in terms of its material culture, as impoverished as much of Italy was at this time. Yet, with the election of Abbot Joshua, San Vincenzo was to embark upon a cathartic experience that would eclipse even Arichis' achievement at Santa Sophia.

5

Abbot Joshua's City

One of the most memorable experiences of the San Vincenzo Project occurred in August 1981 when Roberto Pozzo brought his aged aunt, Rosalinda Iannotta, to the excavations. She was almost blind, and could walk only with assistance, but she was determined to transmit an oral tradition to a new generation who cared for this place. Late that afternoon she led us through the fields, explaining in dialect that a city had existed here. She paused at one point and asserted that a great church had been on the slightly rising slope in front of us. It seemed entirely improbable. No trace of any archaeological remains had yet been brought to the surface by the deep downslope ploughing. We ambled onwards. This, she said, was the 'Valley of the Martyrs' where the Saracens had massacred the monks. Then we climbed around Colle della Torre, reaching the steep north-facing slope in front of which stands Castel San Vincenzo. Roberto pointed to a granite column lying in the field. Rosalinda paused again: this was the 'Piazza Gentile' where the surviving monks had gathered before fleeing the cataclysm overwhelming their city.

Over a decade was to pass before, on 25 August 1992, we discovered the south apse of San Vincenzo Maggiore in a small test-pit, precisely where Rosalinda told us the church had been. It was to be another two years before we came face to face in the crypt of this great church with a portrait of the man responsible for the monastic city of San Vincenzo al Volturno, Abbot Joshua.

The portrait of Abbot Joshua depicts him as a venerable monk with a thin, almost sallow face and neatly trimmed beard in the fashion of the age (Fig. 5.1). The twelfth-century chronicler clearly wanted to make him into the hero of his story. Establishing Joshua's Frankish connections and pedigree was evidently critical to the construction of the story-line. According to John, Abbot Joshua was the brother-in-law of Charlemagne's son, Louis the Pious. It was this familial connection, so the chronicler would have us believe, that led Louis to help Joshua in the construction of the new basilica of San Vincenzo Maggiore by giving him a temple from the territory of Capua (the columns of which were employed in the new church). Louis and his wife supposedly visited San Vincenzo twice. On the second occasion in 808, so we are told, they were present for the dedication of San Vincenzo Maggiore. A great deal of emphasis in the *Chronicon* is

Fig. 5.1. Abbot Joshua – a painting located in the crypt of San Vincenzo Maggiore. (Photo: Sarah Cocke)

also laid upon Louis the Pious as a donor of land to the monastery. Much of this seems to be false, a confabulation created long after the events. Louis never came south of Rome in his life, and indeed for all Joshua's rule (792-817) the king of Italy was not Louis, but first his brother and then his nephew, Pippin and Bernard, respectively. Moreover, there is no reason why he should ever have had rights in the plain of Capua. Indeed, after 791 no prince of Benevento, given the family's hostility to the Carolingians, would have consented to such a thing, nor would the Carolingians have been able to enforce it against the prince's will. But Joshua and Louis may have met at the synod of Aachen in 816, by which time the latter had inherited the throne from his father, Charlemagne. Perhaps Joshua's participation in this historic meeting, together with his Frankish ancestry, led his successors to embroider his pedigree, to account for the otherwise inexplicable scale of his achievement.

As we shall see, Joshua, like the contemporary abbot of Monte Cassino, Gisulf, belonged to a moment of great change in European history, and fully exploited the opportunity.

5. Abbot Joshua's City

The architect's plan

Joshua and his brother monks may have been responsible for the construction of the new church, as the chronicler asserts, but it seems likely that they had the assistance of an architect (Fig. 5.2). Some years previously Pope Hadrian I, for example, had commissioned the services of Walcharius, Archbishop of Sens, an engineer by training, when he was engaged in refurbishing many of Rome's churches. There is much to indicate that Joshua's adviser did not come from so distant a part of the empire, as we shall see.

The heart of the new monastery was San Vincenzo Maggiore. The old abbey church, even with its grand new ambulatory, was modest by contemporary European standards. Huge new basilicas were being constructed in the heart of the empire, of which Abbot Ratger's church at Fulda, the great new abbey church at St Denys, and the new cathedral at Cologne were the most ambitious. Most of these new churches were brashly conceived enterprises designed as much as anything to increase the status of their cult in growing competition to win pilgrims and donors. The cult

Fig. 5.2. Illustration from the *Chronicon Vulturnense*: Abbot Joshua offers a model of San Vincenzo Maggiore to St Vincent. (Photo: courtesy of Biblioteca Apostolica Vaticana)

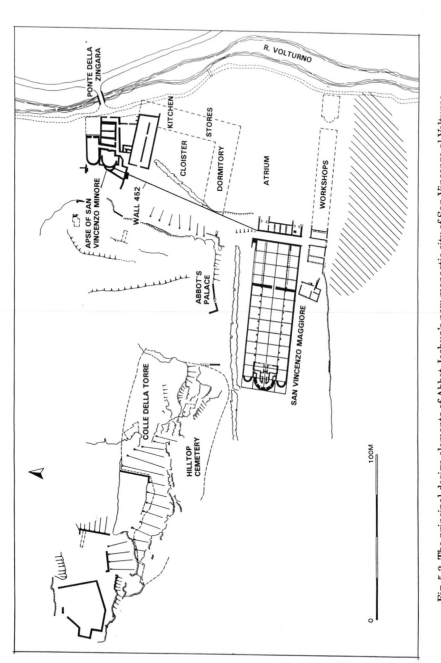

Fig. 5.3. The principal design elements of Abbot Joshua's new monastic city of San Vincenzo al Volturno.

R. VOLTURNO

PONTE DELLA ZINGARA

KITCHEN

STORES

CLOISTER

DORMITORY

ATRIUM

WORKSHOPS

APSE OF SAN VINCENZO MINORE

WALL 452

ABBOT'S PALACE

SAN VINCENZO MAGGIORE

COLLE DELLA TORRE

HILLTOP CEMETERY

100M

0

of the saints was the key to a monastery's range of influence, and consequently the building in which it housed the saint's remains was a prominent manifestation to all of the importance of the cult and the status of the monastery. As we shall see, at San Vincenzo the cult led its monks to seek its saint's remains in Spain at the time the new abbey church was under construction. New technology made the vaunting ambition of these clerics feasible. The knowledge of how to mix lime mortar, for example, was reintroduced to all parts of Europe. The superior quality of lime-based, rather than clay-based, mortar meant that building works might be undertaken on a far grander scale than before.

Abbot Joshua and his architect began with a plan in mind (Fig. 5.3). The new abbey church was to occupy the south-facing flank of Colle della Torre, more than 100 m south of the existing monastery. This became a critical feature in the overall lay-out of the new monastic city. Here, where fields covered earlier remains of the Republican period, the church would have been highly conspicuous to travellers taking the Via Numicia, the main road for the increasing numbers of pilgrims bound for the Lombard shrine at Monte Sant'Angelo on the Gargano peninsula, and afterwards the Holy Land. To enhance its scale, making it a truly commanding monument, it was constructed on a podium, set apart from the south side of Colle della Torre rather as if it was an ancient temple. (Further excavations are necessary to determine whether the complex was actually built on a later Samnite and Republican temple and theatre.)

Once the lay-out of San Vincenzo Maggiore had been established on the ground (and, as we shall see, problems arose as soon as the construction commenced), there was a reference point around which the rest of the new monastery could be planned. In a topographical sense the plan of San Vincenzo was quite different from the plan of St Gall. The St Gall plan brings to mind a Roman legionary fortress. Nevertheless, the architect at San Vincenzo created a plan comprising many different modules or sectors, similar to those planned for St Gall. Distinguished guests occupied one module, the monks another; a sector was reserved for monastic craftsmen, and so on. The challenge facing the architect was to graft the old monastery onto the new one, as well as to design the thoroughfares which connected and simultaneously separated these modules. Hence a critical feature of the architect's plan was a long corridor stretching from the old abbey church to the new one. To be more precise, it appears that a line was drawn from the apse of San Vincenzo Minore to the proposed north-east angle of San Vincenzo Maggiore. Either side of this line a corridor was created. The western corridor on the upper side of the line served lay visitors; the eastern corridor served the monastic community. In plan these long axial corridors appear to imitate the great corridors connecting Charlemagne's palace at Aachen to his cathedral. This imperial complex had been constructed a decade or so earlier in the 790s. At San Vincenzo the corridors also served to connect the old monastery to the

81

heart of the new one. In practice, the architect's plan had to be modified once the building works began.

A decision must have been taken about the design features of the monastery at an early stage. Unlike the earlier monastery, the new plan was invested with a spirit of hierarchy. Reinforcing this spirit was a complex iconography. The new plan involved a focussed ideal, as well as a great deal of collaboration to realize it. The project clearly separates two zones of social space with markers that are often ambiguous to our eyes. It was the epitome of a world of sacred liminality, where monks, as strangers to the deeds of the world, often likened their circumstances to both death and being in the womb. Emphasis was given to creating an asymmetrical arrangement of spaces, one entered from the other. This arrangement was reinforced by a hierarchy of building styles: timber buildings, pisé (cob) buildings, buildings with poorly mortared walls, and buildings containing conspicuously-placed *spolia* robbed from antique buildings – marble blocks, ashlar and mouldings. The use of *spolia* as design features within the buildings was also an important factor in the evolution of the new monastery. This involved many tons of extemely heavy Roman pieces being located and brought to San Vincenzo. (Of course, this was not especially remarkable in Carolingian Europe: marbles plundered from Rome were taken as far north as the monastery of Centula overlooking the English Channel, and to the palace of Ingelheim in the Rhineland.) There was also a hierarchy of floors: beaten earth floors, mortared floors, tile pavements and elegantly made *opus sectile* pavements. A decision must also have been made early on to decorate the greater part of the new buildings. Remains of paintings occur in all the corridors as well as most buildings. Invariably the ornamentation articulated boundaries and limits for those existing within, while lay visitors were also addressed by powerful images. The art is one of entrances, doorways, stairs, capitals and cornices.

Given the highly underdeveloped nature of Italy around 800, the logistical arrangements involving artists, craftsmen and materials must have been complex.

Following the planning and designing of the new concept, there were practical issues to be resolved on the ground. Many matters still baffle us about the construction of San Vincenzo Maggiore. Was there some preceding shrine or an earlier Republican temple in this area? Was there a liturgical necessity for a complex measuring 103 m in all? Unless we are particularly fortunate, the answers to these questions are unlikely to be found in the excavations. We can only put forward hypotheses. At present it seems that the architect laid out San Vincenzo Maggiore on a grid each four paces square. The exact length of a pace varied throughout the regions of early medieval Europe. Here the architect appears to have employed a Beneventan measure for each pace of about 1.76 m.

The builders seem to have started work on at least two fronts. The construction of the raised podium on which San Vincenzo Maggiore was built involved massive earthmoving before the first walls were raised. Meanwhile, the old monastery was renovated. San Vincenzo Minore was transformed into a palace. South of it the corridors were made, and then the cloisters were built. At the same time, new ranges and a graveyard were made on the slopes of Colle della Torre, while the river was canalised, new bridges were built, and a village for the monastery's servants was constructed on the east bank of the river. For reasons which we shall describe below, it seems that the building works probably began in about 800 and lasted well into the 820s. Joshua was not to live to see the completion of his great enterprise.

San Vincenzo Maggiore

The chronicler tells us that San Vincenzo Maggiore was consecrated in 808. He continues: 'The power of the Lord so affected the heart of the king [Louis the Pious] with love of his work, and strengthened the devotion of the monks and the hands of the labourers, that in a short time the church was constructed with outstanding workmanship and with great columns.' The church was 36 paces long, 16 wide and 12 high (to the roof beams). Inside were 36 columns taken from a Roman temple in the vicinity of Capua. A great inscription was set on the front of the church which read as follows:

> *Quaeque vides ospes pendencia celsa vel ima,*
> *Vir Domini Iosue struxit cum fratibus una.*

Whatever lofty structures you see here, traveller, extending from low on high, were built by the servant of the Lord, Joshua, and his brother monks.

The excavations show that the construction spanned at least two generations. The complex consisted of a basilica with an annular crypt in its central western apse, an atrium of some kind, and an eastern entrance or eastwork. The model seems to have been St Peter's, although the basilica itself took a Lombard rather than a Roman form, as we shall see.

First the terrain was landscaped. Large amounts of earth were removed from the western end where the crypt was set below the ground surface. Next, the footings for the basilica were laid out. Large water-rolled boulders were employed, set within a shallow trench. Gradually a free-standing podium, in places nearly 4 m high, was made, leaving a gap of nearly 10 m between the north side of the podium and the steep sloping south flank of the hill. Coursed stone was used for the upper parts of the podium walls upon which rested the large re-used blocks which formed the walls of the church. Tips of soil were placed within the podium to stabilize it. These tips contained numerous sherds of abraded Republican pottery, suggesting that the builders were removing soil from other parts of the ancient *vicus*.

Fig. 5.4. Fragments of the monumental inscription (the settings of the bronze letters) once situated over the façade of San Vincenzo Maggiore (reconstructed by Don Angelo Pantoni). (Photo: Ray Manley)

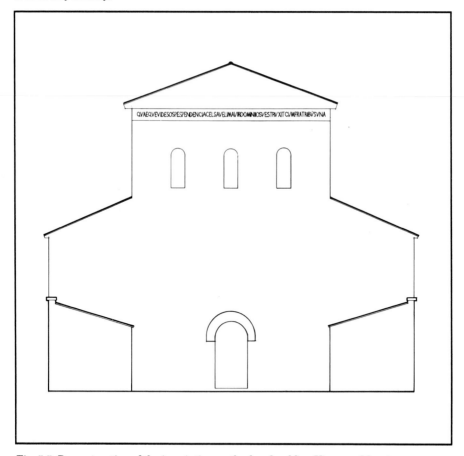

Fig. 5.5. Reconstruction of the inscription on the façade of San Vincenzo Maggiore.

The basilica was 63.5 m long (more than three times the length of San Vincenzo Minore) and 28.3 m wide. The façade wall was 1.5 m thick, while the north and south walls were 0.55 m and 1.17 m across respectively. The nave was 15.3 m wide, the north aisle 5.5 m, and the south aisle 5.7 m. Its exterior was decorated with wide pilasters set at intervals in the fashion of the age. (Pantoni's excavations of St John, the contemporary abbey church at Monte Cassino, revealed that the exterior walls were decorated with pilasters.) San Vincenzo Maggiore was built on a grid of nine squares (each being four paces square) and four squares wide. On the façade was set the inscription commemorating Joshua's achievement. Fragments of the inscription have come to light in the excavations, while others were later used in the floors of the twelfth-century abbey church (Fig. 5.4). Given the size of the letters, the inscription would have run across the entire façade, high up, under the base of its gable in the manner of an inscription on the front of a Roman temple (Fig. 5.5).

To date, the bases of two columns of the nave colonnade have been uncovered, showing that these were 0.68 m across. The distance between the twelve columns separating the nave from the aisles was about 4.1 m. Fragments of columns have been retrieved from the site over the years. These seem to have been of pink Aswan and black Egyptian granite,

Fig. 5.6. Third-century capital from the north aisle of San Vincenzo Maggiore. (Photo: Sarah Cocke)

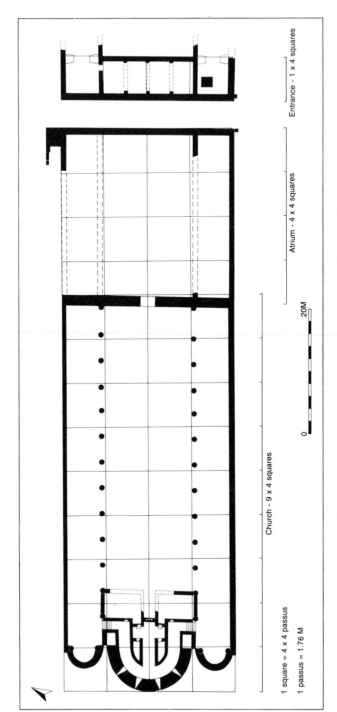

Fig. 5.7. Plan showing the grid system used to construct San Vincenzo Maggiore.

Entrance - 1 x 4 squares

Atrium - 4 x 4 squares

Church - 9 x 4 squares

1 square = 4 x 4 passus

1 passus = 1.76 M

0   20M

perhaps set alternately. A fine third-century Corinthian capital, which was almost certainly located on one of the columns which flanked the northern apse, was discovered where it had fallen in the north aisle (Fig. 5.6). Apparently, the architect's plans were flawed. The building would not stand up, and it seems that he realised it immediately. The side walls of the church, even with the colonnades, were not sufficient to carry the huge weight of the roof. An extraordinary compromise had to be made. The spaces between the columns had to be walled to support the roof. The nave, as a result, was effectively walled off from the aisles flanking it. But was this an idiosyncratic design feature? Interestingly, Pantoni discovered precisely the same use of internal division walls within Monte Cassino's ninth-century abbey church, St John.

Despite this compromise, the grandeur of its decoration, fittings and, above all, its crypt will have left no visitor in any doubt of the importance of San Vincenzo Maggiore. Many sections of the pavement survive in the nave, suggesting that it once had had an *opus sectile* floor made of a great variety of marbles. The original decoration of the walls of the church has been found *in situ* only at the western end of the north wall. From this it is clear that the lower reaches of the aisle walls were painted with at least two different schemes. The main theme was a painted imitation of a

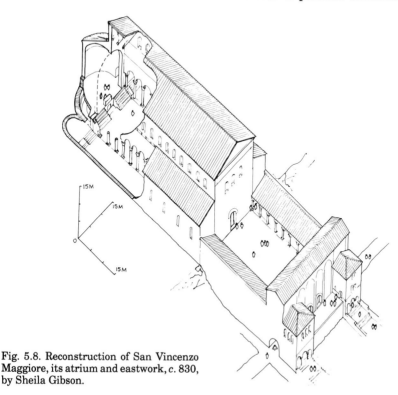

Fig. 5.8. Reconstruction of San Vincenzo Maggiore, its atrium and eastwork, *c.* 830, by Sheila Gibson.

Fig. 5.9. The annular crypt of San Vincenzo Maggiore. (Photo: Eugenio Monte)

sumptuous marble revetment in *opus sectile*: pink imitation porphyry discs were set above a frieze of inverted palmettes. At the eastern end of the wall, this scheme gave way to a panel painted to resemble a stone screen. The dado must have formed a strong and rich base to the figurative scenes on the walls above. The decoration may also have found a powerful echo in the silken hangings in the church. The *Liber Pontificalis* describes the gold-studded silks with central disks and fringes in either purple or gold, which were given as gifts to Rome's churches during the pontificate of Leo III.

The principal focus of San Vincenzo Maggiore was its great west end (Fig. 5.9). It possessed three apses: a central apse 15 m in diameter, flanked by two side apses. The remains of the north apse illustrate how the architect worked. The line of the apse was constructed out of ashlar blocks. The wall was approximately 1.1 m across, and followed what is almost a U-shape as opposed to a finely rounded curve. The first course of the apse, however, took a slightly different alignment, following a near perfect semicircle, treating the ashlar base as a kind of plinth.

Within the apse was an annular crypt, with a central passage, which the architect included in the original design. The crypt was entered from steps leading down from the north and south aisles (Fig. 5.10). The marble

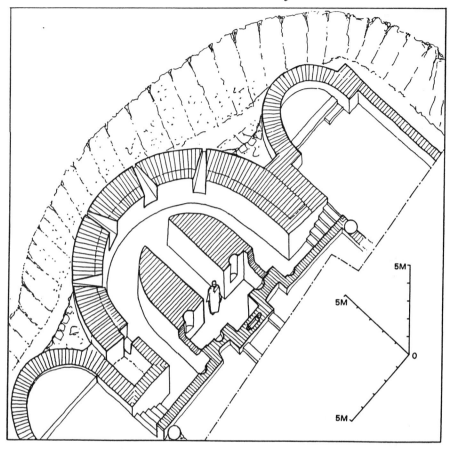

Fig. 5.10. Reconstruction of the annular crypt, by Sheila Gibson.

cladding of the steps themselves had been removed when the basilica was demolished. The passage itself was 1.9 m wide, and must have been vaulted. It was lit principally by four splayed windows. At the apex of the corridor, an axially-aligned central passage, 1.95 m wide, led back to a large cruciform relic chamber. This was evidently a point of great importance. Four almost U-shaped niches were cut into the faces of the walls of the chamber: two facing eastwards, and two opposing them. The east-facing niches had marble bases and each was decorated with a painted abbot in an attitude of prayer. The upper parts of the heads of these two figures have been destroyed, and the surviving plaster surfaces in the north niche are poorly preserved. However, the painting in the south niche is in a relatively good state of preservation. This individual has a carefully trimmed grey beard streaked with white. His companion is depicted as a younger man with a somewhat shorter light brown beard. Their faces are

89

pink and are strongly lighted with white. The eyes of both figures are for the most part destroyed, but enough survives to show that the lower parts of the eye sockets were defined as large curling areas of shadow. This, like the hollows under the cheek, is a special feature of pictorial practice at San Vincenzo in the early ninth century. Another local feature is the elegantly expressive hands. The two figures were originally named in inscriptions, but these are mostly lost. However, we can readily surmise who they were.

The presence of these figures in such a privileged location in the crypt indicates that they are likely to have been holders of high office, probably abbots. Presumably these were the abbots who were responsible for the construction of the crypt and, of course, San Vincenzo Maggiore. If this is correct, it is likely that the older figure is Abbot Joshua and the other is his successor, Abbot Talaricus (817-23) under whose direction, we might now suppose, the great project was completed. If this is correct, then the crypt was not completed until after Joshua's death. Certainly the paintings are consistent in style with this date. Abbots in an act of prayer depicted in this way are known from other ninth-century churches in Italy: there is a funerary image of an abbot at Farfa of around 800, and in Rome a portrait exists of St Cyril over his tomb, in the church of San Clemente. The images of St Quiricus and St Julitta can be seen in the mid-eighth-century oratory of Theodotus in Santa Maria Antiqua, also in Rome.

The niches in the crypt seem to have been designed to hold reliquaries. The fragments of two splendid Roman urns in white marble, with spiral-fluted decoration, one with handles in the shape of Dionysiac panthers, were found in a small room created in the angle between the central and the southern apses of the basilica. This fashion for using fluted urns as containers for the display of important relics in the early Middle Ages is best illustrated by the vase which is still *in situ* in Rome over the entrance to the chapel of San Zeno in the great early ninth-century church of Santa Prassede.

The west-facing niches were set at a higher level and were slightly smaller; each contained the painted image of a saint. Beneath these were the remains of small projecting bases for altars.

The focus of the crypt lay at the centre of the east wall of the relic chamber. A recess was almost certainly designed to take an elegant tomb, probably set within an arcosolium like other grand tombs found at San Vincenzo. Equally important was the small tile-lined window some 0.33 m wide, through which the chamber might have been viewed from the nave above. Either side of the little window were sunken niches in which the remains of numerous glass lamps were discovered. This must have been the focal point of the cult: the place where the relics of San Vincenzo were kept and where, following Benedictine interpretation of the Book of Exodus (27:20), an eternal flame provided a visual presence of God's protection.

The sanctity and status of the chamber were evident from its decoration and fittings. The complete absence of painted decoration on the bottom half of the wall suggests that it was hung with silk curtains (*vela*), as was the case in the crypt of St Peter's. Indeed, an iron staple to hold a curtain survived in the south-east corner of the eastern relic recess.

The crypt paintings reveal a complex iconography. Hurried though the execution was, the artists were bound to a structure. The sequence of panels around the walls is more or less symmetrical, with rectangular compositions alternating with roundels, or *rotae*. The composition seems to have been designed to be experienced by entering from the north stairs, and, after viewing the relics in the central relic chamber, leaving by the south stairs. The rectangular panels display an extraordinary variety and richness of motif and invention. The ornamental vocabulary constitutes a varied and subtle idiom involving a limited number of elements which are seemingly endlessly inflected, rearranged and recombined into striking new formations. On the one hand, there are certain basic concepts such as the repeated chevron/zigzag, the small diagonally divided particoloured field, and the arrangement of colours in counterchanged sequence, which recur again and again in different forms. On the other hand, there is the use of certain stock formulae or motifs, such as the perspective meander, the circular fan with concertina surfaces and the particoloured scales in overlapping sequence. It is as though some elaborate argument is being worked out in abstract ornamental terms. The artists even seem to have attempted to imitate particular Roman marbles and stones including porphyry, *rosso antico*, *africano*, perhaps *pavonazzetto*, *cipollino*, *giallo antico*, alabaster and a grey striated marble. The radiating arcs of some of the roundels seem to give the effect of coloured glass panels transmitting light which strikes their surfaces at varying angles of incidence. These discs may have been designed to compliment, and in part to imitate, stained glass screens with prominent circular designs in the church above. Many of the panels were designed around grids of lines snapped or incised into the plaster, but the inexactitude reveals the speed at which the artists were working. Quite clearly they were using the pictorial vocabulary of a well-established workshop tradition which they adapted to the newly-made crypt.

But where did Joshua and his successor, Talaricus, find the artists? The tradition is clearly Lombard as opposed to Roman, although it owes much to the prevailing idiom of using antique motifs best-known within the Carolingian Empire. John Mitchell, after studying the arts of San Vincenzo for more than a decade, favours the Beneventan court as the source of these artists. Under Duke Arichis II the duchy had flourished. The construction of Arichis' cathedral of Santa Sophia – an architectural and artistic achievement of international importance – was a manifestation of the growing power and prosperity of the region. This prosperity can also be witnessed in the lavish decoration of Arichis' palace recently discovered at Salerno. A bronze inscription was placed on its façade; inside the

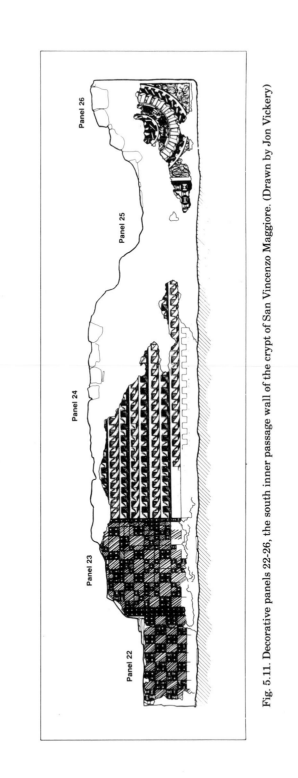

Fig. 5.11. Decorative panels 22-26, the south inner passage wall of the crypt of San Vincenzo Maggiore. (Drawn by Jon Vickery)

surviving section of the *opus sectile* pavement includes tesserae fashioned from green glass and thickly surfaced with gold. The idiom of the decoration of the crypt is geometric, perspectival and in some respects, palatial, highly reminiscent of the rich decor in the arts of the Emperor Justinian's Ravenna. A modest reference to this idiom can be found in a painted panel in the east side of the atrium of Pope John VII's church of Santa Maria Antiqua in the Roman Forum. These early eighth-century painted decorations, greatly influenced by a Byzantine tradition, reinforce the late antique origins of the chromatic illusionism. Mitchell's interpretation obviously leads us to a number of new conclusions, not least that the secular and ecclesiastical élites were sharing the great artists of the age. Above all, we can justifiably conclude, fifty years after Arichis, Beneventan artists were capable of masterpieces as remarkable as any from Carolingian Europe.

But why was the painting of the crypt completed in such haste? One possibility is that either Joshua or Talaricus had come into the possession of the bones of St Vincent of Saragossa. Writing some time after 858, Aimoin of St Germain des Prés, near Paris, recorded how monks from his monastery, then known as St Vincent, some years previously had set out to Valencia in Spain to seek the martyr's bones. On the way the Frankish monks heard that 'the body of the blessed martyr St Vincent had been transferred from the city of Valencia to Benevento ...'. Aimoin came to believe that the monks of his monastery had been deluded, because he later accepted the tradition spread by the monks of the Aquitanian monastery of Castres that they had the body of Vincent, and indeed he wrote the *Historia translationis Vincentii* for them.

Whatever the true story, there can be little doubt that San Vincenzo al Volturno believed that it possessed the body of the saint. This much is made clear by Sigebert of Gembloux, writing between 1050 and 1060, who recorded the acquisition of the relics of the saint by Dietrich I, bishop of Metz (965-84). Dietrich accompanied his cousin, the Emperor Otto I, to Italy in 970. According to Sigebert's account, Dietrich met a cleric of the bishop of Arezzo called Crisulf who had taken the relics from a monastery near the Tuscan hilltop town of Cortona. Apparently, Dietrich, much intrigued by these circumstances, enquired about the history of the relics at Capua. Here he learnt how the body of Vincent was brought secretly by two monks from Spain to San Vincenzo al Volturno to be held 'in the greatest veneration for a long time, until the monastery was devastated by the pagans, and the body of the saint was then taken to ... Cortona'. Sigebert continued his tale, recording how Dietrich decided to take the relics back with him. However, Bishop Ambrose of Bergamo had other ideas. Because his cathedral was dedicated to St Vincent, he made plans to snatch the body, only to be thwarted by the vigilant Dietrich who arranged for it to be removed by clerics to Remiremont.

The cult of a saint was of paramount importance in this period. A saint's corpse was seen as the *pignora*, literally the security box left by the saint upon death as a guarantee of continuing interest in the earthly community. The popular desire for contact with holy men had been reinforced by the gradual introduction of the Roman liturgy throughout Latin Christendom, and in particular by the increasing practice of including relics of saints in altar stones when dedicating churches. Even parish churches were expected to possess relics. A Carolingian capitulary of c. 802 ordered that 'each priest should build his church with great diligence, and should look after the relics of the saints with the greatest diligence at night vigils and the divine office'. Every effort was made to introduce a common standard as a wedge with which to separate the masses from paganism and magic. Did Joshua embark upon his great construction before he had obtained the saint's bones? If so, whose relics were housed in the altar in San Vincenzo Minore? Why was this altar destroyed and the relics removed, as we shall see, around the time that the new crypt was completed? Such questions lie beyond the scope of the sources to resolve. However, one matter is quite clear. The great basilica with its annular crypt, to which was added in Abbot Epyphanius' time an atrium and eastwork (see below), were in arrangement an imitation of St Peter's. San Vincenzo Maggiore's crypt is a close copy of the great annular crypt built by Pope Gregory the Great in the late 590s, and ranks as one of the major crypts of Dark Age Europe. The plan of the basilica follows a Lombard rather than a contemporary Roman form. San Salvatore at Brescia, San Salvatore at Spoleto and San Salvatore at Monte Cassino were smaller versions of the same triple-apsed form (Fig. 5.12). But we must not overlook the grandiosity: above all, the great earth-moving operation, twenty or more years of construction works, the transport of massive amounts of monumental *spolia*, and the vast task of decorating the completed building. The most appropriate parallel is Abbot Ratger's monstrous new abbey church at Fulda, designed to house the bones of St Boniface, and to serve as the 'St Peter's of the North' (Fig. 5.13). Was Joshua's intention to create a 'St Peter's of the South', close to a major artery for European pilgrims, at a point almost upon the Carolingian frontier, and just inside the territory of Benevento? Given the scale of the rest of his enterprise, such a vision is quite consistent with this remarkable man's energy and determination.

The builders' yard

The architect appears to have defined the dimensions of San Vincenzo Maggiore at the outset. The eastern part of the complex, as we shall see, took the form of a raised atrium and eastwork built during the 820s. But this was not constructed until the basilica and its crypt were completed. In the area east of the church, then, the architect gathered his craftsmen. A small part of this builders' yard was excavated between 1992 and 1993.

Tile- and brick-makers seem to have been the first craftsmen to have

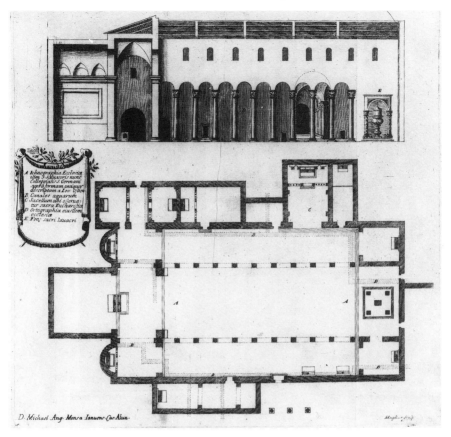

Fig. 5.12. Eighteenth-century print by Don Erasmo Gattola of San Salvatore at Monte Cassino.

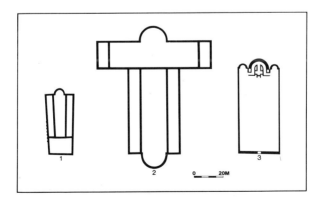

Fig. 5.13. Comparative plans of (1) Abbot Gisulf's renovated abbey church of St John at Monte Cassino; (2) Fulda; (3) San Vincenzo Maggiore.

Fig. 5.14. Tile with the inscription *Livtperti svm* from the assembly room. (Photo: author)

worked here. Sections of a large brick-built kiln with long parallel flues were uncovered. The vaulted flues were about 0.9 m wide. Roman bricks and fragments of *dolia* were employed in the construction of the kiln, indicating the paucity of materials available. The kiln measured several metres in length, and was almost as wide, with several flues underlying the pierced tile-made floor of the furnace on which the tiles and bricks were fired. Here, for example, were made the distinctive floor tiles with incised initials cut into their surfaces (Fig. 5.14). Over a third of the tiles laid in early ninth-century pavements carry script or ornament or both, and a similar proportion of the *tegulae* and *imbrices* from the roofs were marked with inscriptions and decorative motifs, all drawn free-hand into the hard green clay before firing. These record the names of over a hundred individuals, although only one tile, found in the Assembly Room (see below), records a full name: LIVTPERTI SVM (I am Liutpert). These contracted names include ALIP (Aliperti or Alipardi), ge, GVN, Io (Iohannis), LAN, Li and L (Liutperti), me, Sa, TEVP (Teuperti) and VR (Victoris). In addition, some graffiti show attempts to imitate script in a scribbled fashion. Such was the power of writing at San Vincenzo that even illiterate members of the community were emboldened to practise it. Sometimes the inscribed tiles are embellished with compass-drawn designs of intersecting circles and arcs, or with reiterated undulating lines which apparently imitate the diagonally veined marbling of the painted dados of all the principal rooms of the monastery. The tiles bearing names are seemingly set in a random sequence, with no consistent orientation of the letters. The inscribed tiles seem to be concentrated in areas frequented by distinguished guests of the monastery, and in the immediate approaches to these quarters. Fewer came to light in the excavations of San Vincenzo Maggiore. This association suggests that the monks prized their inscribed tiles, and considered them a fitting accompaniment to the richest architectural, sculptural and painted work that they could command, as a means to dazzle guests and prospective patrons of the monastery.

The initials probably belong to the army of tile-makers who throughout Joshua's age floored and roofed his new monastery. These men evidently had an overt passion for the art and display of writing. It is clear that the tilers were literate, at least to the extent of being able to write their own names. None of the hands is hopelessly unpractised, and some of them appear to have been well-trained and fully conversant with the conventions of contemporary scribal practice. The abbreviations 'ge' and 'Sa', for instance, were both made by men well-acquainted with pre-Caroline script. Don Angelo Pantoni found similar tiles at Monte Cassino in his excavations of the church of St Benedict, which was enlarged by Joshua's contemporary, Abbot Gisulf (796-817). He also published a group found in the church of S. Maria delle Cinque Torri, a remarkable centrally-planned church built by Gisulf's predecessor, Abbot Theodemar (778-96), which was destroyed in 1944. These tiles include names either spelt out in full or contracted in large letters: MAVRICI or MAV, PET, CA, IO, GISEPERT, TOMICKI, BO. There are also tiles with a prominent stamp bearing the name IOHANNES. These must have been inspired by Roman brick stamps. Very little of Monte Cassino has been scientifically excavated, but it seems likely, on the basis of these few finds, that its tile-makers shared the fashion for displaying script. Both groups of artisans might have reflected upon their shared Samnite past when tile-makers tended to mark their products in this distinctive way.

Overlying the brick-kiln was a mortar-mixing level, suggesting that San Vincenzo Maggiore, some 40 m to the west, was well under construction. The next period of activity in the builders' yard is notable for a diversity of metal-working furnaces. Traces of a small T-shaped bronze smelting hearth, partially destroyed by the later eastwork, were found. Nearby was a tile-lined pit, 0.9 m square and 0.66 m deep, for copper-smelting. Numerous fragments of copper alloy slag as well as large amounts of charcoal were associated with these kilns. A little to the west of the copper-smelting kiln, a virtually complete jar covered by an inverted bowl had been buried in the ground. This may have served as a reservoir of water for the smithing operations. Several small pits for storing materials were also associated with the furnaces.

South of the furnaces, a characteristically deep, clay-lined pit for making a bell was found. The pit was 3 m deep and 1.4 m across, similar to others known from places as diverse as Pavia and Winchester. The bell was made using the lost-wax process. After firing the bell-mould in the pit in order to melt the wax, the stone structure of the furnace, the vaulted flues and the remains of the fire would have been removed quickly, as the twelfth-century German writer, Theophilus, describes in his treatise, *De diversis artibus*. Next, the pit would have been re-filled with earth and clay, packed around the prepared mould. During the excavation of the bell pit, large amounts of carbonized wood and burnt material, including clay, tile and travertine fragments, were found. During the casting process, the molten bronze was probably channelled from a crucible at ground level rather than being poured in by hand. A clay-lined pit close by probably functioned as a water reservoir. Later this pit was backfilled with rubble, bronze crucibles, burnt clay and fragments of bell-mould. The *regione* of Molise today boasts a celebrated family of bell-makers, the Marinelli, who for centuries have maintained a foundry at Agnone, 100 km east of San Vincenzo. On hearing of our discovery the family visited the excavations and, having seen the well-preserved bell-mould fragments, declared that the ninth-century bell was between 45 and 50 cm in diameter, and would have weighed around 50 kg. In size it was worthy of the *turricula* at Aachen that Charlemagne's biographer, Einhard, tells us was built as a bell-tower in the royal palace a decade or so before this example was made at San Vincenzo.

After the metal-working period, a small workshop with simple rubble-built walls was erected in this area. Inside a glassmaker set up his furnaces. This is one of the outstanding discoveries of these excavations because we know so little about the art of glass-making before Theophilus wrote *De diversis artibus*.

The glassmaker's house was approximately 8.5 m long and 6.5 m wide. A hearth with a chimney above it was sited in the north-west angle of the building. In the middle of the building was a circular brick-built kiln with a diameter of 1.7 m. This appears to be the base of an upright structure like the brick-built furnace illustrated in the Cassinese copy of the ninth-century *De Universo* of Raban Maurus dating to c. 1023. This kiln had three stages: the furnace at the bottom, the fusion chamber, and an oven on the top. Two pairs of possible stoke holes or ash pits extended from one side of the kiln. These contained immense amounts of glass waste in the form of moils (ends knocked off the glass-blowing pipe), clippings and reticelli rods. The central position of the kiln, together with the finds associated with it, shows that this was the glassmaker's main furnace. The absence of any adjacent structures suggests that the three processes of refining, founding and annealing were carried out in the same structure. A likely parallel for this was found on the Venetian island of Torcello in excavations made beside Santa Maria Assunta. Here a large circular structure for seventh-century glassmaking was found in excavations made by a Polish team in the 1960s. In the San Vincenzo case, the kiln was reconstructed on two further occasions, indicating that the output was measured in tons of glass.

The glassmaker's workshop was a well-made building, not a temporary *bottega* of the kind discovered in excavations made, for example, in the ninth-century Adriatic port of Pescara. The artisan was working within an established tradition, which involved building a workshop of some considerable size. He was an exceptional craftsman, making wafer-thin vessels in opaque, pale blue and very pale green glass, many of which were elegantly decorated with trailing white or yellow lines. His output consisted primarily of bowls, dishes, lamps with characteristic vertical handles and small flasks. Lamps constituted by far the bulk of his output. Following Benedictine tradition, glass lamps, filled with olive oil, were used to keep the churches illuminated day and night. Lighting San Vincenzo Maggiore must have posed the glassmaker a considerable challenge which, to judge from the staggering volume of glass waste, he met.

By the standards of the glassmakers working in north-west Europe, the range of forms and the quality of the decoration are exceptional. The glassmaker also made distinctive stemmed chalices. Other examples of these intricately made vessels have been found at the port of Aquileia, the gothic palace of Monte Barro near Como, and at the monastery of Koper in Slovenia (Fig. 5.15). The glassmaker may also have been responsible for making the monastery's window panes. Nearly every building, as we shall see, was glazed, though as yet we have not found the workshop in which the panes were made.

The most striking feature of the workshop is the quantity of waste glass which littered the environs of the workshop. Normally, glassmakers were extemely economical with this precious material, re-using every scrap. This was not the case here where droplets, Roman coloured tesserae, trimmings and broken vessels – some of which are Roman – and reticelli rods were found in remarkable numbers. There were even fragments of gilded vessel glass decorated with foliate and lozenge designs in gold leaf. These are also likely to be of Roman origin. Evidently, the glassmaker had access to sizeable amounts of glass cullet (waste glass), which he then worked into vessels. Where he found this remains a mystery. But given his professionalism in every aspect of his practice, it seems likely that he had contacts who knew of old Roman sources of such waste, perhaps in Campania, where Pliny the Younger tells us there were good sands for making glass. Alternatively, the glass may have come from the great Roman glass factories of the Near East in either Syria or Egypt, which were regularly plundered for cullet up until the high Middle Ages. The glassmaker was also able to persuade the monastery's potter to make him wheelthrown crucibles in large numbers. Given the prominence of glass throughout Joshua's monastery, it seems likely that the glassmaker, like

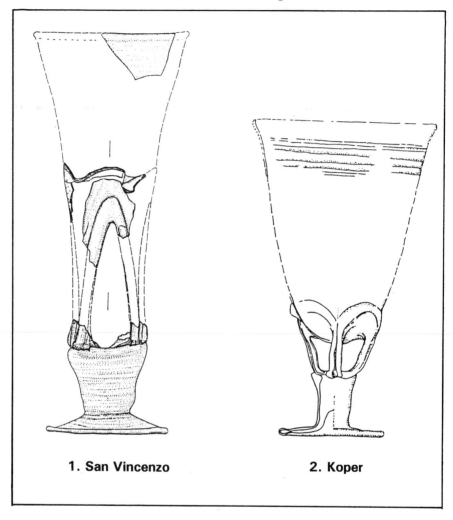

1. San Vincenzo   **2. Koper**

Fig. 5.15. Glass chalices from San Vincenzo and Koper, Slovenia.

the architect of the new 'city', was one of the great personalities of the community.

In the 820s, when work was set to begin on the eastwork in front of San Vincenzo Maggiore, the glass workshop was systematically demolished and a concrete mixer was set up close by as the foundations for the new building were made. New workshops were now constructed along the south side of the abbey church (see p. 131 below).

The builders' yard had existed for a generation. During this time the tiles for the basilica roof as well as the floors and roofs of other buildings were made. There then followed a phase in which the metal fittings of the monastery were made here. Finally, the lamps and tableware were produced in a purpose-built workshop. But we must remind ourselves that only a fraction of the builders' yard has been discovered in these excavations. The greater part of it remains sealed beneath the atrium of San Vincenzo Maggiore. Here, we might surmise, are archaeological levels of rich promise illustrating all those other crafts that were essential to the creation of Joshua's enterprise.

The distinguished guests' palace, the cloisters, the lay cemetery and the *vicus*

As the basilica was built, other parts of the monastery began to take shape around it. A new marble bridge, the *pons marmoreus*, was made across the river Volturno in front of the abbey church. Another bridge, situated a kilometre upstream, may also date to this time. As the bridges were built, the river was canalised, presumably to control the flow of water passing the monastery. The original bridge, the Ponte della Zingara, dating from later Roman times, now served the northern part of the monastery.

The eighth-century monastery situated directly in front of the Ponte della Zingara was extensively rebuilt. San Vincenzo Minore was partially demolished, and the remaining western apsidal end with its altar was incorporated within a much larger building which we believe to have been the palace for distinguished guests. The interpretation is based simply upon the amenities provided in this new complex, which comprised a stable, a store, a possible servants' quarter, a chapel, sumptuously decorated apartments, a private garden and an associated refectory. Could it also have been the abbot's residence? The ninth-century reformer, Abbot Haito of Reichenau, informs us that '[the] auditorium of the abbot lies between the claustrum and the gate ..., so that he can receive in conference the brethren without inconvenience to the guests, and the guests without inconvenience to the brethren'. Placed directly in front of the Ponte della Zingara and next to the cloisters, the hall seems to have served this purpose. The abbot himself, we believe, inhabited a fine building on the south flank of Colle della Torre which overlooked San Vincenzo Maggiore and had direct access to it.

The palace was conceived on two levels; an outer staircase on the south side provided access to the upper level (Fig. 5.17). On the ground floor a chapel at the west end was separated by a cross-passage from three simple undercrofts, one of which was a cobbled stable. Above were grandly decorated apartments. Apart from San Vincenzo Maggiore, here existed the only other example of an *opus sectile* pavement in the ninth-century monastery. The central section of the first-floor hall appears to have had dados painted in imitation of intricately laid *opus sectile* revetment in red porphyry and red speckled granite, with segments of plain colour juxta-

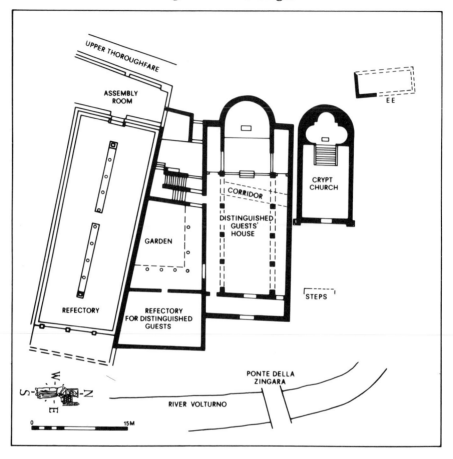

Fig. 5.16. Simplified plan of the northern sector of the monastery including the distinguished guests' complex, *c.* 830.

posed in such a way as to suggest an arrangement of cut marble panels. From the central and perhaps the eastern part of the palace came evidence of a scheme of overlapping parti-coloured semicircular scales similar to those found in the assembly room (see p. 109). Fragments of drapery and traces of figurative painting similar in style to the wall of prophets found in the assembly room provide an idea of the original splendour and significance of this room.

Along the north side of the palace, the eighth-century chapel remained unaltered. This was reached by a ground-floor cross-passage that separated the truncated apsidal end of San Vincenzo Minore from the undercrofts. Curiously, access to the undercrofts, including the stable,

Fig. 5.17. View of the palace looking eastwards, showing the ground-floor room: the chapel with the altar in the foreground, a cross-passage, and three undercrofts. (Photo: author)

involved passing from the Ponte della Zingara in front of the chapel. On the south side of the palace lay a peristyle garden flanked on its eastern (river) side by a range which we have interpreted as a refectory for the visitors accommodated in the hall (Fig. 5.18). The garden is particularly interesting. In form it resembled the atrium of a Pompeian house. In front of the guests' refectory stood a peristyle supported by re-used fluted columns of antique date. Ninth-century capitals delicately carved in fine white limestone bore the weight of the porticoed roof. The back wall of the portico (the front wall of the guests' refectory) was decorated with a frieze depicting a colonnade, echoing the fluted columns supporting the portico itself (Fig. 5.19). Painted plants, one of which was in a pot, were depicted between the columns. The Pompeian idiom, however, was tempered by the painting on the wall at the south end of the east portico. Here traces of one or two painted figures, either saints or prophets, were found. These would have gazed down the length of the portico at visitors passing from the hall into the door of the refectory. It is tempting to believe that the Pompeian atmosphere was completed by the presence of a large marble vase of first- or second-century date which had stood either between the columns, as at Pompeii, or in the centre of the garden itself. On one side of the vase was a fresh-faced Apollo. But we should not be deceived that the ethos belonged to the late Republic or early Empire. Unlike gardens of that age, which facilitated access to all the rooms around, this garden was used to control visitor-flow.

Fig. 5.18. View of the garden court with the palace to the right. (Photo: author)

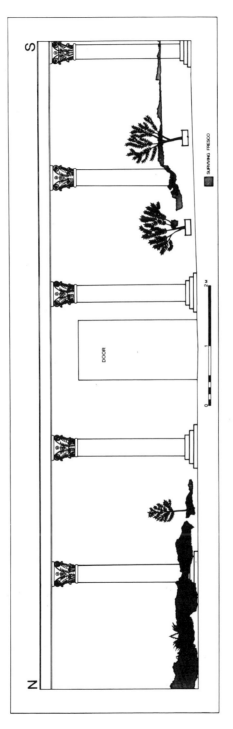

Fig. 5.19. Schematic drawing of the paintings on the east wall of the garden.

Little of the guests' refectory survived the catastrophic sack of 881. However, fragments of the painted dado feature bands painted with Egyptian blue made from cobalt. Such tiny details illustrate the sumptuousness of a room that has been virtually lost to us. A tile-lined chute, almost certainly a simple toilet, was set into the bench against the western wall. Like the other refectories found at San Vincenzo, this one had had a roof made of thatch or shingles which would have retained the warmth in the winter, and proved cooler in summertime.

On the west side of the garden lay the entrance hall and a staircase by which the first-floor rooms of the palace could be reached. Beyond it was situated an open courtyard that we have termed the vestibule. From this courtyard a staircase led up to the upper thoroughfare which ran southwards to San Vincenzo Maggiore. In the south-west corner of the vestibule at ground-floor level was a wide doorway that led into the lower thoroughfare, the main artery serving the cloisters.

The complex once again illustrates the eclecticism of the architect. The transformation of San Vincenzo Minore into a sumptuously decorated palace, given the ambitiousness of the new basilica of San Vincenzo Maggiore, remains an interesting curiousity. The model was a triclinium, a later Roman palatial form now fashionable in Carolingian Europe. The king of Asturias, for example, built such a palace at Naranço that still stands today (Fig. 5.20). The Lateran palace, according to the author of the *Liber Pontificalis*, was adorned on a wondrous scale: a marble floor, various white and porphyry columns, marble sheeting around the walls, a mosaic in the main apse, and paintings in the other two apses. A king of Mercia built a timber version at Northampton, which was later rebuilt in stone. The garden, as we have seen, was an imitation of a Campanian house of later Republican or early Imperial date. In a sense it is a classic illustration of the Carolingian Renaissance movement. The complex as a whole provides an illustration of ninth-century standards of regal grandeur. Town-houses of the aristocracy in ninth-century Gaeta and Naples tended to be dwellings of two floors, each about 6 m square. Often these houses had wings for further accommodation, and were built around colonnaded courtyards. The palace complex at San Vincenzo would have possessed many features familiar to a Beneventan aristocrat. Indeed, it brings to mind a passage in Ammianus Marcellinus' history of the later Roman Empire where he describes how the 'parasites admire the beauty of columns in a high façade or the brilliant sight presented by walls of coloured marbles, and extol their noble owners as more than mortals'. Like the later Roman aristocrat, Abbot Joshua carefully defined the architectural context in which his public encounters took place. As in late antiquity the host was raised to the status of hero, while guests, in Ammianus Marcellinus' sense, were parasites.

The baffling aspect of these new works is that the complex was fitted, often awkwardly, within the pre-existing buildings. It is almost as though

Fig. 5.20. The ninth-century palace of Santa Maria de Naranço, Oviedo.

there was not time to build from scratch, and there was an urgency to provide facilities for visitors drawn to San Vincenzo by the scale of the works. Much the same can be concluded from the excavated parts of the cloisters.

Only one part of the cloisters has been excavated. This is a section of the long corridor connecting the distinguished guests' complex to San Vincenzo Maggiore, which we have called the assembly room, and the refectory. In the later eighth century a corridor connected San Vincenzo Minore to a large building which we proposed was a refectory. Whether there was a cloister square at that time, as in the Frankish monastery of Altenmünster at Lorsch, remains a matter for speculation. In Joshua's

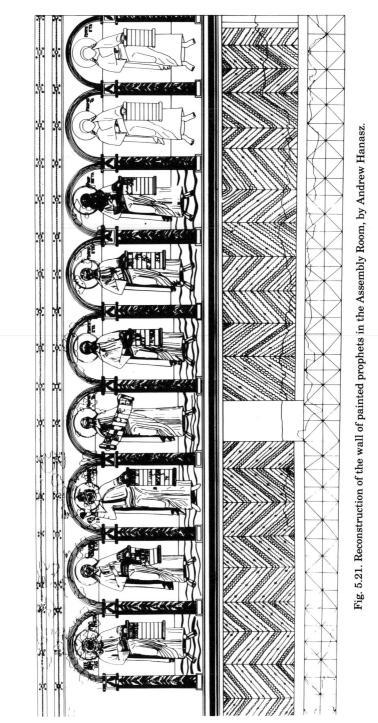

Fig. 5.21. Reconstruction of the wall of painted prophets in the Assembly Room, by Andrew Hanasz.

plan, however, a great deal of room was provided in which a square of buildings consisting of a refectory on the north side, a kitchen and stores on the east (river) side, a dormitory on the south side, with a long passageway on the west side, could be fitted within the riverside area between the distinguished guests' complex and San Vincenzo Maggiore. A geophysical survey of the unexcavated parts of this area shows that it is certainly contains the remains of buildings. The assembly room appears to be an enlarged version of the earlier corridor, created by excavating the hillside up to the wall that separates the lower and upper thoroughfares (the axial line that ran from the apse of San Vincenzo Minore to the north-east corner of San Vincenzo Maggiore: see above, p. 81). Likewise the refectory was an enlarged version of the earlier eighth-century building. Its west wall was extended into the space created by the excavations to make the lower thoroughfare. But its east wall runs on an altogether different axis, aligned to the front of San Vincenzo Maggiore. In sum, the cloisters marked the point where the old and new monastic plans were fused together.

The first section of the lower thoroughfare consisted of the assembly room, a waiting room where monks gathered before entering the dining room. The room was trapezoidal in shape. It was floored with tiles, most of which bear the initials described above. The benches along the walls were painted with particoloured overlapping designs as well as a scheme of composite squares and lozenges. Both designs were intended to imitate a revetment in *opus sectile*. Traces were found of a wooden benchtop that was burnt in 881. The dado around the wall depicted marble panelling. Even the little metal clamps to hold the panels in place were painted by the artist. The most important discovery in the room was a midden of 5,000-10,000 fragments of painted plaster which had fallen onto the tiled floor from the west wall (the wall running notionally from San Vincenzo Minore to the north-east corner of San Vincenzo Maggiore). The extraordinary jigsaw puzzle to put these fragments together produced a line of seven figures identified by their accompanying *tituli* as prophets (Fig. 5.21). Each holds a long unfolded scroll and is set within elaborate arches. The seven figures all stood frontally, staring straight ahead. Each prophet, except King David (number 5), wore a long loose garment which reached his ankles, with deep triangular sleeves and with red *clavi* on the breast, and over this, a cloak worn on the right shoulder. Certain pictorial formulae were employed by the artists. The most obvious of these formulae are the wide arching foreheads lit with a spreading area of highlight; the great curling shadows below the eyes; the combs of brilliant white lights set either beside or below the eye; the small mouths with pursed pendulous lips; and the scalloped contours of the prophets' beards. The artists have produced a vivid impression of life and energy. The differences between the prophets show that the figures were the work of more than one person. Prophet 1, for example, is elegantly painted; whereas prophet 2 displays

109

a less proficient hand working to the adopted formulae. Prophet 4 is identified as Micah; parts of all but one of the letters beside prophet 5 show that he was David; and John Mitchell has, with clever detective work, identified prophet 7 as Jeremiah.

A painted scroll from the north-west corner offers a possible interpretation of the function of the room. The theme is assembly and the gathering of the weak and persecuted, while the text displayed by the fourth prophet ('Feed thy people with thy rod, the flock of thine heritage, which dwell solitarily in the wood, in the midst of Carmel: let them feed in Bashan and Gilead, as in the days of old': Micah 7:14) reminds the onlooker of God's feeding of his chosen people, dwellers in a harsh sylvan wilderness. Both would appear to have been appropriate to the ante-room to the refectory.

On the east wall of the assembly room, either side of the door into the refectory, little survives of the scheme of decoration. From the few fragments, however, John Mitchell has proposed that the twelve figures of the apostles were arranged symmetrically on either side of the doorway, painted in the same idiom as the prophets, each beneath an arcade.

These paintings represent an important chapter in the history of San Vincenzo. They are clearly earlier in date than those in either the crypt of San Vincenzo Maggiore (see above) or in the crypt of Epyphanius (see below). On archaeological grounds they should be dated to around 800-10, as Abbot Joshua initiated his great enterprise. As we have seen, the wall on which the prophets were painted was axiomatic to the lay-out of the new monastery. As to the origins of the artists, this is certain to lead to much debate. The ruddiness of the hues, the intensity of the features with the distinctive white highlights emphasizing eyes and beards are all strongly reminiscent of other early ninth-century painting in the Lombard abbeys of San Salvatore in Brescia and St John, Mustair. But we must be cautious not to exaggerate the northern Lombard connection. The discovery of similar paintings in the church of Seppanibile on the Adriatic coast south of Bari illustrates the rich artistic intercourse between the Lombard territories on the eve of the Carolingian Renaissance.

The refectory was almost certainly decorated in the same idiom (Fig. 5.22). Sadly, the sack of 881 left it in ruins. The monks entered through a wide central door, made from ornamented pieces taken from a Republican tomb. The marble threshold, like the smaller version set in the doorway of the distinguished guests' refectory, was also taken from a Roman building. The refectory was approximately 32 m long and 14 m wide. More precisely, it seems to have been 18 paces long and about 7.5 paces wide. Modifying the earlier, late eighth-century refectory, to create the new one may account for these odd figures. A narrow spine divided the building down the centre, set within which were bases for a row of columns to support the roof. The remains of the roof, destroyed in 881, show that it was thatched and its timber framing was pinned together by numerous nails about 14 cm long. The exact profile has been a matter of debate. We have used local

110

Fig. 5.22. View of the remains of the monks' refectory looking westwards. The pulpit lay in the far corner of the building. (Photo: author)

thatched barns as a guide to its shape and volume, but a question-mark will always hang over this.

The building was floored with tiles laid on fine sand. Some 912 remain of an estimated 1,740, of which 429 had some kind of decoration or maker's signature. Benches with footrests were built along all the walls except in the north-west corner of the room. In this corner there is a gap which may have been designed for the wooden crockery cupboard (which can be seen on the plan of St Gall). A lock mechanism was found in this area. Benches also ran along either side of the central spine. The terminal at the west end of the spine was an early Roman inscription prominently positioned to attract the attention of all who entered the building.

The refectory was built in a hurry. Noticeably, it was not constructed on a level base, but, instead, slopes nearly a metre from one end to the other. The fabric of the building was poor and at several points buttresses had been inserted to reinforce the wall. All the walls had been painted, but unfortunately these were too scorched to interpret. The two long walls were each pierced by about fourteen windows. These were glazed with a combination of blue, green and clear panes, set in H-shaped lead cames within wooden transennae. Reconstruction of these panes shows that the intention was to create a mosaic of different lights, once again in imitation of *opus sectile*.

Just inside the door, tucked in the south-west corner, were the remains

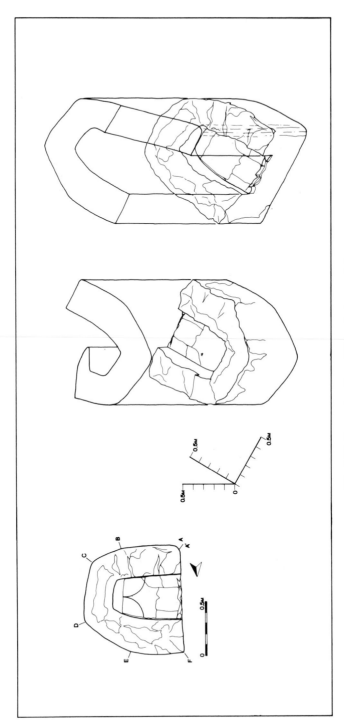

Fig. 5.23. Reconstruction of the refectory pulpit.

of a pulpit (*analogium*) (Fig. 5.23). Here a monk read to the assembled community throughout each meal. This pulpit was horseshoe-shaped, made of brick and tile which was then plastered and painted. In form it followed the pattern of late antique pulpits known from the eastern Mediterranean: a rounded front, gently bowed sides, and a straight back; and in its original state it must have risen to a peak at the fore edge and sloped down to the rear. The exterior surfaces were decorated with a striking scheme of painted marble revetment, consisting of broad and narrow undulating red veins framing prominent hollow ring-discs. The painting appears to imitate carved relief, showing that the artist was well aware of the tradition of church furniture involving elaborately carved stone panels, which was widespread in Italy at this time.

The monastic refectory in Carolingian times was intended to accommodate the entire ecclesiastical community at mealtimes. The plan of St Gall places the abbot's table close to the pulpit and has sufficient tables for 120 monks, and yet more space for visiting monks. As is stated on the plan: 'Haec domus adsistit cunctis qua porgitur aesca' (This hall, where the food is laid out, has a place for everyone). The refectory at San Vincenzo could easily have accommodated two long tables either side of the central spine that divided the room. Benches on either side of these tables as well as those along the walls would have provided sufficient seating for 335-40 monks, a community more than twice the size of St Gall (Fig. 5.24). The thatched roof has been the subject of some debate as such buildings are uncommon in Italy in modern times. In Ardo's biography of St Benedict of Aniane, emphasis is given in the description of his monastery to its 'simple walls and the use of straw to cover the roofs' as an illustration of the monk's humility in an era of grandiose building. At San Vincenzo the use of thatch as an expression of humility is hardly tenable. More practical

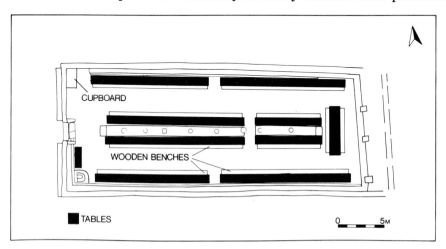

Fig. 5.24. Reconstruction of the seating in the refectory.

explanations need to be sought. Above all, this type of building retained the heat in winter. At the same time a thatched building was easy to construct, as all the materials were readily available (Fig. 5.25). This would have been a significant factor if the number of monks grew rapidly to several hundred in a short space of time.

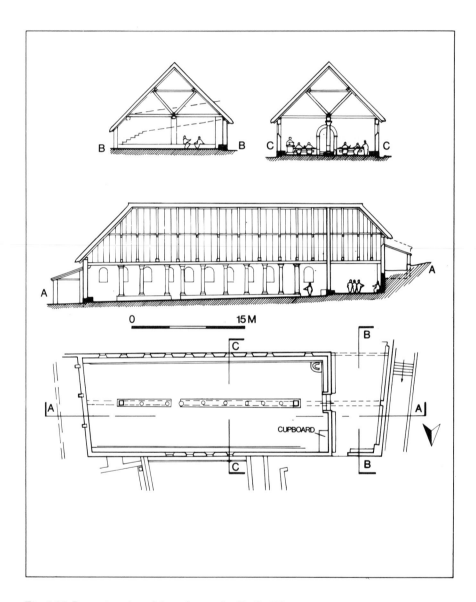

Fig. 5.25. Reconstruction of the refectory, by Sheila Gibson.

Fig. 5.26. Two rock-cut arcosolia in the hilltop cemetery. (Photo: Catherine Coutts)

We must imagine that the kitchen and stores alongside the river, and the dormitory to the south were constructed in the same frenzy of building. The drop of 80 cm in the floor level from one end of the refectory to the other, as well as the bowed walls and poor quality wall-construction, reinforced with buttresses in places, illustrates a haste to make provision for the new community.

Many other traces of the monastery belong to this era. A terrace further up the east-facing slope behind the thoroughfares almost certainly dates to this age, as does a large building overlooking San Vincenzo Maggiore, quite possibly the abbot's residence. Further up the hill is a large, sprawling cemetery. This appears to have evolved around two prominent rock-cut arcosolia (Fig. 5.26). Hundreds of graves have been found here, many of them grouped together in small cells. The small-scale excavations of the cemetery have brought to light a minimum of 76 skeletons belonging to males, females and juveniles. Only one infant has so far been discovered. Given this range of individuals, it seems probable that this was the cemetery for the monastery's lay population, situated where it might overlook the new basilica as well as the fields they had worked on the Rocchetta plain. Yet further remains of a church and associated buildings have been found on the summit of the hill. The hilltop was certainly terraced at this time, making it appear almost like an acropolis.

More of the monastery has been found on the east bank of the river. A scatter of ninth-century debris, including pottery and window glass, has come to light in the ploughsoil between a point opposite the Ponte della Zingara and the likely location of the *pons marmoreus*. Yet further remains have been discovered in the area of the present abbey, towards the eastern edge of the Rocchetta plain. Immediately south of the Republican ditch (see p. 45), in two excavations made within the precinct of the twelfth-century abbey, evidence of large post-built structures has been found. Post-holes were also discovered during excavations within the abbey church itself. The post-holes vary considerably in size from 0.15 m to around 1 m in depth with a similar range of diameters. Most have either a U-shape or funnel-shaped profile. The structures were orientated on a north-east to south-west axis. The irregularity of the building method brings to mind the barns used in the locality until recently, as well as the poorly constructed Dark Age timber buildings at Luni (Liguria), Montarrenti and Poggibonsi (Tuscany) and Piadena (Lombardy). Timber buildings in Italy were primitive structures in comparison to the precisely made dwellings of the Anglo-Saxon, Danish, Frisian or Carolingian world. These post-built buildings appear to cover several hectares. As yet no floor surfaces or associated features have been found, and it will be some time before we have fully analysed these remains. A few sherds of ninth-century pottery pinpoint the chronology of these buildings, which are probably barns or animal sheds. Similar buildings were found when the Carolingian *vicus* of the abbey of St Denys near Paris was excavated some years ago. The topography of the village of servants who provided the vital support for the monastery at San Vincenzo remains to be reconstructed. The first intriguing indications suggest that the servants lived close to the river, while their barns lay grouped in the area behind the village. Traces of a mill, found beneath the Republican bridge over the rock-cut ditch, may also date from this era. A monastic community of more than three hundred necessitated a lay community of a similar size, comprising the dwellings of dozens of families – the *pars rusticus*. The archaeology of the dwellings of these families, now that we have discovered their tombs, will provide an invaluable counterpoint to the archaeology of the monastery. Here, after all, those who featured in the history of the age encountered those who have left no written record.

Joshua's achievement

The new monastery covered between six and ten hectares. Its population probably increased from a hundred or so in the late eighth century to as many as five hundred or even a thousand strong by *c*. 820. The new community was probably gathered from all over central Italy, and perhaps further afield as well. The aristocracy probably provided their sons as monks, while new servants were acquired along with the many donations of estates that Joshua received in the early ninth century. The size of the new community necessitated the alacrity with which the architect set about his work. The accommodation for the distinguished guests who, as patrons, furnished San Vincenzo with its new-found wealth was an essential pre-requisite to sustaining the mighty ambition of completing San Vincenzo Maggiore. Another essential pre-requisite was the provision of amenities to house and feed the community. The new plan, therefore, involved expedient decisions as well as bold, inventive ones. While San Vincenzo Maggiore was constructed from scratch, makeshift alterations were made to the old monastery, and at the same time the cloisters were hurriedly reconstructed. The vital ingredient in this enterprise was a group of skilled professionals who provided the decoration, the floors, the glassware, the tiles and, in all probability, the books that underpinned Joshua's ambitious intentions.

It is tempting to compare Abbot Joshua's enterprise with the ill-fated attempt by Abbot Ratger to rebuild Fulda. Ratger's grandiose plans were eventually thwarted by his community who felt that they were excessive and extreme. But, as we have seen, the basilica of San Vincenzo Maggiore was only one aspect of the new plan. In effect, Joshua set out to build a city. In size and complexity it brings to mind the great monasteries of later Merovingian and Carolingian France. Contemporary chroniclers describe Fontanella (St Wandrille), St Riquier (where in 831, 2,500 houses were grouped into specialized quarters around the monastery) and St Denys as monastic cities with numerous chapels and shrines as well as quarters for craftsmen and servants. *Eulogimenopolis*, the suburb at the foot of the hill crowned by Monte Cassino, is a likely Italian parallel nearer to San Vincenzo. The result, however, was no less impressive than the new papal towns such as Centocelle which date to the mid-ninth century, or the Beneventan new town of Sicopolis near Capua, founded at the same time. The effect was to transform the eighth-century retreat into a centre of civilization, putting San Vincenzo on the international stage as one of the great places of Carolingian Europe.

6

San Vincenzo at its Zenith

Good fortune served Abbot Epyphanius. His portrait, identified by a painted inscription, survives in the crypt of the palace chapel (Fig. 6.1). The figure kneels in a supplicatory pose before Christ. The artist shows him as tonsured and bearded with large, melancholic eyes. This is not a portrait in the modern sense, but it is recognizably a tall, young to middle-aged man. The artist has taken care to emphasize the features of his face, the folds of his garments and the demeanour of an important, living person. By contrast, a deacon depicted in an adjacent panel of the cycle of paintings is almost a caricature of a monk. Similarly, the crucifixion towering above Epyphanius is strikingly painted, as are the nativity

Fig. 6.1. Abbot Epyphanius (824-42). (Photo: James Barclay Brown).

and the martrydom of St Lawrence, but the figures are plainly stereotypes, as are the line of Vestal Virgins and the archangels which grace other parts of the crypt. Their pale faces stare directly at us without a hint of the individual highlighting – the thick streaking of white paint – that distinguishes the abbot.

Abbot Epyphanius took office in 824. Unlike his eminent forebears, he was from Marsica, the region to the north. Clearly, he was familiar with San Vincenzo, its European strategy and its Beneventan power-base. In less than a decade he had enlarged the monastery's properties still further. As we have seen (p. 33), the chronicler records that he built two churches in the monastery. But it is his completion of the monuments of Joshua's age which must have caught the imagination of visitors.

The completion of San Vincenzo Maggiore

Abbot Epyphanius presided over the completion of San Vincenzo Maggiore. The basilica itself had been completed by Epyphanius' predecessor, Talaricus; the next stage in the project was the creation of an atrium and entrance modelled upon St Peter's (Fig. 6.2). As yet only the entrance leading to the atrium has been excavated; the atrium itself awaits investigation.

The atrium was designed as a square structure of approximately four squares (each of four paces) which was butted up against the basilica. East of this lay a ground-floor corridor which connected the upper thoroughfare to the workshops created by Epyphanius along the south side of San Vincenzo Maggiore (see below). West of the corridor lay the porters' lodges. The exact arrangement of this complicated conclusion to Joshua's project will remain a matter of debate insofar as the demolition team in the late eleventh century removed several features critical to our interpretation.

The architect began his work in this area by demolishing the workshops in the builders' yard described in Chapter 5. Next, the foundations of the the atrium were laid out. Large boulders were deployed for the first course, just as they had been for the basilica. The foundations extended from the front of the basilica and ran up to a north-south line where the east wall of the glass workshop had been situated – a line which was to become the façade of the imposing eastwork. No account was taken at this stage of constructing the north-south ground-floor corridor which was to connect the nucleus of the monastery to the workshops. Next the architect worked on two separate building blocks: the square atrium, and the façade comprising three elements: a raised landing and two flanking porters' lodges. Eventually, the architect fused together the two building blocks by constructing some kind of entrance immediately behind the façade over the top of the corridor, creating a tunnel at ground level and the eastwork above it.

A large courtyard almost certainly lay in front of the complex in the area

119

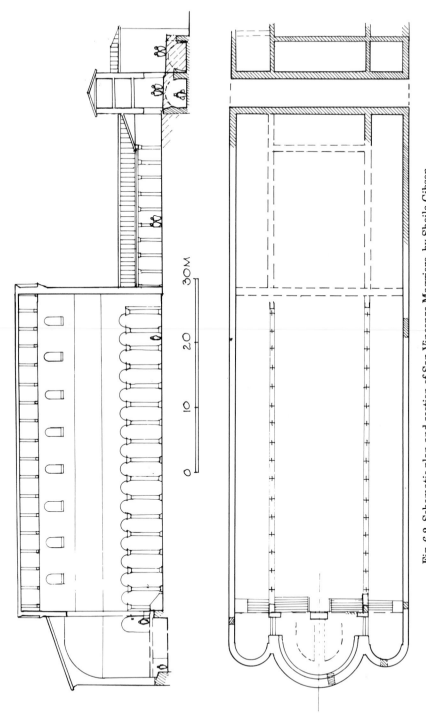

30M

20

10

0

Fig. 6.2. Schematic plan and section of San Vincenzo Maggiore, by Sheila Gibson.

between the church and the river Volturno. We are not certain how those approaching the church were separated, but it seems likely that monks entered by way of the north porter's lodge, whereas pilgrims entered through the south porter's lodge. A painted canopy extended beyond the door of the north porter's lodge; a dentilated Corinthian cornice was used as the lintel of the door itself. As one entered, on either side of the door, were small triangular hearths. The decor once again reinforced a sense of grandeur: painted panels imitating marble veneering ran around the walls. The western half of the room was filled by a staircase supported on a vault, which took one up to an exterior landing directed in front of the façade. Much the same arrangement existed in the south porter's lodge. A line of pilasters decorated the façade, just as pilasters decorated the exterior walls of the basilica. We have no evidence of the doors leading into the complex, nor of the building situated over the ground-floor corridor. The corridor is strongly reinforced at its north and south ends, suggesting that it had supported a powerfully made vault. In Sheila Gibson's reconstruction (Fig. 6.2), we have proposed a narrow entrance chapel layer directly behind the façade, beyond which lay an atrium with flanking porticoes.

Remains of the upper parts of the south wall of the atrium show that this supported a monumental dentilated cornice. The effect would have been imposing – a massive version of the dentilated cornice along the sides of the eighth-century Tempietto di Clitunno, near Spoleto, where the intention was to re-create the ethos of an ancient temple. A rise of more than four metres separated the old ground surface from the ground level in front of the atrium.

The architect created this raised contained space for a purpose. Much of it was used as a graveyard for the monks, buried in layers. At least four layers of tombs have been identified, indicating that hundreds, if not thousands of the monastic community were interred here during the ninth century. To those who had known the earlier abbey church, San Vincenzo Minore, with its associated cemetery beyond its apse, the adoption of the new cult of the dead by the living – a Carolingian fashion – would have been most apparent. This was the 'paradise', mentioned by the chronicler, directly in front of the holy shrine to St Vincent. All in all, in an age noted for its undistinguished timber construction, it called for an ambitious feat of engineering to conclude Joshua's project.

The architect's models for this ambitious project were close at hand. The author of the *Chronica monasterii Casinensis* describes an entrance chapel in front of the atrium before the ninth-century church of San Salvatore at Monte Cassino. In his excavations of St Benedict's shrine on the summit of Monte Cassino, Don Angelo Pantoni discovered a cemetery directly in front of the façade of Abbot Gisulf's early ninth-century abbey church. Nevertheless, we must look to Rome for the source of this architectural arrangement. A drawing of St Peter's by Martin van Heemskerck of 1532-35 depicts a high vestibule in front of the atrium leading to the Constantinian basilica. Closer inspection shows a flight of steps leading to the landing in front of the vestibule. A high central doorway was set within three wall arches, possibly part of a lost vaulted porch. Above the the door was a mosaic donated by Pope Paul I. The vestibule itself was tall and narrow, and contained a chapel, Santa Maria in Turri. This entrance, although overshadowed by the basilica, nevertheless made a grandiose initial impression and served as the first shrine in the complex constellation of shrines culminating in the relics of the saint held in the crypt.

The completion of the monastic city

Elsewhere in the monastery the architect deployed the same techniques used in completing San Vincenzo Maggiore. For example, the distinguished guests' palace was completed with several grandiose additions, in which the use of vaulting occurs for the first time. Similarly, the complex access to the atrium may have provided ideas for rearranging access to the upper and lower thoroughfares at the north end of the monastery.

The alterations to the palace for distinguished guests probably occurred because the relics in the altar of San Vincenzo Minore could now be transfered to the new basilica of San Vincenzo Maggiore. This offered the occasion for large-scale changes. The eighth-century altar was rudely demolished: a crow-bar was inserted into the relic-chamber, presumably after the relics had been removed, and the upper part of the altar was ripped away from the lower. The painted altar, only three generations old, was consigned to oblivion. Tips of rubble were then thrown over the broken parts. Images evoking memorial were commonplace in the new monastery, and it is strange to see the insensitive way in which this special monument – the container of the monastery's cult – was treated.

The old apsidal end of the palace was levelled off to the height of the first floor in its nave. Then a new, third apse was constructed which reached onto the terrace above. This necessitated demolishing part (if not all) of the old late Roman tower (used as a graveyard in the eighth century), once situated on this terrace. The third apse would have dominated the northern roofline of the monastery. Attached to it, on its north side, was a small tower. The ground floor accommodation was altered too. Vaulting was inserted to support the first-floor apartments. The central ground-floor room which once served as a stable was walled in. With these alterations, the ground-floor accommodation and stabling was probably transferred to a new range built immediately north of the crypt church.

Alterations were made to the other parts of the guests' complex. A bench was added to the eastern portico beside their garden. A colourful scrolling plant was painted along its length, with large round red flowers (or fruit) and two-lobed heart-shaped flowers like those in the crypt of the crypt church. Opposite the guests' garden, alterations were made to the en-

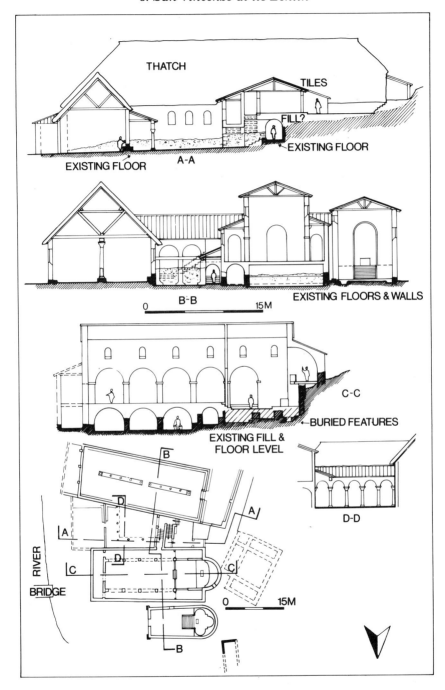

Fig. 6.3. The distinguished guests' complex and refectory, *c.* 830.

123

trance hall, the main access to the distinguished guests' apartments. The early ninth-century entrance hall to the palace was aggrandized with a new façade. At ground floor level this was decorated with two blind arcades. Above, to judge from a fallen arch preserved beneath the rubble of a later destruction, were three arches at first-floor height extending between the monks' refectory and the palace. These echoed the lower arches, but almost certainly contained windows, giving the appearance of a loggia. The building now resembled the grand façade of San Vincenzo Maggiore. A parallel for this portico has come to light in recent excavations in the forum of Nerva in Rome, where a similar four-arched portico was added to a ninth-century building alongside the Via Argileto.

The vestibule, the small courtyard beyond the entrance hall, connecting the cloisters to the distinguished guests' complex, was remodelled. The open courtyard was made into a room, and as in Joshua's time, no wall went undecorated. Visitors passing between the cloisters and distinguished guests' complex now traversed a covered yard. Rather more ambitiously a first-floor passage bridged the vestibule. Lay visitors could now go from the first-floor of the entrance hall (and thus the first floor apartments of the palace) directly to the upper thoroughfare in the direction of San Vincenzo Maggiore. In the centre of the vestibule, dominating the floor, was a decorated tomb. The tomb was closed by five re-used blocks of building stone, three bearing traces of painted plaster. An inscription served as the head of the grave: a large floor tile had been purloined for this purpose and on it was a cross flanked by three lines of roughly incised lettering which read: CRVX XPI CONFVSIO DIABOLI EST ('The cross of Christ is the confusion of the devil'). It was the work of an inexperienced scribe: initially he omitted the A of Diaboli and subsequently had to convert the B into an A, eliding the B with the A before inserting a small pointed O onto the slant in the space between B and L.

From the fragments of painted plaster found in this room, we can deduce that the vestibule had been splendidly decorated. Close to the corner of the room had stood a fresh-faced saint (Fig. 6.4). He was one of at least two saints dominating this space, each of whom carried a bejewelled book. His head is surrounded by a large yellow halo. His title and name would have been painted close by; but the surviving fragments offer us no clue. The saint's red eyes stare out beneath steeply arched brows. His nose and mouth are concisely defined, as in the portrait of Epyphanius. The face is modelled with a soft purplish brown and thick brushstrokes form a brilliant impasto. His tunic is striped with blue and white, and in his left hand he holds a large book on the cover of which are five great jewels in pearled settings. Parallels for this figure can be found in many paintings from Rome and central Italy. The image of San Prosper in the lower church of San Clemente, Rome, and the figures of St John and St Paul from Santa Maria in Via Lata, Rome, bear a passing resemblance to it. Even to the uneducated eye it is clear that this colourful figure was

Fig. 6.4. Head of a young saint from the vestibule, *c.* 830. (Photo: John Mitchell)

125

painted in a different tradition from the ruddy coloured prophets who gazed flat-facedly outwards across the adjacent assembly room in the lower thoroughfare. In the new paintings the artists used a wide range of colour to attract attention.

The art of the age of Epyphanius is best judged by the crypt in the crypt church, the little church situated on the north side of the palace. The celebrated crypt, in which Abbot Epyphanius' portrait is to be found, belongs to the remodelling of the distinguished guests' complex. The crypt was entered on its south side by a narrow door. Recent restoration demonstrated that the crypt was not hewn out of the rock, as was once thought, but constructed of ashlar and rubble. It has a tricorn shape which irregularly imitates the tricorn presbytery above (see below). The cycle of paintings is beautifully preserved; below it is a painted dado which boldly imitates the marbling found commonly in the excavations. Here the medieval imagination in all its complexity can be confronted. We are witnessing the apocalypse, as defined by Abbot Ambrosius Autpert in his eighth-century treatise, *Expositio in Apocalypsin.*

On first entering the visitor instinctively glances up at the vault above the stairs. Confronting us are the remains of a large figure seated within a red double mandorla against a blue sky filled with stars. This figure is often identified with the risen Christ. He stretches out his left hand towards a book which is held up to him by a second, smaller, individual. On the wall immediately ahead of the steps are two virgin martyrs holding crowns, and four more virgins process along the wall ahead. These were originally identified by inscriptions, but only the name of Anastasia, second in the line, has survived. On the wall opposite is an image of the Virgin Mary, crowned and regally robed, seated on a throne, with the child Christ sitting before her. A small figure, probably a deacon, kneels before the Virgin and grasps her left foot in adoration.

A large figure of Christ seated on a sphere fills the vault where the three arms meet at the centre of the crypt. In the apex of the vault of the western arm, the principal axial arm of the crypt, the Virgin Mary is shown a second time seated on a magnificent jewelled throne. Below her, in the rounded apsidal end of this arm of the crypt, is an archangel holding a sceptre. Below him is a diminutive figure dressed in a long red garment in suppliant attitude. Facing the apse is a deep arched niche (or arcosolium similar to that in the crypt of San Vincenzo Maggiore) lit by a narrow, rectangular *confessio* window. Here the Annunciation is depicted with the archangel Gabriel and Mary separated by a little window. On the two flanking walls the Nativity is represented in two parts. On the northern wall Mary reclines on a bed and Joseph sits beside her. On the southern wall are two scenes: above, the Child Christ is depicted wrapped in swaddling clothes; below, two midwives bathe him in a large chalice-like bath.

The cycle on the northern arm of the crypt is the most familiar. On the east wall is a crucifixion flanked by Mary and St John, with Abbot Epyphanius kneeling in supplication at the foot of the cross. Beyond this is a deep round-headed niche above which the crowned figure of Jerusalem sits weeping. Behind the figure of Jerusalem is the Resurrection, two Marys who approach an angel seated before the Holy Sepulchre. Further along is a standing figure of Christ. On the wall opposite the martyrdoms of St Laurence and St Stephen are vividly depicted. Another niche separates the two violent martyrial scenes; in it stands another deacon, his hands raised in an attitude of prayer. Finally, high up at the end of this arm of the crypt, beside the round-headed splayed window is the Right Hand of God, signifying the active part played by God in all the services held here.

The programme is obviously complex. One likely interpretation is that this is an Apocalyptic epiphany, in which a dead person stands before the Almighty, in the person of the angel of Revelation 7:1-3, who will set a seal on his/her forehead to mark him/her as one of the elect servants of God. The dead person is shown here at the moment in which he/she passes from Purgatory into Paradise and is enrolled into the number of the elect, the moment in which his/her name is entered into the celestial Book of Life. The Virgin's humility and subsequent exaltation is one of the principal themes in the programme, centering on the powerful image in the vault in which she displays the text from the third verse of the Magnificat, and continuing in the episode of the midwives bathing the newborn Christ. The kneeling figures of Abbot Epyphanius and the unidentified deacon bring the programme to a focus. They imitate the humility and good service of Mary at the Annunciation and that of Christ at the Crucifixion, and, like the midwives who bathe Christ, hope for subsequent exaltation. These kneeling postulant figures would make good sense in a funerary context, since it is at death that the issue of the imitation of Mary and Christ becomes of vital importance.

Who, then, was the enigmatic person for whom the crypt was made? Was it Abbot Epyphanius? John Mitchell proposes an alternative: the vaulted niche below the *confessio* window, he believes, holds the key (Fig. 6.5). Here was the small tomb described by Domenico Notardonato to Nicola Padula in March 1832 (see p. 4). It is 1.44 m long and 38 cm wide. As it is too small for an adult, Mitchell proposes that the scion of a major family was interred here – a family already closely connected with the monastery. The extraordinary prominence given to the Child Christ on the flanking wall would seem to reinforce this hypothesis. It is a contentious solution to a riddle that cannot be solved. Perhaps, to follow this hypothesis further, the family was responsible for other alterations to the church. Its nearest parallel, in some respects, is the Zeno chapel in S. Prassede at Rome – an oratory sumptuously decorated in bright glass mosaic, rather than painted, made by Pope Paschal I (817-24) for his mother Theodora Episcopa.

Fig. 6.5. The tomb in the east niche of the crypt church. (Photo: James Barclay Brown)

The making of the crypt accompanied significant alterations to the chancel of the eighth-century church. A central stairway led up to the chancel, all trace of which has disappeared. The apse, preserving the line of the Roman one, remained in place. Inside this a triconch was made. The architect carefully fitted the triconch into the space, and packed the gaps between the old and new walls with plenty of rubble and mortar. Then these walls were painted. Some painting has survived in the central apse of the triconch. Here we can see a painted *velum*, or curtain, decorated with concentric circles set within framing squares. It was a pinkish orange colour, and the ground against which it hung was blue-grey sprinkled with irregular clusters of tiny red flecks. The flecking may be an imitation of some rare variegated stone.

Changes were also made to the east end where a simple atrium was made within the pre-existing sunken profile of this area (Fig. 6.6). Visitors proceeded down two steps to a metre-wide marbled pavement, before crossing several block-built tombs and ascending several steps to the nave of the church. The atrium served as a small graveyard for adult individuals, distinguished neither for their youth nor age. The most important tomb was situated directly in front of the door into the nave (Fig. 6.7). This tomb was plastered and contained the body of a young man aged about

128

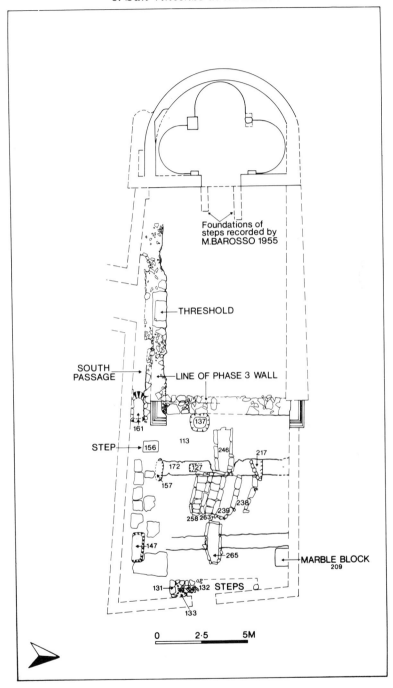

Foundations of
steps recorded by
M.BAROSSO 1955

THRESHOLD

SOUTH
PASSAGE

LINE OF PHASE 3 WALL

161

137

113

STEP

156

246

217

172

127

157

238

239

258 263

147

265

MARBLE BLOCK
209

131

132 STEPS

133

0   2·5   5M

Fig. 6.6. Plan of the crypt church in the age of Epyphanius.

129

Fig. 6.7. Grave (246) and skeleton of a young man interred in front of the door to the crypt church. (Photo: author)

twenty. The remains of a painted inscription, written on the surfaces flanking the niche for the head of the dead man, were found in place in the excavation. The text, written in elegant, well-formed red capitals, concluded with the formula 'Et vitam eternam'. Positioned as it is beneath the threshold, was this the body of the deacon depicted in the crypt paintings, the monastery's officer responsible for these new works? Modest though this cemetery was, its very creation within the nucleus of the monastic buildings illustrates its significance. It is tempting to regard it as a simple imitation of the atrium in front of San Vincenzo Maggiore.

The grandest tomb found so far, however, occupies an arcosolium within the ground-floor passageway leading between the crypt church and the ground-floor passages of the palace. An arched door, midway along the corridor that in Joshua's time opened into a chapel (formerly San Vincenzo Minore) of the palace, was blocked when the chapel was demolished. The arch was made into an arcosolium which still bore traces of painted plaster when we discovered it in 1980. (In shape and form it resembled the two large arcosolia in the hilltop cemetery (see p. 115). The arcosolium provided a canopy for a plastered and painted tomb which was unquestionably that of someone distinguished. The sense of the scheme of decoration seems to be primarily protective. The dead man was surrounded on all four sides by the cross, the most effective of all Christian apotropaic symbols. A large pink cross is painted on each of the four interior walls of this tomb and vine scrolls with large red blossoms spread out along each of its longer sides. The cross at the head of the tomb is flanked by the words of a protective inscription which we have already encountered elsewhere: CRVX XPI CONFUSIO DIABOLI ('The cross of Christ – the confusion of the Devil') (Fig. 6.8). The form of the four crosses is peculiar. Long bars run across the ends of the four arms of each cross, and from the ends of these bars extraordinary triangular serifs project upwards. John Mitchell compares it to crosses in painted tombs in the cemetery of San Tecla, the old cathedral of Milan. On stylistic grounds the tomb belongs to the middle or the third quarter of the ninth century. Could this be the tomb of Epyphanius himself, who died in 842?

The collective workshop

The atrium of San Vincenzo Maggiore necessiated the demolition of the workshops which had occupied this area for a generation or so (Fig. 6.9). This provided the occasion for building a new collective workshop of the kind depicted on the St Gall plan. Traces of similar workshop complexes have been discovered in excavations of the monasteries at Augsburg and Corvey. Craft waste, kilns, kiln debris and so forth were found. The author of the *Chronica monasterii Casinensis* records the existence of workshops either side of San Salvatore at Monte Cassino. At San Vincenzo an undeveloped area immediately south of the atrium of the abbey church

131

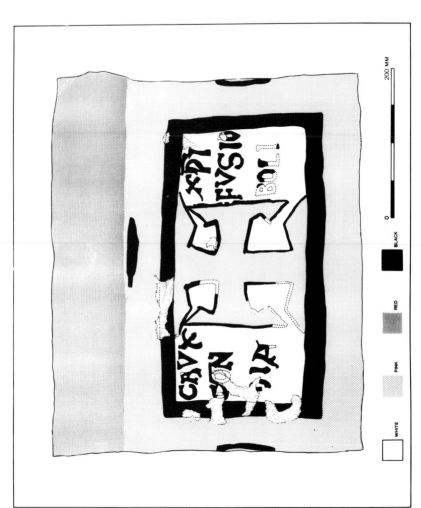

Fig. 6.8 'CRVX XPI CONFVSIO DIABOLI': the north end wall of a painted tomb below the distinguished guests' palace. (Drawn by Barry Vincent)

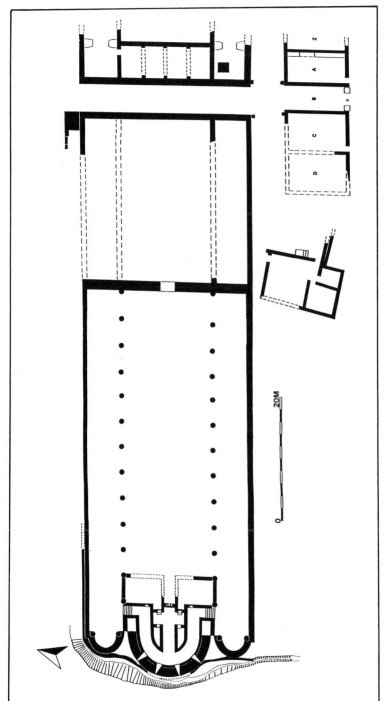

Fig. 6.9. The location of San Vincenzo Maggiore and the remains of the collective workshop.

was chosen for the new buildings. A Republican building was levelled, the ground was landscaped, and a long building was erected, separated by a passageway from San Vincenzo Maggiore. Only a part of this complex has so far been excavated, including four workshops, A-D. These were six paces wide, but the length of the collective workshop is not yet known. A separate refectory was made for the craftsmen.

Benches ran around the two walls of workshop A; it also had a tile pavement. Amongst the objects found in this room were several lengths of gilded beaded wiring, two Beneventan silver deniers, and a Hellenistic gem (evidently intended for re-use as a setting). The most remarkable discovery was an elegant enamelled plaque with silver trays in the form of palmettes similar, in some respects, to a ninth-century enamel plaque discovered in a thirteenth-century craftsmen's shop at St Denys, Paris. Several small crucibles with pinched lips probably purpose-made for pouring molten silver were associated with the workshop. The combination of evidence indicates that this was an enamel-maker's workshop. In the past some scholars contended that the craft was lost in the West after the Barbarian invasions, to be reintroduced in the ninth or tenth centuries. David Buckton, however, has argued that some Dark Age workshops continued to operate in Italy throughout the period. These workshops, in his opinion, nurtured the craftsmen who, in later centuries, revived to produce in enamel-ware for Byzantium. The evidence from San Vincenzo appears to confirm his hypothesis.

Workshop B began life as a passageway leading from the corridor below San Vincenzo Maggiore to the yards south of the workshops. After *c.* 848, however, it was transformed into a smith's workshop, possibly for making cavalry equipment. Workshop C was a glassmaker's workshop to begin with. Remains of a tile-built kiln (the base of a tripartite tile-built kiln similar to that found in the earlier workshop?) were found in the corner of the room; outside, sunken into the yard, were traces of a bowl-furnace for working glass similar to the Migration Period kilns of Helgö, Sweden and, perhaps more pertinently, the thirteenth-century kiln excavated at Santa Cristina, near Germagnana in Tuscany. Once again glass waste littered the area, including fragments of distinctive constricted bases of hanging oil lamps and bottles with in-sloping mouths which were not produced in the earlier workshop located in the builders' yard.

Only a corner of workshop D has been examined. Here an iron-working furnace was found.

These workshops were producing luxury goods – commodities designed not only for use within the monastery, but also on its estates and within the households of its benefactors. Enamels, cavalry equipment, and glassware were made here. Pottery, leather goods, everyday metal equipment as well as ivories and bonework must have been made in other workshops.

Set back from the workshops, lying at an angle, is a remarkable building with two annexes (Fig. 6.10). The main building has pisé walls,

Fig. 6.10. View of the craftsmen's refectory under excavation. (Photo: Catherine Coutts)

though the two annexes appear initially to have been post-built timber structures. The building was burnt down in 881 – an arrowhead was found in the fire layer – and it seems that it had a thatch or shingle roof. Attached to the east wall of the main building is a curious set of steps which appear to have risen to a point in the centre of the room. The clay and rubble walls are too poorly made to support a first floor, reached by an exterior staircase. A simpler explanation is that the steps led to a pulpit situated in the middle of the room. If so, this is the third refectory to have been discovered at San Vincenzo. The remains of an oven in the western of the two annexes tends to confirm this interpretation. The two annexes were later rebuilt with mortared walls. Situated almost against the south wall of San Vincenzo Maggiore, though 4 m below the pavement of the atrium or basilica, this poorly made structure reveals the telling architectural hierarchy within the monastery. The fabric of the building resembles the simple peasant structures found in the early medieval village of Colle S. Giovanni di Atri (in the Abruzzo) and in ninth-century Pescara. Indeed, small farmhouses with clay and rubble walls were built in the Abruzzo until recently. Its construction was manifestly inferior to that of the adjacent workshops. Yet the existence of the pulpit reveals the daily intervention of liturgy in the lives of the lay brethren or artisans who assembled here to eat. Using the formula for calculating the seating capacity of the monks' refectory, this building was designed for about fifty craftsmen to eat at long tables.

135

The material culture

The ninth-century levels are rich in artefacts which illustrate the moveable wealth in the monastery. Here are a few illustrations:

A milky white jade sword chape or pommel might seem an unlikely discovery in a monastery (Fig. 6.11). This is nephrite jade, an exceptionally hard stone which sometimes occurs in Alpine districts, but mainly comes from the vicinity of the river Karakash in Khotan, to the north of Tibet. The form of the object is not at all European. An interesting parallel is a very hard Egyptian stone (lapis lazuli) pommel from a Sassanian sword which has been re-used as the chape of a scabbard belonging to a Hunnic warrior found in a grave in south Russia. The San Vincenzo object was almost certainly associated with a collection of horse-gear and a set of sword-belt mounts made in workshop B after *c.* 850 (Fig. 6.12). The finest piece is a large trefoil brooch made of iron and inlaid with a trailing silver ornament. The same vegetable ornamentation also occurs on two oval mounts and a distinctive D-shaped buckle. An illustration of a warrior in the ninth-century Vivian Bible, a Carolingian book, shows a trefoil used as part of a weapon-fastener. In Viking Scandinavia, however, trefoil brooches were worn by women as funerary attire. Examples are also known from Great Moravia – like Scandinavia and the Duchy of

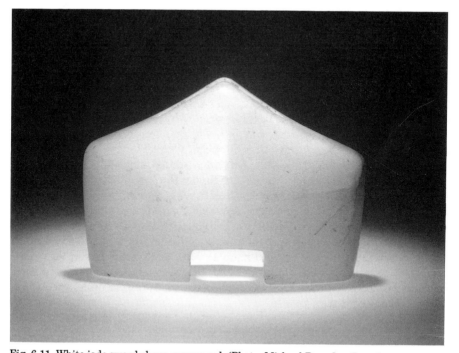

Fig. 6.11. White jade sword chape or pommel. (Photo: Michael Brandon-Jones)

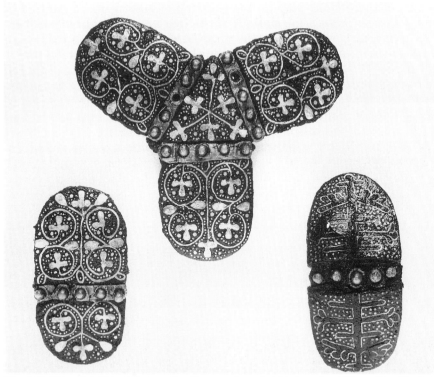

Fig. 6.12. Silver-inlaid trefoil strap-distributor and two baldric brooches. (Photo: Ray Manley)

Benevento, a territory just beyond the bounds of the Carolingian Empire. The decorated trefoil from San Vincenzo is only the second example known from Italy, the other from Rome is now in the British Museum. The horse-gear almost certainly forms part of the collection. This consists of a cruciform four-way strap distributor, a silvered strap slide, an iron snaffle-ring from a horse-bit and a rein-shackle. The fine spindly-plant ornamentation is distinctly Italian, similar to the trailing vegetation found in the paintings in Epyphanius' crypt. Similar plant motifs also occur on the altar panels from Santa Maria in Avenino at Rome, and on capitals at Santa Agata dei Goti at Rome. Significantly, three identical buckles and two more rein-shackles have been found in the east room of the ninth-century collective workshop at San Vincenzo. These discoveries indicate that the set was in fact made in the workshop, in its heyday before the sack by the Saracens. Why these pieces should have ended up in a later deposit remains a mystery.

From the late ninth-century midden behind workshop B comes an ivory head of a monk (Fig. 6.13). The fragment consists of the head, neck and part of the draped shoulders of a tonsured man. It has been sawn across

137

cleanly at the bottom, perhaps to re-use it as a setting of some sort. The front face is cut with some mastery, but the surface has not been polished. The eyes are set with small blue glass beads. Only one other example exists of this mixture of materials, the Genoels-Elderen diptych (now in the Musées Royaux d'Art et d'Histoire, Brussels). Accents of glass figured prominently, however, in the architectural stucco embellishment of the Lombard oratory of S. Maria in Valle, at Cividale. But the closest parallels are to be found at San Vincenzo itself and the pictures of tonsured figures

Fig. 6.13. The ivory head of a saint, with glass eyes, made in the monastery workshops. (Photo: James Barclay Brown)

such as Abbot Epyphanius in the crypt. In our present state of knowledge, there is some reason, therefore, to believe that San Vincenzo al Volturno was an unique centre for ivory carving in Italy.

The midden also contained pieces of bonework including a complete comb. This was possibly designed for liturgical purposes. By comparison with the ivory, the workmanship is crude.

Kitchen waste makes up the bulk of the refuse. It contains, for example, over twenty thousand fragments of animal bone, showing an emphasis upon pork in the monastic diet. Fragments and even complete pots come from the same dump. Most belong to a central Italian tradition, including red-painted pitchers and early green-glazed wares. One type merits attention, however. It has a distinctive collar rim. The form is otherwise unknown in Italy; instead, it is the standard container used in the Paris and Loire valleys. A few sherds of green-glazed pitchers occur in the later ninth century, almost a century after this type made its reappearance in later eighth-century levels in Rome. Pots were also brought from much more distant sources. Two lustreware dishes of Abbasid derivation have been found, attesting to Arabic connections. Less exotic are the thin-walled sherds of soapstone found in the workshop sector in later ninth-century layers. One complete vessel shows how skilfully the Alpine craftsmen worked with lathes to make these jars.

Perhaps the most improbable finds from the workshops are prehistoric implements. Numerous beautifully worked Mousterian flints have been found in these levels, as has a small polished stone axe of Neolithic date. The blades and scrapers had not been used in any functional sense. Their finely chipped edges showed no secondary working. These objects, we surmise, were collected by the craftsmen either as beautifully made talismans belonging to another age, or possibly, as Michele Mercati records in his ground-breaking study of lithics in *Metallotheca Vaticana* (1717), as extraordinary products of nature, made by lightning striking stone.

The earthquake of 848

In 848 a violent earthquake shook central Italy. Recent excavations in the Campus Martius at the Cripta Balbi have found large seismic cracks in the buildings dating from this time. According to the *Chronicon Vulturnense*, several buildings in Isernia fell down. The chronicler further reports that the earthquake caused serious damage in the monastery. San Vincenzo has the misfortune to be situated close to a fault-line; our experiences of two strong earthquakes at San Vincenzo in 1984 left us with no illusions about the horrors of these periodic natural events.

Great cracks, fist-sized fissures, in the façade of San Vincenzo Maggiore show that the vaulted basilica was badly shaken. The undercroft below the vaulted landing was filled at this time, to reinforce the weakened structure. It is difficult to tell how the façade itself was repaired, if at all. We have identified no evidence of any damage to the basilica. But given its curious construction, with pillars reinforcing the columns supporting the roof, it seems probable that it survived unscathed. The distinguished guests' palace, another vaulted structure, was also damaged. Its south wall curved outwards, leaving fist-sized gaps between it and the cross-walls separating the ground-floor undercrofts. Nevertheless, the building remained standing and the seismic cracks were patched up. Some of the buttresses around the walls of the refectory may also have been built after 848.

The earthquake will have most gravely affected the superstructure of the buildings rather than the lower parts, judging from the effects of the 1984 earthquakes in Castel San Vincenzo. The real impact of the 848 earthquake, therefore, is difficult to gauge. One indication of its severity may be reflected in the changes made within the workshops. Room B, a thoroughfare up until this point, was made into a workshop. A strong door was inserted to close its south side, and a wooden partition was erected to close off the north end. This was the occasion for the laying of a new floor in room A, and room D was apparently abandoned at this time.

The most far-reaching changes were made to workshop C (Fig. 6.14). This was transformed into an apartment. The formerly open glassmaker's room was divided into three parts: a door was cut through the south wall (leading to the yard beyond), this gave access to a narrow passage with a

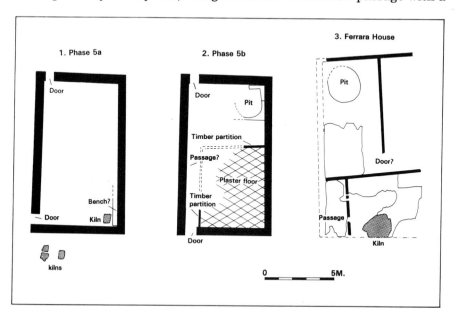

Fig. 6.14. Workshop C in phase 5a (glass workshop) and 5b (an apartment), and a comparable dwelling excavated at Ferrara.

wattle-and-daub partition wall; from this one could enter the front (south) room or a room at the back. The front room possessed a hard mortar floor; its walls were plastered and painted. Little of the back room has been excavated, but beyond the timber partition wall lay a toilet. Decorating the south front of the building was a line of terracotta consoles: moulded corbels decorated with plant motifs and plaques which would have given a classical impression to anyone crossing the beaten pathway to the door. The arrangement and size of the apartment brings to mind the tenth-century tenements constructed in timber, found during excavations in the Corso Porta Reno at Ferrara. In particular, the use of partition walls supported upon sleeper beams is common to both places. We might sur-mise as a result that, notwithstanding the decoration of the erstwhile workshop, this was a fairly normal-sized dwelling of the period.

Who lived in workshop C? One possible answer can be found by refer-ence to the St Gall plan. The plan depicts accommodation for a chamberlain in the great collective workshop. This senior figure, belong-ing to the executive of the monastery, was responsible for the production and maintenance of the monastery's material supplies and tools including the community's footwear. With a community of more than three hundred monks, and hundreds of servants, it was an awesome charge. Added to this, the far-reaching changes of the Carolingian age brought new respon-sibilities. At the synod of Aachen in 816 it had been decided that craftsmen should 'be instructed to perform their work henceforth not without as heretofore, but within the monastic enclosure'. The chamberlain, in other words, was responsible not only for the commodities made in the monas-tery, but also for their distribution to the outside world. As we shall see in Chapter 10, these commodities were critical means for winning the mu-nificence of secular donors.

It is unlikely that San Vincenzo invented the role of a chamberlain as late as *c*. 850, after the earthquake. Before this his apartment presumably was situated elsewhere within the collective workshop. It appears that he was installed in new rooms, as part of large-scale modifications to the workshop quarter. Some hint of alterations made to all the workshop buildings, not just those found in the excavations, has come to light in the deep midden of rubble and rubbish which was first deposited in the corridor immediately behind workshop B, and then, over subsequent years, collected there. Apart from some building debris, the excavated deposits contain over 20,000 fragments of animal bone, and the waste of craft activities as diverse as glassmaking and ivory carving. In short, the midden reinforces the suspicion that the devastation caused by the earth-quake was more extensive than can be detected, and necessitated considerable reconstruction of the workshops.

Nevertheless, the apogee of San Vincenzo had passed. Tell-tale vignettes reveal the onset of the monastery's decline. The painted plaster on the benches in the assembly room went unrepaired, and a mound of

Fig. 6.15. Fragment of ninth-century sculpture. (Photo: Michael Brandon-Jones)

kitchen waste more than a metre deep accumulated directly behind the façade of San Vincenzo Maggiore. In effect, the age of architectural invention and ubiquitous decoration was at an end. Few who visited the monastery in the 860s and 870s can have failed to be struck by its recent opulence and its waning fortunes.

On the other hand, San Vincenzo's eclipse should not be exaggerated. The animal bones show that the craftsmen ate well in the adjacent refectory. Of the ten thousand fragments of animal bone which could be identified, nearly half were of pig. A third of the bones were of sheep/goat,

142

while a smaller amount of the assemblage was made up of cattle bones. The assemblage also reveals a well-balanced pattern of managing the stock. At the same time San Vincenzo's craftsmen continued to make fine enamels, glassware and metalwork up to October 881.

7

The Sack of San Vincenzo,
10 October 881

Tybia nunc dicat, mea luctu corda recisa,
Quis subito miseris, funera tanta tulit.
Et populis varios clamores reddat ab alto,
Quos faciat casus posse referre suos,
[Huc] pariter Muse gemit redeant resolute,
Dulce quod est nimium dicitur exicium.
Carminibus planctum propriis coniungere tantum,
Ut simul astra sonent, cantica tristia dent.
Cum domus ista perit, multos [h]ac peste peremit,
Ethnica iam venit, querula turba fremit.
Fert monachis bellum, tulit unde reflexa flagellum,
Et dedit arma super femineamque fidem.
Rustica servorum facit hoc manus impia donum,
Percutit ipsa suos hac nece sic Dominos.
Castra petunt forts, concurrunt ocius hostes,
Corruit alta domus, menia cuncta ruunt.
Non etas tempus, iuvenis, puer, atque senectus
Excipitur, cuius vivere sit placitum.
Funditur hic sanguis, iaciuntur corpora campis,
Spiritus et celo dant modo iure Deo.
Fit rebus finis, non bellis, armaque viris
Sanguine resperis, signa fuisse Dei.
Et procul Emathios ostendunt florida campos,
Cespis purpureum continet ipsa decus.

This planctus recounting the sack of San Vincenzo in 881 is still sung at San Vincenzo on 10 October each year. The neums dotted across a page of the chronicle offer little idea of how it was actually sung, though musicologists have attempted to reconstruct it as a gregorian chant. Rather like a folk song recounting an ancient injustice, the planctus reminds the listener of the calamitous fate dealt to the monastery. Are we to believe the composer? Chroniclers, especially monks, often exaggerated attacks on monasteries by Arabs and Vikings.

We never expected to find archaeological evidence of this infamous day. It seemed likely that the sack had been exaggerated by the twelfth-century chronicler, even though local farmers eagerly retold the story as if it had

144

occurred yesterday. All the farmers knew about the battle and the pillaging of gold, and spoke of it with greater animation than the fierce battle fought here in the harsh winter of 1943-44. The present monks of Monte Cassino were especially concerned that we might uncover martyrs of 881 in our excavations. In their view these would be relics, to be treated quite differently from archaeological objects. It came as a great surprise, therefore, when we realized how closely the excavations corroborated the chronicler's account.

As we have seen, Arabs first appeared before San Vincenzo in 861. The band was led by Sawdan, the emir of Bari, by this time a powerful potentate in the politically highly fragmented world of southern Italy. He extracted 3,000 gold solidi from the monastery in return for not 'burning the buildings'. This was common practice north of the Alps where Danegeld was paid by kings and abbots to buy off Viking marauders. San Vincenzo's treasury, if it matched the great treasury of its neighbour, Monte Cassino, was well able to meet the ransom. Besides the ornaments, oriental exotica and myriad gifts made over by Beneventan aristocrats in San Vincenzo's treasury, there was almost certainly a fine library full of bejewelled books. Tradition has it that Sawdan returned twenty years later. This is unlikely: first because he would have been an old man, and secondly because the fateful sack of 881 stemmed from a coalition of forces involving the bishop of Naples.

The story of the Arabs in ninth-century Italy, like that of the Vikings, must be treated with some caution. Christian chroniclers were tempted to depict them as dastardly heretics who brought devastation wherever they went. In practice, as Federico Marazzi has shown, the geo-political situation was more complex than the black-and-white story of the sack of San Vincenzo might suggest. The Arabs had been occupying almost all of Apulia, as well as much of Basilicata and Calabria since 845. The corsairs, in short, had settled down, much as many Viking bands were doing in northern France, England, the western Isles and Ireland. The Carolingians were well aware of the threat posed to the integrity of Latin Christendom by these new settlers. As early as 847, the Emperor Lothar had said 'May our dearest son go down to Benevento, with all the hosts of Italy, France, Burgundy and Provence to put to flight the enemies of Christ, Moors and Saracens, both because our people there are awaiting our help, and because we are most certain of the fact that, if those lands fall into the hands of the infidels, they will be able to invade the region of Rome and then, may God spare us this, the great part of Italy'. The Arabs, nevertheless, successfully resisted two Carolingian expeditions, finding alliances to safeguard their future.

San Vincenzo's fate seems to have been sealed by the debilitating avarice of bishop Atanasio, duke of Naples. Two years after winning power, Atanasio unleashed a decade of bitter struggle to win the rich soils of the Terra di Lavoro around Capua in northern Campania. Erchempert, a contemporary Cassinese chronicler, has left a description in his *Ystoriola Longobardorum Beneventum degencium* of this struggle, of which, in some part, he was an eye-witness. In 879 Atanasio allied himself with Pandenolfo of Capua against Pandenolfo's cousins, with the secret intention of ousting them all and winning control of this territory. In 880 Atanasio's Neapolitans together with Arabs and troops from the port of Gaeta attacked *castrum Pilense*. Quite how many Arabs were involved remains unknown. Erchempert informs us, by way of illustration, that Duke Docibile I of Gaeta always kept a core body of Saracens near him, which in 884 was 150 strong, and which in the past had numbered as many as two and a half thousand. Notwithstanding such numbers the attack on *Pilense* failed, but in 881 a new campaign was launched on a larger scale and succeeded. Erchempert himself was taken prisoner. Exactly at this time we learn that Guaiferio, the old duke of Salerno, who shortly before had taken holy orders, died. The monks of Monte Cassino wished to bury him in the monastery, but on reaching Teano, near Capua, were compelled to bury the old duke there because the route northwards was menaced by maurauding Arabs. The Arab mercenaries had gone on a rampage in the Volturno valley, and further afield as well. Venafro, Isernia and Boiano, the homes of minor counts, were attacked. Marazzi believes that, together with the Neapolitans, they now began to menace the principate of Benevento, an adventure occasioned by the death of the Beneventan prince, Gaideris. It was also the context for the sack of San Vincenzo.

Bishop Atanasio's part in the destruction of the monastery did not escape the scrutiny of San Vincenzo's twelfth-century chronicler. Prefacing his account of the destruction with the text of chapter 44 of Erchempert's narrative, he was well aware of the complex alliances between the Neapolitan bishop and the Arabs that had sealed San Vincenzo's fate.

In 880 San Vincenzo was in decline. There are many tell-tale signs. The tunnel below San Vincenzo Maggiore connecting the workshops to the heart of the monastery was now blocked by refuse. On top of this were small bronze-working furnaces. Another sign was found in the vestibule, the court connecting the cloisters to the distinguished guests' complex. Fine alluvium had accumulated on the floor: it was as though animals had been kept here, or at least as though an inundation of flooding had not been cleared up when the Arabs arrived.

The marauders almost certainly approached up the Volturno valley, ascending the Rocchetta plain by the principal road to the monastery. Forewarned, the monks prepared themselves. They hid the monastery's treasure. Then, leaving the old monks, they gathered at the *Pons Marmoreus* to confront the Arabs. (Don Angelo Pantoni interpreted an eighteenth-century place-name to suggest that the bridge lay near the source of the Volturno, 2 km from the monastery. In our opinion, the bridge lay directly in front of the abbey church. This would place the main battle with the Arabs some hundred metres upstream from the present Ponte

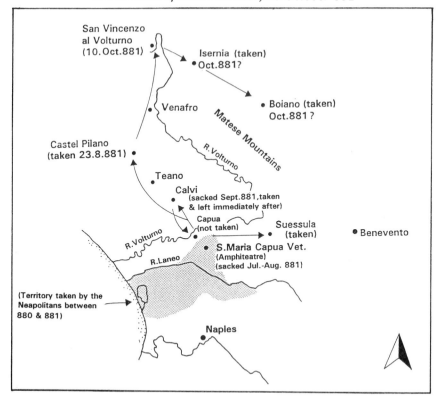

Fig. 7.1. The movements of the Arab band in the Principality of Benevento in 881.

della Zingara.) A ferocious battle ensued in which many of the attackers lost their lives. With weapons and stones the monks, so the chronicler recounts, held off the assault. But at a certain point, some of the monastery's servants, wearied by the struggle, quit the battle and sought out the 'king of the Saracens ... asking [him] for their liberty and their lives'. After making this unholy pact, the slaves, unknown to the monks, led the Arabs by another route into the monastery. The monastery was put to fire. The monks, exhausted, realized that their fate was sealed; and the slaves showed the Arabs where the treasure was concealed. Then the Arabs ran riot, destroying the monastery's wealth, and throwing its stores into the river. After the struggle was over, the chronicler records, Sawdan committed heinous sacrilege, drinking from the sacred chalices. The author of the *Chronicon S. Benedicti Casinensis* picked up the story, adding: 'the squalid tyrant [i.e. Sawdan] sitting above a pile of dead ate like a foul dog'. While the Saracens debauched themselves, the surviving monks, led by Abbot Maio, fled to a *castrum*, before departing for Capua.

The buildings on the east bank of the river Volturno would have been

147

the first to fall prey to the marauders. After this, they fired the distinguished guests' refectory and monks' refectory, both roofed with thatch and ideal targets. The windows of the refectory burst outwards into the distinguished guests' garden, many of the panes distorted by the fierce heat. Inside these buildings everything was reduced to ash, and decorations were scorched beyond recognition. A fierce fire also occurred at the front of the distinguished guests' palace. The tell-tale veneer of charcoal could be traced to the atrium of the crypt church, and then along the ground-floor passage of the palace to the vestibule, where a wall had collapsed blocking the door into the assembly room. In the assembly room itself, situated beyond the refectory, the wooden bench-tops were burnt, yet the paintings depicting a line of prophets on the back wall of the room were barely scorched.

The focus of the attack, however, was San Vincenzo Maggiore. The basilica appears not to have been damaged, but its atrium and porters' lodges were fired. The timber beams supporting the porticoes exploded causing the dentilated cornices to tumble outwards, down upon the craftsmen's refectory below. An arrowhead embedded in the floor of this refectory – another thatched building – shows that it too was fired. Its timber posts and wooden thresholds were found carbonised in their original positions.

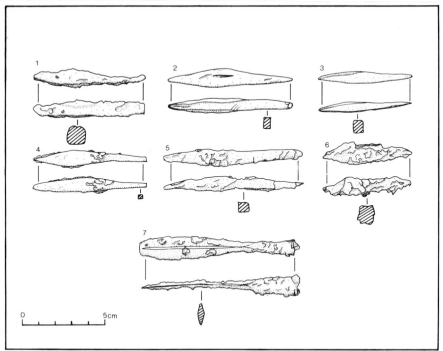

Fig. 7.2. Arrowheads from the sacked buildings at San Vincenzo.

148

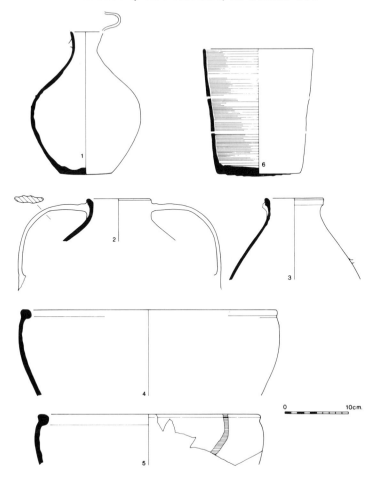

Fig. 7.3. Broken pots (1-5) and an Alpine soapstone jar (6) from the burnt remains of workshop B.

The most vivid episode of this fateful day involves the adjacent work-shops where fine metalwork was made. Heavy arrowheads were fired from short, reinforced composite bows, significantly heavier than those com-monly used in Lombard Italy (Fig. 7.2). This weapon, in many respects a forebear of the crossbow, is best known from the later Turkish and Mongol periods in the Middle East. The weighty arrows almost certainly carried flaming torches. Nowhere was this concentrated fire more apparent that at the entrance to workshop B. The lock and key to the door of the room lay within its clearly defined, carbonised remains. Fire arrows forced it to collapse in flames, bringing down shelves behind it on which pots had been stored (Fig. 7.3). The fire engulfed the workshop, reducing the north

149

timber wall of the workshop to charcoal, and then the chamberlain's apartment next to it. Excavation of the spread of charcoal revealed what the raiders were after. A fragment of gilded bronze – at a distance, to the uninitiated eye, splendidly worked gold – remained undetected in the destruction. Several lengths of gilded beaded wire were found in the burnt layers in the staircase within the north porter's lodge. Associated with these was a wafer-thin silver denier issued by Prince Guamerius of Salerno (880-901). This unique coin seems to have been newly minted when it was lost in the conflagration.

An associated hoard of metal offcuts and other objects was found in a shallow hole cut into the floor of the upper thoroughfare beside the distinguished guests' palace. These had all been deposited in an iron-bound wooden chest. The chest had been ransacked and torched. A small, simple bronze crozier, the blue glass setting for a fine ring, and tiny bronze rods for filigree work were found in thick charcoal. Two other objects were dislodged from this deposit in the eleventh-century rebuilding. One was a small fragment of gilded bronze virtually identical to the piece described above from the workshop, the other was a battered, gilded and enamelled plaque (Fig. 7.4). The plaque, now torn on two of its sides, had been part of an icon or the lid of a reliquary made in the monastic workshop. What survives is a buckled triangle measuring 16 x 10.5 cm. The remaining piece consists of a copper back-plate round the edges of which a secondary plate has been riveted. The secondary plate carries low, double-walled partitions which clasp tiny sunken chains of beaded wire and divide the surface of the object into a series of variously shaped cells. These cells held images and decorations in cloisonné enamel. The one surviving enamelled field shows an exotic flower on a turquoise stem set against a deep azure background. The flower has red, yellow, white and green petals. The edge of the plaque is framed with gilded beading, some of which has been bevelled for attachment to a wooden frame. In its original state it must have been similar to two other well known ninth-century enamels: Pope Paschal I's cross reliquary (in the Vatican) and the Fieschi-Morgan staurothek in New York. Spectrographic analyses of the cobalt blue glass used in the enamelling, undertaken at the British Museum, show that it is identical to the blue window glass and the blue vessel glasses made at San Vincenzo. The plaque, it seems, was made in the monastery's workshops.

The chamberlain, or perhaps the enamel-maker himself, seems to have sped from the workshops, losing some of his materials in the north porter's lodge, and attempted to conceal the rest near the palace. But in the mayhem he failed in his mission. Apart from the silver coin of Prince Guamerius, we found only those pieces discarded during the plundering. Fine and intact objects were removed. This episode illustrates the panic that swept through the community that day. In the layer of mud over the tiles in the assembly room and vestibule were trampled potsherds, a few

Fig. 7.4. The buckled remains of an enamelled plaque, probably destroyed in 881. (Photo: John Mitchell)

broken fragments of window glass and odd pieces of bronzework. A smashed fragment of an elegant tombstone was left on the carbonised wooden benchtop in the assembly room. The smashed glasses in the distinguished guests' refectory as well as the absence of objects other than

151

the lock and key among the charred debris of the main crockery cupboard in the monks' refectory are two small vignettes of the orgy of looting.

The bodies of the dead were almost certainly left where they fell. In the course of a few hours that autumn a curtain came down on the community. The impact of the sack upon the courts of the region is difficult to judge. It was a brutal manifestation of the breakdown of law and order in the old principate. At Naples, Bishop Atanasio's conscience, it would seem, was

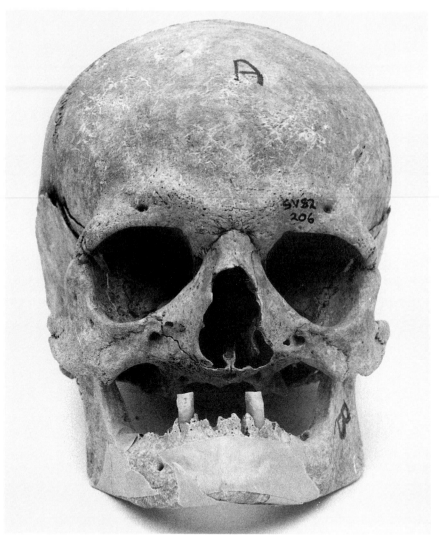

Fig. 7.5. The grossly deformed skull from Tomb 10 in the crypt church; possibly a victim of the Arab sack. (Photo: Michael Brandon-Jones)

gravely pricked. In 883 the bishop was responsible for San Vincenzo acquiring houses and warehouses in the port; he himself was present at the signing of the agreement concerned with one property. We can only speculate on how this wily individual made his excuses for the calamity which had befallen the community of San Vincenzo. Nonetheless, that same year Monte Cassino suffered the same fate. On Tuesday, 20 October 883, the Arabs arrived at Monte Cassino and repeated the desecration. San Vincenzo's chronicler records the sack in copious detail, reminding the reader of how Abbot Bertarius was brutally killed at the altar of S. Salvatore.

8

After the Arabs

When Abbot Godelpertus led his monks back to San Vincenzo in 916 they found it in ruins. Many buildings had been destroyed; many more were damaged. San Vincenzo Maggiore was derelict. The chronicler leaves us in no doubt that this state of affairs outlasted the turn of the millennium. Indeed, it seems likely that successive abbots chose to spend the greater part of their time at Capua, rather than in the ruins of the abbey. Even so, according to Sigebert of Gembloux's account of Bishop Dietrich's visit to Capua in 970, the monks 'appeared to be few in number'. Only after c. 1000 did the rhythm of revival and rebuilding begin again. But is the chronicler's record of San Vincenzo's dismal plight accurate?

The abbey church of San Vincenzo Maggiore remained untouched until the eleventh century. Untended, the huge edifice fell into disrepair. Signs of this were found in the north porter's lodge: the brick-built vault supporting the staircase had collapsed onto the layer of burning dating to 881. Understandably, the task of repairing a building exceeding 100 m long was beyond the capabilities of a small band of monks. The chronicler tells us that the monks now used San Salvatore, the church constructed by Abbot Talaricus (817-23). Was San Salvatore the church on the crown of Colle della Torre – a place readily defended if raiders of any kind returned?

The northern part of the monastery, the original eighth-century settlement, provides more clues to the state of affairs in the tenth century. The crypt church had been little damaged. Being on the northern limits of the settlement, furthest from the abbey church, it perhaps escaped the raiders' full attention. Its crypt and chancel were unharmed. Its atrium had fared less well. Alluvium had built up around its small sunken graveyard, presumably brought in by inundations of the river Volturno when it was unattended in the period 881-916. Several poorly made graves were cut into alluvium within this area. One contained the disarticulated bones of several individuals; another consisted of a line of tiles, in Roman fashion, on which a young woman with a fifth-century bronze coin had been laid to rest. In comparison with the stoutly made ninth-century tombs in the atrium graveyard, these were plainly makeshift.

The palace had also survived the sack more or less intact. The fire had spread along its ground-floor corridors, and several of its colourful windows had been blown out. Doubtless its first-floor rooms had been

Fig. 8.1. Rubble and tile (from the sack of 881) in the garden of the distinguished guests' palace. (Photo: author)

ransacked, but painted plaster fragments from the palatial apartments exhibit few signs of scorching, suggesting that the main hall at least escaped the worst of the conflagration. In the apse two graves were cut into the floor. Both contained disarticulated skeletons: one held a jumble of nine individuals including five children, the other five adults. Each of the undercrofts beneath the palace was used in this period. A deep deposit extending out and along the south corridor (overlying the distinctive veneer of burning) unmistakably comes from stabling animals. The undercrofts accommodated humans as well, to judge from the presence of kitchen waste comprising animal bones, broken pottery and glasses.

The wide door from the south ground-floor corridor of the palace leading into the garden was still passable. But a charred beam lay across the portico immediately beyond it, and remained where it fell until it was covered over by deep tips of rubbish in the mid-eleventh century. The distinguished guests' refectory had been completely destroyed. The peristyle garden itself had also been damaged, perhaps irreparably. The Roman ornamental vase associated with it (p. 104), found in pieces in an eleventh-century level, was perhaps wantonly smashed in 881. Nevertheless, it was still possible to walk along the north portico of the garden beside the south wall of the palace towards the entrance hall.

The entrance hall itself was utterly transformed (Fig. 8.2). The old passage from the garden leading up to the vestibule was filled by two large

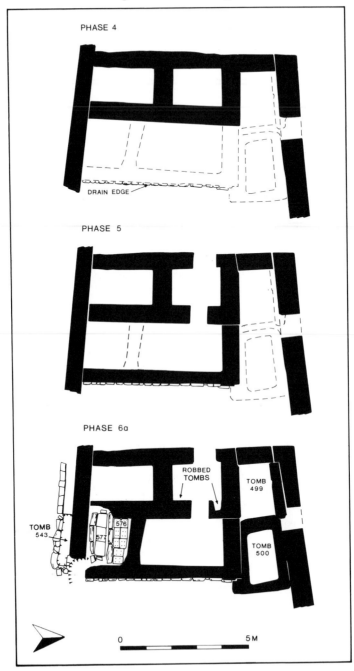

Fig. 8.2. Phase plan of the entrance hall, showing (4) the early ninth-century building; (5) the building in the age of Epyphanius; (6a) the tenth-century mausoleum.

tombs. These were intended to be seen by visitors. The first (tomb 500) contained a single male who was notably old. The grave itself was painted, though the plaster had deteriorated badly before the excavations. A simple marble step had been wedged against the tomb, enabling viewers to slip through a window in the south wall of the palace. The larger tomb (496) was a small mausoleum. Visitors might have peered down upon it from an opening in the vestibule or from a window in the ground-floor passage of the palace. The jumbled remains of eight males and one articulated woman were found when the tomb was opened. Niches cut into the sides of the old stairwell were intended to hold lamps to light the grave.

Visitors were directed into the ground-floor rooms of the entrance hall itself by a large Republican inscription. The inscription records a votive offering by Afinia Phieris, a priestess presumably associated with San Vincenzo in ancient times (see p. 45). The rough-hewn back of the huge marble inscription, once set into a monumental building, now retained the tumbled rubble filling the vestibule. It drew the visitor first into a narrow room in which the traces of two tombs can be seen. Both tombs – perhaps sarcophagi – were removed in the tenth or eleventh century. The door led to a badly burnt room beyond which were two more tombs, tightly wedged into the available space. Each contained the disarticulated remains of several aged adults (Fig. 8.3). Beyond these a hole had been rudely chopped into the refectory wall. The hole is tomb-sized, but any tomb has long since gone. Next to it, however, inside the refectory, was yet another

Fig. 8.3. Tenth-century tombs, possibly of 'martyrs', in the entrance hall. (Photo: author)

157

tomb. This tomb had been rudely inserted into the refectory bench, cutting through the burnt layer. The tomb lay more or less in line with those in the monumental staircase. Sealed within it were the remains of a particularly old woman. The derelict entrance hall had become a cemetery.

Many other tombs were found in the passages around the entrance hall. The upper thoroughfare led from the monumental staircase towards the old Roman tower. This had probably been a graveyard in the eighth century, before the construction of San Vincenzo Maggiore. Now several more tombs, most containing the disarticulated remains of more than one person, were constructed here. Immediately below this passage, at the end of the ground-floor south corridor of the palace, and beside the monumental staircase, a young boy and a woman had been buried in shallow graves. Both lay barely below a spread of kitchen waste and animal muck that extended from the undercrofts.

When the entrance hall was demolished during the eleventh century (see below) a number of outstanding objects was found. Several may have belonged to the dead interred there, disturbed when the structure was dismantled. Other objects had been brought from ninth-century tombs elsewhere in the monastery. Two fine tombstones, for instance, belonged to monks who had almost certainly been buried in the monks' cemetery close to San Vincenzo Maggiore. A long narrow one was made for Tamfrid (Fig. 8.4). Its elegantly carved inscription tells us that 'Although the limbs of the priest Tamfrid lie buried in this tomb, his soul seeks the stars'. The spirit of the couplet brings to mind the brightly painted stars on the vaulted roof of the crypt, painted in the age of Epyphanius. The other tombstone, more elegant still, records a certain Teudelas (Fig. 8.5). The face of this tombstone bears a cross with arms that flare out to form impressive terminals rather as in the painted grave described on p. 131. The carefree discarding of these memorials, as so often in the history of San Vincenzo, reveals a lack of interest in its material past.

The ravaged condition of the monastery is best revealed by the state of the monks' refectory. The door leading from the vestibule to the assembly room in the lower thoroughfare had been blocked by fallen rubble. An improvised door was smashed through the north wall of the refectory beside the monumental staircase. The refectory itself was a burnt-out shell. In its north-west corner, where the crockery cupboard had once been, traces of a beaten-earth floor were found overlying the debris. The floor approximates to the size of a small dwelling of this age, but its purpose is quite obscure.

The chronicler recalls that Abbot Rambaldus built a church by the gate soon after the monks returned. Is this a reference to the crypt church or to a new church situated by a bridge directly in front of San Vincenzo Maggiore? If it was the crypt church, it might explain the activity focused upon the palace and the entrance hall immediately next to it. After all, the palace had probably been the grandest monument in the ninth-century

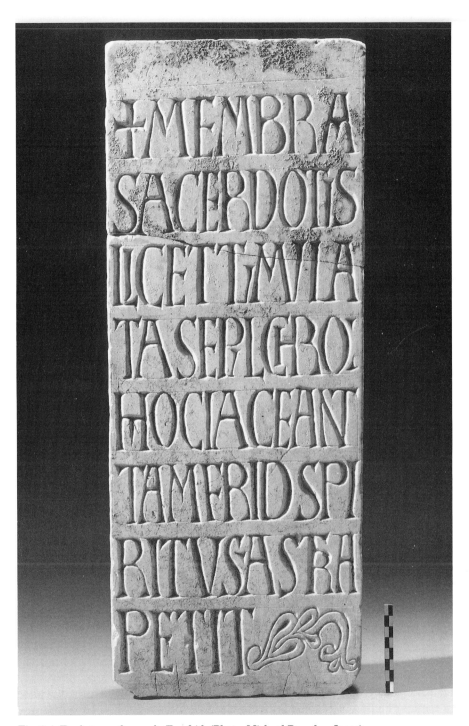

Fig. 8.4. Tombstone of a monk, Tamfrid. (Photo: Michael Brandon-Jones)

Fig. 8.5. Tombstone of a monk, Teudalas. (Photo: Michael Brandon-Jones)

monastery after the abbey church. It was, therefore, a natural focus in the decades after the sack. Distinguished visitors were perhaps once again accommodated here, although in humbler conditions than had previously existed. The ground-floor rooms were clearly put to use. The continued presence of visitors may explain the makeshift cemetery in the entrance hall. The prominent positioning of the inscription to Afinia Phieris indi-

160

cates that the cemetery was designed for restricted pilgrimage. Was the intention to create a martyrium – a memorial to the disaster that had befallen the abbey? Were these the victims of the Arab sack and, perhaps, the remains of desecrated tombs from the monks' cemetery in the atrium of San Vincenzo Maggiore?

In these ramshackle conditions successive tenth-century abbots drew up foundation charters for villages such as Castel San Vincenzo, Vaccherecchia, Cerro, Colli and *Olivella* (see Chapter 9). A rational spirit, it would appear, lay behind the revival of the Val Volturno. The fruits of this enterprise, if we interpret the chronicle correctly, are to be found in the phase of rebuilding at the turn of the millennium.

Renewal

Abbot John IV (998-1007) restored Joshua's abbey. A little later Abbot Ilarius (1011-45) paved and decorated it with paintings. He also added a bell-tower, and set about restoring the churches of Santa Maria Maggiore, San Pietro and San Michele in the monastery. Finally, Abbot John V (1053-76) built a new chapter house as well as a new internal and external cloister. Over three generations, a new Romanesque monastery began to take shape, only to be demolished when Abbot Gerard (1076-1109) decided to build an entirely new monastery on a level, fortified site on the east side of the river Volturno.

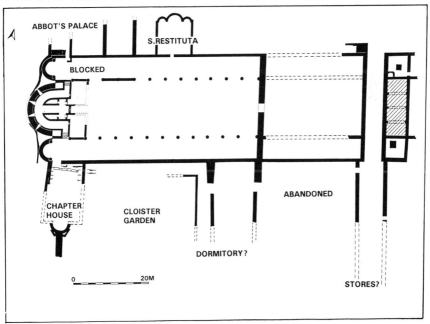

Fig. 8.6. Plan of San Vincenzo Maggiore and associated buildings in the eleventh century.

161

The excavations of San Vincenzo Maggiore confirm the chronicler's account. The eastwork and atrium were restored, as were those parts of San Vincenzo Maggiore which had fallen into disrepair. The old porters' lodges were turned into flanking towers, either side of the façade. New staircases were made in each tower. In the southern tower were the enigmatic remains of six small furnaces, possibly for heating glass to repair San Vincenzo's celebrated windows. The atrium was restored, but it is doubtful that the eleventh-century version emulated the monumentality of its ninth-century forebear. The north-east angle of the basilica had partly collapsed, and this had to be repaired. Two huge buttresses were erected against the south wall to prop it up. Inside the church itself the columns in the nave and aisles were reduced from twenty-four to twenty. The four westernmost columns were removed and replaced by walls to create a partly enclosed choir. Entry to the crypt from the stairs to the north aisle was now no longer possible as this doorway was blocked. An alteration was made to the south apse too: the area immediately in front of it became a separate side chapel, in which the only doorway to the crypt was located.

Abbot Ilarius may have been conscious of the limitations of his predecessor's works. It is likely that he made a bell-tower, a *campanarium excelsum* within the south porter's lodge. It remains a mystery as to how the church was entered, since, in the ninth century, the north and south lodges had been the principal means of access into the church. The atrium lying beyond the façade may have been the inner cloister described in the *Chronicon*. Monks and abbots were probably still buried here.

Abbot Ilarius' greatest achievement was the redecoration of the basilica. Unfortunately, the painted decoration of the eleventh-century church perished when it was dismantled around 1100. However, a number of blocks bearing painted plaster fell from the upper walls during this demolition. These were found during the excavation of the crypt and they throw some light on the nature and extent of the lost scheme. Fortuitously, several blocks which fell into the annular crypt seem to derive from the central apse. Prominent among these is the left half of a great, over-life-sized, frontal head. Although it was found in the southern quadrant of the annular corridor, it would appear to derive from a large frontal image of Christ in the centre of the apse. The figure had great glaring eyes, features powerfully contoured in black, an elegant little sweeping moustache, quite delicately defined red lips, and striking red hair. Strong green shadows defined the nose, the eye sockets and the outer edges of the face, and the cheeks displayed prominent roses. This was clearly a large and extremely impressive head. In design and style it can generally be compared to advanced painting of the early eleventh century elsewhere in Italy.

Under the central section of the apse the middle part of another head and a related eye were found. The face is of a young individual, half turned to the right. It is painted in a striking pale green, shaded with darker green, with features brilliantly defined in red, pink and black, and delicately lighted with white. Again there is a striking pink rose on the surviving cheek. To judge from the scale and manner of painting, these fragments must have come from the same scheme as the first head. Various fragments of wings were found in related contexts. These suggest that angels figured prominently in the decoration of the apse, probably flanking a dominant central figure of Christ. Part of a head, clearly by a different hand but related in style, was found in the southern part of the annular corridor.

A remarkable passage of drapery, apparently from the knee and lower leg of a figure, was recovered in the northern stair passage of the crypt. This is painted in two shades of green with highlights in elegant configurations of white, and other folds defined in red and black. Particularly striking is the circular comb-light on the knee. Also from the western end of the north aisle is another passage of drapery, equally impressive to the eye, although rather different in design. Part of another head was found in the same area. This was rather more linear in conception than the other eleventh-century work. By contrast, a fragment of another rather smaller head, which was found in rubble at the foot of the south wall of the church, was a much finer and more sophisticated piece of work. This shows the nose, moustache and mouth of an elderly man, half turned to the right, and is the work of an artist who was fully in command of the means of representing the three-dimensional human figure. Another large fragment seems to show a haloed head, flanked by a large, rounded and elaborately lit configuration of red drapery. This is flanked by an elaborate border with a concertina fan-design in four colours, which recalls one of the motifs employed in the early ninth-century dados of the crypt. Finally, there are various ornamental motifs which clearly derive from the eleventh-century phases of the church.

Other passages of painting were preserved in the chapel which had been constructed in the western end of the south aisle. At the foot of the south wall of the aisle, part of a large haloed head and part of the halo of a neighbouring figure were found. This is a striking face, with furrowed brow, painted in green, modelled with ochre and with the features articulated in deep red. Eyes and nose were deftly defined with quick sketchy strokes of the brush. There is a tendency to form little angled accents. The haloes are yellow and contoured in white. This is distinctively eleventh-century painting. The idiom employed is different from that of the paintings from the central apse, although in both, green is the predominant colour in the representation of flesh. The decoration of this room evidently included large figures of saints standing in close, overlapping order.

It is clear that more than one phase of work is represented in these fragments. However, all of them must belong to the eleventh century, and the majority are likely to be from the period of Abbot Ilarius' decoration of

Abbot John's newly refurbished basilica. The great head of Christ and the associated fragments of angels bear vivid testimony to the ambitions of the abbot and his monks in this period. Although a trifle rustic in execution, they are in line with contemporary developments in other parts of Italy. In general terms, the conventions used in the representation of faces are similar to those employed by the artists responsible for the painted decoration of the church of Sant'Orso at Aosta between *c.* 1015 and 1020. Other comparisons can be found in paintings at sites which lie geographically much closer to San Vincenzo: in the Grotta di San Michele at Olevano sul Tusciano, in the hills just to the east of Salerno; in the Grotta delle Fornelle and in the Grotta dei Santi at Calvi, in northern Campania; in the later paintings in the Grotta di San Biagio at Castellammare di Stabia, and in the crypt of the church of Santa Maria del Piano near Ausonia, which lies about half way between Monte Cassino and the Gulf of Gaeta.

The abbot's house, chapter house and cloisters

With the completion of the new abbey church, other buildings were constructed around it. A new monastic plan was being created. Less ambitious than Joshua's monastic city, Ilarius' was nevertheless a major enterprise. New sectors were designated within the monastery, to judge from the remains found so far. The abbot resided alongside the north side of the basilica; the cloisters now occupied the south side of San Vincenzo Maggiore; the workshops were relegated to a yard covering the old northern parts of the monastery. But before the new monastery could be made, enormous earthworks accompanied by considerable engineering took place. The great chasm on the north side of the building, including the storm-water ditch, was filled in. Limited landscaping also occurred on the south side, involving the demolition of the ninth-century workshops. Traces of the building operations have been discovered. A mortar-mixer was found overlying the ninth-century workshop yard. Evidently this provided mortar for building the cloisters. Similarly, a lime kiln was found immediately outside the east wing of the cloisters, occupying the ground which in the ninth century had served as an east-west passage separating the abbey church from the workshops.

At least three buildings were erected on the north side of the church. A stone dwelling of some size was made at right angles to the old apse, using the old north nave wall as its downslope, end wall (Fig. 8.7). Here, a marble staircase led up to the ground floor of the building, and then upwards to a first floor which no longer survives. A mortar surface covered part of the ground floor, concealing the ninth-century storm-water ditch which had passed outside the nave wall. A layer of occupation debris, including fragments of ceramic kitchenwares, was found in the rich layer of debris overlying the floor. This ground-floor room may have been a kitchen for the occupants who inhabited the floor(s) above. Who lived here? The

Fig. 8.7. The remains of the later eleventh-century abbot's house attached to the north apse of San Vincenzo Maggiore. (Photo: Will Bowden)

probable answer is the abbot. Situated opposite the apse of the abbey church, it was convenient for attending services, and at the same time discreetly concealed from the main body of the monastery.

East of it, separated by a passage, lay a building with thick walls which has yet to be excavated. East of this, again separated by a passage, lying approximately at the centre of the north side of the basilica, there are the substantial remains of a large triple-apsed side chapel. Part of its splendid painted decoration is preserved on the lower walls. This is the remains of a dado painted in imitation of a *velum*, or curtain. The *velum* is yellow with staggered rows of red crosses and was punctuated by six large medallions, three of which survive in a fragmentary state. One carries a striding figure in a short tunic, the second a large griffin and the third, another magnificent and fabulous beast. The painting is exotic, bold and expert in execution. In the late eighteenth century the chapel was ruinous and known locally as Santa Restituta.

Major buildings now flanked the south side of the basilica. The most impressive lay immediately south of the south apse. The so-called chapter house is a room with the remains of a fine mosaic floor. The room was built at a slight angle to the pre-existing church, allowing access to the two ninth-century tombs probably to be associated with abbots (see above). A screen may have separated the tombs from the room. The room itself was floored with a combination of *opus sectile* and mosaic, only part of which has survived.

The design of the pavement consisted of small *rotae* made up of concentric bands of mosaic tessera and little sections of cut marble, with the central disc in mosaic in the one completely preserved example. An obvious more or less contemporary parallel is the pavement in Santa Maria in Patira, in Calabria, in which *opus sectile* and mosaic are combined in the same fashion. The room was reached by a narrow doorway in the south wall of the south aisle. A low bench ran along its west wall. Fragments of green heads, smaller in scale than the ones from the chapel in the west end of the south aisle, but painted in a very similar idiom, were found in this room. These have the same characteristic furrowed brows, with prominently defined lateral lobes and puckered eyebrows defined in dark red.

Separating the chapter house alongside the south apse from the cloisters which extended out from the atrium (or inner cloister) was a peristyle garden. Little remains of the cloisters. The ninth-century cloisters had been largely destroyed in the Arab attack of 881. The old workshops were first raked over for roofing tiles which might be re-used; broken ones were then stacked against the ninth-century walls. Dumps of material were tipped over the old buildings, raising the level of the new cloister up by over a metre on a low terrace. The cloister range was constructed on this terrace. With walls approximately 1 m thick, an east wing was made extending from the south entrance of the ninth-century ground-floor corridor (behind the façade), to a point *c*. 35 m southward. Remains of door thresholds were found in its west and east walls. This wing, situated nearest the entrance to the monastery, probably served as the stores, and possibly the kitchen. The south wing lay at right angles to the east one. Nothing of this has yet been excavated. Normally, this would be the site of the refectory. The western wing formed the third side of the quadrangle, running up to join two buttresses, dating to Abbot John IV's refurbishment of the basilica. This huge building presumably served as the monks' dormitory. As a rule, inside the quadrangle there would have been a secluded cloister garth. In this case, though, it seems that the ruins of the ninth-century craftsmen's refectory, as well as the dentilated cornice blocks which in 881 had tumbled here from the atrium above, remained. It is possible that these ruins, covered by brambles, were barely visible in the eleventh century. Nevertheless, it is curious that this island of dereliction, a monument to the fateful sack of 881, escaped the programme of renewal.

At the other end of the monastery the crypt church was restored in the eleventh century, while the buildings immediately south of it (the palace, entrance hall, vestibule, assembly room, refectory, etc.) were demolished.

The sunken atrium of the crypt church was entirely filled in and a visitor might now walk across levelled ground to the door of the nave.

166

Bodies were still interred in this open space at the east end. One tomb contained a badly disfigured adult, his skull cracked by a heavy object, possibly a sword. Were these still more victims of 881, strategically re-buried where they might attract most attention?

The palace, with the exception of its highest apse, was systematically levelled to a height just below its first floor. It was taken apart section by section. Much of its stone, marbled pavements, sculpture and window glass was evidently carefully saved. Nevertheless, a heap of mortar and rubble tumbled downwards to fill the undercrofts. The upper thoroughfare was likewise levelled to ground level and the rubble used to fill the lower thoroughfare. The first floor of the entrance hall was toppled into the garden. One of the three first-floor arches survived in a toppled pile above the littered tiles that had already slipped from its roof down into the guests' garden. Several tombs were removed from the entrance hall, as were some marble steps, before it was buried with rubble which filled the ground floor and spread outwards into the garden. Still more layers of rubble created from levelling the refectory were added to these tips. As the levelling proceeded, some of the columns from the central spine of the refectory were smashed. Monks must have rooted through the piles of window glass blown out in 881 to salvage the precious lead cames with which the panes had been fixed in the windows. Further up the hill, on terrace 3 immediately behind the crypt church, yet more demolition work went on. The early eleventh-century church situated here and the adjacent passage were knocked down, and most of the stone and marble was taken away. The extent – and indeed the brutality – of the destruction was quite extraordinary.

Meanwhile, on the eastern side of the old garden the monks set up a mortar-mixer (Fig. 8.8). This was a shallow bowl about 2 m wide. The paddles which mixed the mortar were attached to a central spindle which was itself attached to a high rectangular frame embedded in the garden. Within the frame oxen or donkeys were harnessed to rotate the paddles as they walked round the mixer. The mortar was of poor quality, being bulked out with crushed tile, large lumps of charcoal and pieces of limestone.

The northern part of the settlement – the original nucleus of San Vincenzo – was made into a yard. This covered the area formerly occupied by the distinguished guests' refectory, the refectory and the lower thoroughfare. Post-holes cut through this surface indicate that simple timber buildings occupied the yard. A small kiln (Fig. 8.9) was made on the yard surface, set against the back wall of the old assembly room (the room itself lay buried beneath a metre of rubble). The kiln comprised a simple circular oven, nearly 2 m in diameter, and a stokehole about 1.5 m long. Its firing chamber was constructed from smashed tiles lined with clay. Inside the chamber were traces of a horseshoe-shaped stand on which the contents once stood. The stokehole was made from wattle and daub. As far as we could tell, the kiln had barely been used. It was too solid for a bread oven,

Fig. 8.8. Remains of an eleventh-century mortar-mixer. (Photo: author)

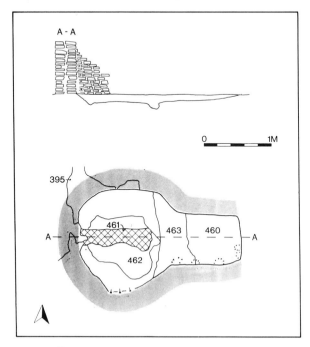

Fig. 8.9. Eleventh-century potter's kiln.

168

and too small for a tile or lime kiln. No traces of metal or glass were found around it. We must conclude, therefore, that it is a rare example of a potter's kiln. The form of the furnace is consistent with others known from this date in France, the Netherlands and West Germany. A potter – *figulus* – was one of the signatories to the agreement made between San Vincenzo and the neighbouring village of Cerro in 989. Did one of his descendants work for the monastery? None of his work, unfortunately, has survived.

One vestigial feature here, however, merits description. A metre above the line of the south corridor of the old south church a gateway, mostly made from re-used blocks, was created directly in front of the Ponte della Zingara. This opened onto a narrow passage which led towards the surviving apse of the ninth-century distinguished guests' hall. What was the purpose of this makeshift arrangement? Was the original locus of the cult at San Vincenzo, more than a millennium old by this time, once more sanctified?

After the savage sack in 881, the monks must have been preoccupied by their vulnerability. Yet the first fortifications were surprisingly slight. A short tract of walling immediately south of the cloister is interpreted as a section of an enclosure wall. The use of large blocks in its construction closely resembles the remaining fortifications designed by Abbot Gerard and his successors around the new twelfth-century monastery. When were fortifications first erected around the old site? Was the wall built around the cloister during John V's time, or was built at an earlier date, making it necessary to fit the new cloister into an already defined space? A likely date is soon after the Borrelli family sacked part of the monastery in 1042 and occupied the. *turris*. No other traces of the fortifications have been identified. The compact form of the Romanesque monastery, so different to the extensive ninth-century settlement, made it more readily defendable.

The Romanesque achievement

The eleventh-century refurbishment of San Vincenzo Maggiore took three generations to complete. For the most part it seems to have paralleled the more famous building operations at Monte Cassino, on which, as our analyses of the excavated results continue, it may shed some light. The thrust of the works was to concentrate the monastic settlement in a more tightly arranged plan around San Vincenzo Maggiore. As at Monte Cassino, the abbot's house lay close to the basilica (somewhat closer than its ninth-century precursor which occupied the hillside overlooking the church). The inner and external cloisters were probably connected by passages and staircases, unlike the ninth-century arrangement. Only the workshop zone, in common with the plan of Cluny at this date, was located some way from the church. In some ways, the intention resembled the policy of *incastellamento* (the formation of nucleated villages), practised

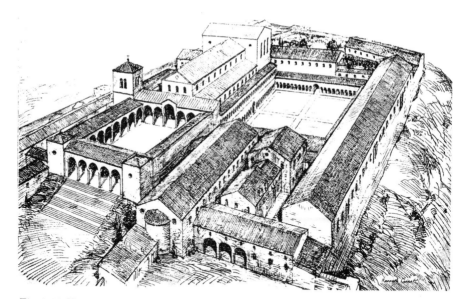

Fig. 8.10. Hypothetical reconstruction of Monte Cassino in the late eleventh century, by K.J. Conant and H.M. Willard.

on the monastery's estates, whereby dispersed farms were brought together inside a fortified enclosure.

By the mid-eleventh century the abbey church of San Vincenzo Maggiore once again had the tripartite form that had been first created in the ninth century. The plan bore some similarities to the proposed reconstruction by K.J. Conant and H.M. Willard of Monte Cassino in the eleventh century (Fig. 8.10). Entry into the atrium (internal cloister?) at present remains a mystery. Was there a central stairway up to the raised landing between the two towers which replaced the ninth-century staircases in the north and south lodges? Or were there staircases flanking the north and south sides of the atrium which have yet to be identified? The atrium area, too, is a matter of speculation. Whether there was an atrium, such as Conant and Willard propose for eleventh-century Monte Cassino, or a galilee, a great eastwork of north European type, such as Conant proposed beyond the façade of the abbey church at Cluny II, dating to *c*. 1043, is a matter which only excavation will resolve. The basilica itself was still a grand building, to judge from its decorations. Its paintings, in particular, are of the highest quality, and illustrate the innovative skills of San Vincenzo's artists in the second quarter of the eleventh century.

The building history closely resembles what was happening at Monte Cassino. Abbot John III (997-1010) of Monte Cassino began the process of renovation following the Arab sack of 883 when he completed a circuit of fortifications. Meanwhile, Abbot John IV, his contemporary at San Vin-

Fig. 8.11. View from the 'valley of the martyrs' past the site of San Vincenzo Maggiore (left) to the new abbey-church. (Photo: Ray Manley)

cenzo, launched a programme of renewal, beginning with the basilica. Abbot Atenolfus of Monte Cassino (1011-22) erected a campanile, as did Abbot Ilarius at San Vincenzo. Atenolfus also refurbished Monte Cassino's abbey church. His successor, Theobaldus (1022-35) pursued these works, and laid out an atrium flanked by two towers. Abbot Richerius, by birth and education a German, continued the construction of Monte Cassino's eastwork, seeking to make an atrium that was partly inspired by St Peter's and partly by Ottonian models. Abbot Desiderius (1058-87), in a celebrated campaign of works, then rebuilt the entire monastery. John V's works at San Vincenzo in the 1050s and 1060s were somewhat more modest, but nevertheless he enhanced the monastery significantly. Desiderius' ambitious programme at Monte Cassino, which went on into the 1080s, must have been the inspiration for Gerard, originally a Cassinese monk, who was elected abbot at San Vincenzo in 1076, to abandon the four-hundred-year-old site of San Vincenzo and establish an entirely new monastery on a level, readily fortified site (Fig. 8.11).

Demolition

When Gerard decided to move the monastery to a new site he needed materials. The existing monastery served as a quarry. San Vincenzo Maggiore was systematically demolished, just as the buildings in the north part of the monastery had been razed a few decades earlier. The destruction started from the ground level in the church. Hence, at this

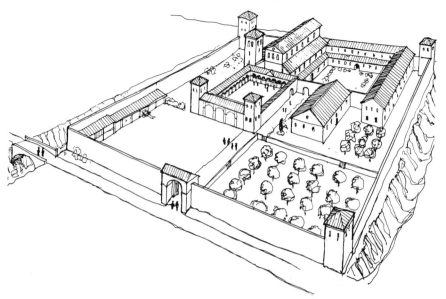

Fig. 8.12. Interim reconstruction of Abbot Gerard's monastery, by Sheila Gibson.

level, much of the east and west ends were left, as they lay well below the surface. The workmen progressed across the gently rising artificial terrace, dragging the tips of mortar and rubble downslope. Among the objects found in these tips are two silver coins of the Emperor Henry III (1046-56), minted in Pavia. For the most part, the workmen efficiently transported away everything that might be re-used. Only broken marble and small sherds of glass were left in the tips. Cut into the upper parts of the west wall of the corridor beneath the old entrance (i.e. on the eastern side of the atrium) was a large lime kiln, evidently deployed to provide materials for Abbot Gerard's new project. A second kiln was located directly in front of the north lodge. Most pavements were lifted; coloured marbles were rarely left behind. Only some of the white Proconnesian marble was overlooked by the workmen. Once again, the fragments of saints' faces, lost in the piles of rubble, painted only a generation or two before the demolition, call into question the clinical manner of the destruction.

Not all the church was dismantled at once. Although the crypt was filled in, it appears that the central apse remained standing on its own. This may have served as a focus for the cult of San Vincenzo until the new abbey church was consecrated on 20 April 1117. At this point the old apse was finally knocked down. An interesting parallel exists for this. The demolition of the northern part of the monastery to provide materials for Abbot John V's new claustrum (see above) had been comprehensive except for the apse of the south church, the erstwhile San Vincenzo Minore and later

172

distinguished guests' house, which remained standing until modern times. In the excavations around the distinguished guests' palace traces of a path leading up to this apse were discovered. The sanctity of this spot, which owed its origins to late antiquity, survived the demolition.

With the removal of its apse, all trace of San Vincenzo Maggiore was soon lost. Only the chapel on its north side, known in the eighteenth century as Santa Restituta, survived the demolition. As for San Vincenzo Maggiore, those of its walls which remained served as terraces for nearly a millennium. Olives and vines were cultivated in an aggregate of marble, glass and painted plaster.

Abbot Gerard's monastery

Abbot Gerard (1076-1109), John V's successor, evidently found the old site unsatisfactory. Was it too vulnerable to attack, or was the abbot mesmerised by Abbot Desiderius' great rebuilding of Monte Cassino? Perhaps it was a combination of both that led him to embark upon yet another phase of building works. According to the chronicler, Gerard led the 'transmigration' of the monks to a new site on the opposite side of the river Volturno. He chose a location immediately south of the Republican ditch, and east of the first-century Roman villa where the cliff face of the plateau on its east side provided a second line of defence. The flat site had been occupied by a large group of timber buildings in the ninth century. A smaller nucleus may have existed here in the tenth and eleventh centuries. In an excavation close to the twelfth-century abbot's palace a palimpsest of post-holes was discovered, suggesting that a small community outlasted the ninth-century monastic *pars rusticus*. If so, the peasants were evicted and their buildings razed when Gerard erected his model monastery. In all a precinct covering three hectares was planned. The area was defined by its defences. Besides the massive north ditch, dating to Republican times, a second rock-cut ditch was laboriously excavated to form the south side of the area. This ditch runs from the Volturno to the cliff edge, dropping nearly 11 m along its length. A fortress wall ran around the limits of the zone, stretches of which are visible today.

Inside the precinct a characteristic plan was laid out. This was dominated by the abbey church and an enclosed atrium in front of it. A range of buildings ran along the north side of the enclosure, with garderobes directing the waste into the north ditch. The cloisters were situated on the south side of the church, covering much of the ground between the church and the south ditch. In the south-west corner lay the abbot's palace – a tower-house. Close to this a workshop was constructed for the duration of the building works. Other buildings, yet to be identified, certainly occupied the area.

The chronicler records that the first building to be erected was the atrium. Little remains of this enclosed colonnaded entrance to the abbey.

173

In size (32.8 x 37.2 m) and form it must have resembled the refurbished atrium made by Abbot John V in front of San Vincenzo Maggiore. Here, though, the architect had the advantage of building on flat ground. There were probably eight columns per side, although only the west side is complete. The monumental marble column bases had clearly been brought from the old site, probably from the nave of San Vincenzo Maggiore itself. Their obvious variety reveals that the search for design perfection of the Alberti kind was a far-off goal. Two small lodges appear to have been made in the façade of the atrium; a tile kiln occupied the north lodge, evidently intended to produce the tiles for the roof of the basilica and covered parts of the atrium. Later, a cemetery was made in the north portico.

The precinct was dominated by the new abbey church. The triple-apsed church was 48 m long and 21.7 m wide. Its apse reached to the edge of the cliff, the church dominated the view up the valley to the east past Cerro as far the Via Numicia. All the finest stone and marble, stripped from the old abbey church, was deployed to make this as grand a church as Desiderius' at Monte Cassino. References to San Vincenzo's epic past abounded. According to the chronicler, Abbot Joshua's mausoleum was broken apart and his remains, along with those of Ambrosius Autpert, were transferred here. A local farmer told us how, as a boy, he had crawled into a crypt in the east apse of the church: if it could be found, its comparison with the ninth-century crypt would make a fascinating study. In his report of the excavations of the new church Don Angelo Pantoni makes no mention of this crypt. Instead, he was fascinated by the discovery of fine marble pavements of the so-called Cosmatesque form filling the wide nave and flanking aisles. The floor had been laid directly on top of the post-holes belonging to the earlier timber buildings. The pavements contain marble almost entirely plundered from the old site. Notably, broken pieces of ninth-century tombstones were also used. Here, too, Pantoni found the fragments of the monumental inscription which had graced the façade of San Vincenzo Maggiore, recording Abbot Joshua's achievement (see p. 83). The tombstone of Abbot Ilarius (1011-45) also came to light here. Once again, we cannot ignore the rude treatment of these memorials of San Vincenzo's past. The contrast between this treatment and the chronicler's account could not be clearer. The material record of these two great personalities in San Vincenzo's history apparently had no value whatsoever. Whereas, so far as the chronicler was concerned, these two abbots belonged to the pantheon of the semi-divine, makers of history itself. Memory and oblivion are contrasted in the twelfth-century regard for text and disregard for material culture. History before the Renaissance was an abstract sum of personalities and events, and seldom the material manifestation of those individuals or events.

To the south of the church Pantoni found traces of a cloister walk. Our small excavations in the apple orchard showed that few of these have survived. Traces of substantial buildings, ripped out by ploughing, and tesserae from wall mosaics once covered with gold-leaf were our most notable discoveries. The tesserae were unlike those from the ninth-century workshops which had been looted from classical sites. Perhaps, like those commissioned by Abbot Desiderius for Monte Cassino, these were made by Venetian craftsmen. The ploughing also brought to light a collection of fine coloured window glass. Once again, these panes were quite different to the ninth-century examples from the old site. In plan the new cloisters were as compact as the short-lived ensemble erected by Abbot John V on the old site, and like those nearby at the Benedictine monastery of San Clemente a Casauria in the Abruzzo which partially survive today. The scriptorium where John wrote his history would have been here: we might imagine it to have been well-lit like the surviving twelfth-century scriptorium at S. Pietro Avellana in Marche with its wide splayed windows.

The present restored seminary includes the remains of a medieval tower which in its earliest form was where abbots Gerard, Benedict and the chronicler (later an abbot) John resided. Nineteenth-century photographs show it in a derelict condition. But the building was quite consistent with the tower-houses then being erected all over Italy as the feudal age generated a ubiquitous sense of insecurity. Flanking it are sixteenth-century wings. Excavations in the grounds directly in front revealed a stone building at least 19 m long and 7.7 m wide. This was an open-ended workshop. Initially, a tile kiln occupied the east end, fired with the help of easterly winds. Evidently this was ineffective: the kiln was moved to the west end of the building, where it was rebuilt at least once and then abandoned, a small pottery kiln made of waste tiles was inserted into the remains. The potter was making large water pitchers.

John was writing his chronicle within the largest fort in the region. Its wide ditches and walled defences are an impressive witness to the resources that the monastery could mobilize. Inside Abbot Gerard almost certainly rationalized the earlier plan of the Romanesque monastery at the old site, building on conveniently flat ground. The emphasis was upon a grand ritual centre, with affluent use of *spolia*, wall mosaics and magnificent stained glass. The cloisters and abbatial palace doubtless shared this affluent guise. But, as we have seen, little else occupied the monastic precinct. In essence, this was an extraordinarily grand feudal manor where San Vincenzo's epic history ended. Here, John the monk sought out a romance of the past. Did he write it for his fellow monks, or for visitors, or for wider dissemination? As we have seen, the text is a scrapbook. It mixes a history of individuals and events with fable, which, like the ground around the monastery, will only be understood when it is fully 'excavated' by a scholar who comprehends the material context of this epic.

9

In the Shadow of San Vincenzo

By Greek or Roman standards the remains at San Vincenzo are not impressive. They scarcely compare with Pompeii, Herculaneum or Ostia. But by Dark Age standards they are outstanding. This was a world of timber huts, long-houses and makeshift urban structures inserted into ruined Roman buildings. Being made of ephemeral materials, Dark Age structures are elusive. San Vincenzo is thus an exceptional discovery. But an essential aspect of our project was to establish how exceptional San Vincenzo was to those people living in Central Italy in the later first millennium. This led us to examine the history of settlement in the upper Volturno valley. Our aim was to examine how San Vincenzo's estate evolved. Could the archaeology of the monastery and its villages shed light on the historical debate about monastic economies in the early Middle Ages (see p. 7)?

The classical landscape

Let us begin with a fixed point: the upper Volturno valley in classical times. Classical writers leave us in no doubt about the organized landscape of Italy. From their descriptions we form a picture of country estates worked by tenants and plantation slaves. We also form a picture of a world where entire provinces were devoted to a monoculture. Some regions were evidently arable while others specialized in polyculture (olives and vines) or livestock. Country scenes on mosaics and sculptures augment these descriptions. Rural living was romanticized by the Romans. Horace, for example, wrote glowingly of the large olive-growing estates around Venafro and the rustic mixture of farming in the upper Volturno valley.

The archaeology of the Roman world fleshes out this picture. No one can be unimpressed by the archaeology of its cities. Ancient Rome was the outstanding achievement of the classical state: its road network, civic buildings and scale of metropolitan planning are awesome. But in many respects the mark the Romans made on the landscape around their cities was even more impressive. Archaeologists working every imperial province have traced the vestiges of great ranches and estates with numerous cottages and kilometres of gridded fields. An indelible imprint of empire was left on Europe's variegated landscapes.

Horace's description of the landscape in this part of Samnium offers only tantalizing glimpses of what we now know was there. A survey of about 10 per cent of San Vincenzo's territory, made in 1980-81, yielded a good deal of information. The field survey was led by Peter Hayes whose task was to find early medieval settlements associated with the monastery. In particular we wanted to find out whether some Roman settlements were still inhabited in post-classical times, as in a sense the Roman villa at San Vincenzo was occupied by monks.

Method is important if a field survey is to possess any historical merit. The territory was divided into viable parcels and it was decided to investigate the environs of San Vincenzo in some detail (Fig. 9.1). This meant field-walking as much of the Rocchetta plain as might be reached. But within the rest of San Vincenzo's territory there was only time to examine a swathe of land down the Volturno valley between the present villages of Colli and Montaquila, and a complementary swathe running east-west at right angles across the profile of the hills. Two small mountain basins around the modern villages of Filignano and Selvone in the western sector of the territory were also field-walked.

Each parcel of land was gridded into kilometre squares. A team of four then investigated each square, marching in a line up and down every cultivated field to see what might be observed in the plough-soil. Few fields in western Europe disappoint the archaeologist. The refuse of ages, whether from farms, manure or other less durable activities, litters the landscape. Lithic tools and debris, pottery of numerous types from Neolithic times to the present day, and occasionally metalwork, are staple discoveries. These fossils from past ages are the archaeologist's texts: each must be interpreted to tell its story. Each item is bagged, and its context registered in great detail. From this evidence the succession of settlements and their attendant landscapes can be reconstructed. Just as the excavations at San Vincenzo revealed phase after phase of building, so these surface scatters allow us to formulate a picture of the sequence of sites built on these landscapes. But the Roman age is more richly represented than any other.

The scatters of abraded Roman potsherds tell a story familiar in most parts of the West Mediterranean. The upper Volturno valley was densely settled in the period from *c.* 100 BC until the third century. Between San Vincenzo and the Roman colony of Venafro smallholdings existed every kilometre or so. Interspersed between these cottages at three or four kilometre intervals were larger homesteads – *villae rusticae* – estate centres. The widespread scatter of potsherds, thrown out with the kitchen waste, shows the extent of manuring. The scatters belong to a moment when the morphology of the landscape was being altered. The study of alluviation in the survey zones reveals substantial soil-movement at this time, most probably the result of intensive ploughing. But the most

177

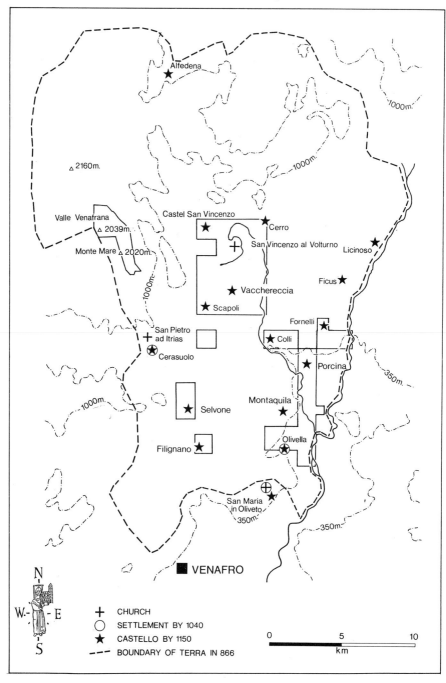

Fig. 9.1. The areas covered by the San Vincenzo survey.

Fig. 9.2. Transhumance cabin and associated pens. (Photo: Fred Baker)

illuminating evidence for the impact of Roman imperial agrarian policy is on Monte Mare.

Two thousand metres above sea-level, on the pastures where shepherds tend their summer herds, the remains of a Roman transhumance encampment were discovered in a survey undertaken in 1985. The outline of the encampment, though partially destroyed by a recent cabin, can still be made out on the ground. Trial excavations in 1985 pinpointed the shepherds' rubbish middens. Among the rubbish were many sherds of coarse cooking pots, as we would expect. But there were also sherds of fourth-century North African tablewares and a few fragments of glass vessels. The assemblage was worthy of a modest villa.

By the fourth century this densely populated landscape was undergoing a major transformation. Sites from the fourth to the eleventh century were virtually absent in those areas examined by the field walkers. In sum, the field survey was totally unhelpful in shedding light on the central issue of the project – the relationship of San Vincenzo to its village communities.

The Roman Empire began to lose momentum in the second century: its distant borders made it difficult to manage. By the third century economic recession had set in. Field surveys document what contemporary sources describe as *agri deserti*, not only in the upper Volturno valley, but in most parts of western Europe. The disappearance of small farms, and the slow decay of villas during the fourth and early fifth centuries, speak eloquently of the malaise that ultimately brought destruction of the empire. But what happened to the farmers?

The whereabouts of the peasantry in later Roman times has intrigued

179

Fig. 9.3. Transhumance cabin on Monte Mare. (Photo: Fred Baker)

Fig. 9.4. A shepherd in his cabin; note the cheeses on the shelves. (Photo: Fred Baker)

archaeologists and historians alike for many years. It is commonly assumed that archaeologists are unable to recognize them. Either elusive new sites were founded or earlier farms continued to be occupied. In the territory of San Vincenzo we hoped to resolve this issue.

The late Roman villa beneath the monastic remains contains ample diagnostic artefacts. With the help of these, we surmised, we would be able to recognize contemporary sites while field-walking. But the distinctive late Roman pottery found at San Vincenzo was absent from the many small Roman farms found in the survey of the upper Volturno valley. This indicates beyond reasonable doubt that the settlement pattern hereabouts was transformed by the fourth century, if not before. The villa at San Vincenzo, including its accompanying churches is our only real clue to the archaeology of the elusive final phase of the Roman state in this region. The villa, as we noted in Chapter 3, was situated on a slope in a rather unlikely position. We can only wonder whether other first- to fourth-century villas were abandoned in favour of similar situations – places which might be detected only by test pitting. In sum, it seems that a new Christianised landscape was created. Its focus was the villa and its surrounding fields, while beyond it, in an outer world, after a millennium of intensive management, a wilderness began to form.

The fifth-century San Vincenzo villa, however, was appreciably smaller than the early to middle Imperial villa and its associated cottages. Seventy persons, we have calculated, lived at, or at least were associated with, the centre. An analysis of the skeletons from the cemetery revealed a notable number of young female adults and infants – indices of regular childbearing. On this evidence, the community was able to maintain its numbers adequately. But the population was small in comparison to the community which had occupied the *vicus* here in Republican/early Imperial times. This settlement had covered as much as ten hectares. Part of this enormous decline over half a millennium owed much to the creation of the colonies at Isernia and Venafro as well as to the redistribution of many families to the homesteads dotted around the Rocchetta plain. But plainly a major demographic decline was in process. The reasons for this, like the decline and fall of the Roman empire itself, are the stuff of historical debates. Nevertheless, two factors merit consideration. Increased taxation may have induced many farmers to emigrate to great towns such as Rome or Naples. Certainly the seaboard towns were booming once more by the early fifth century. (A parallel worth noting is the recent population of Rocchetta al Volturno which dropped from 2,500 in the mid-ninteenth century to about 800 in 1950. The opportunity to emigrate to the New World coupled with harsh standards of living, including high taxation, largely accounted for this.)

A second factor may be loosely described as cultural adaptation to late Roman economic stringency. Jack Goody has recently surmised that attitudes to marriage altered at about this time. The Church, he argues, attempted to regulate reproduction by forbidding marriage between close kin. Late marriage may have been promoted at about the same time, leading to fewer births. Goody believes that the Church stood to inherit estates from childless marriages. This may have been true for the élite in Roman society, but for the population as a whole high taxation, deteriorating political conditions and low expectations may equally have determined the sharp decline in the birth rate.

Goody's thesis is controversial. It accounts for the rarity of late Roman sites, but not the complete breakdown of the settlement system. By AD 550, as we have seen, the classical age in this corner of Samnium had ended. San Vincenzo was deserted; only its graveyard was sporadically used. Other villas hereabouts, we may surmise on the absence of data, were deserted at this time, leaving the population of the valley at its lowest ebb for a millennium.

The latest Roman site found in the upper Volturno valley is also a harbinger of medieval settlement in the region. On the exposed pinnacle of Colle Sant'Angelo, we discovered the precursor of the tenth-century *castello* of Colli al Volturno. A tiny structure, possibly a shrine, about 6 m long and 3 m wide, was created here in the later sixth century, at approximately the time that the Lombards conquered Samnium. A bronze coin of the Emperor Justin II (565-78) was found in the make-up of the floor of the building, while later Roman potsherds and fragments of glass lamps occurred in the associated layers. Like the recently excavated shrine of similar date found at Sant' Angelo di Archi in the nearby Sangro valley, this one was almost certainly placed beside a feeder road linking the trans-Appennine Via Numicia to the roads which forked immediately below Colli a Volturno, south towards Venafro or west towards Sora.

In search of dark age villages

The *Terra Sancti Vincentii* was a block of land given to the monastery by Duke Gisulf. This may have been a pre-existing estate comprising mountain pastures and the upper Volturno valley. It certainly bridged two different eco-systems: the Continental climate of the uplands, and the polycultural zone from San Vincenzo southwards. By 866 the block of land was recognized by the Emperor Louis II. The *terra* covered 400-450 km^2; it was smaller than those of the abbeys of Farfa and Monte Cassino, but larger than Subiaco's. But the chief resource of land in the Middle Ages was its potential for productivity. This, of course, depended upon the workforce tied to the land. The search for this workforce, as archaeologists have discovered throughout Europe, is far from straightforward.

Late Roman villas are difficult to find; Dark Age homesteads are virtually invisible. The only clues in this region, as we shall see, exist in the *Chronicon Vulturnense*. The chronicler tells us that when Paldo, Tato and Taso arrived the *terra* contained *silva densissima*. This was a biblical

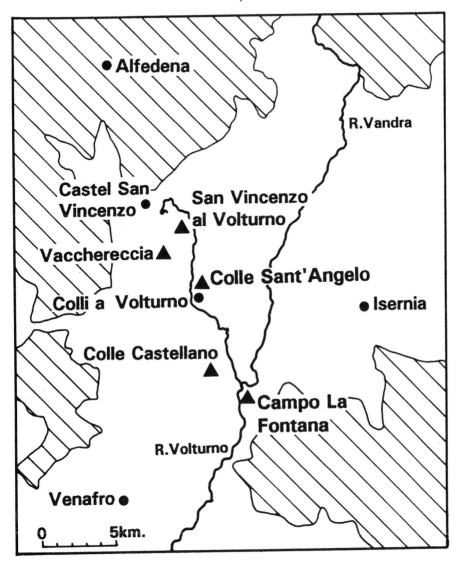

Fig. 9.5. The main sites mentioned in this chapter.

metaphor (see p. 26), laying emphasis upon the opposition of culture/ nature and christian/pagan. Our archaeological enquiries, nevertheless, tend to confirm this transformation of the landscape. A study of the geomorphology of the Rocchetta plain shows that the plateau and most hill slopes had been cultivated in some form or other in the early imperial period. The extent of the cultivation must have been similar to that in the

183

nineteenth century. The decline in the population, as in modern times, must have meant that hill slopes and poorer ground were abandoned to encroaching vegetation. Added to this, the river Volturno would have once again intermittently flooded the plain. When the founders arrived dense woodland would have been the most prominent feature of the landscape.

San Vincenzo's slaves and tenants are, of course, incidental to the chronicler's tale. Nevertheless, he records slaves working homesteads in the territory. These were *condumae*, servile tenant families regarded as a single unit, each with their own plot of land. One such family occupied the Casa Lorenzo, a broad terrace on the edge of the Rocchetta plain only 2 km from the monastery that to this day is still called after the early medieval farm. Systematic field-walking on the terrace failed to find any trace of the homestead itself. Only potsherds of early Roman date were found. A peasant in classical times had evidently occupied the terrace; his Dark Age descendants, for reasons we surmise below, constructed a house on the nearby slope overlooking the old Roman ruins.

The chronicler also records the existence of several clusters of families named in a group of gifts to San Vincenzo made in 807-36. These families lived at the southern end of the *terra*, close to Santa Maria in Oliveto. These are interpreted as clusters of slave families in groups of three to five. Each group gave its name to their block of land, names such as Fracte, Mazzano, and Toro. Such clusters are common in ninth-century documents from south and central Italy. A telling entry occurs in the chronicle as far as San Vincenzo's peasants are concerned is recorded in 854. A group of peasants protested that they were freemen who had come to San Vincenzo to aid its defence (against the Arabs), not to be serfs. From this brief report we may deduce that San Vincenzo was sorely in need of tenants not just to defend the valley, but to work its land. Some small indication of the low population is illustrated by the history of church-building in the territory outside the monastery. Often a group of families supported a small church known as a *plebes*. References to two churches in the *terra*, probably *plebes*, occur in the chronicle. At San Pietro *ad Itias* a chapel was founded in the 840s, somewhere near the later village of Cerasuolo, and another called San Eleuterio was founded in the 850s near the later village of Filignano. The fact that they were recorded at this time may suggest that the number of tenant farmers in these parts was growing. Until recently, the form of these churches remained a mystery, but a surviving early medieval church in the *terra* of San Vincenzo offers us an impression of the world of the Dark Age peasant.

The church is beside the Roman bridge known as the Ponte Latrone, close to the modern hamlet of Campo La Fontana (Fig. 9.6). It survives almost to its full height, though today it is used as a stable. The church is located beside the south end of a massive Roman bridge known as the Ponte Latrone – a motorway-sized bridge as much as 60 m long supported on at least eight to ten arches. In early medieval times the bridge provided

Fig. 9.6. The eighth-century chapel at Campo La Fontana. (Photo: Ray Manley)

a crossing over the Volturno connecting San Vincenzo to the heartlands of the kingdom of Benevento. By the eighth century, though, at least one Roman pier had collapsed and the makeshift route over the river involved taking a rough steep pathway carved up through a standing pier to reach the original Roman bridge level. It is staggeringly primitive in contrast to the scale and ambition of the original bridge.

The little church is dwarfed by the Roman monument. It measures 6.5 m long and 5.04 m at its widest. It is an elegantly made triconch, with a small nave, resembling in many ways the ninth-century crypt church at San Vincenzo. Although its walls are made of poor river boulders, the fluid lines of the triconch betray the work of a masterful architect. Its first roof was a small dome, which was subsequently replaced by the vault which survives today. Its position and size suggest that it may have housed no more than a shrine. Symbolically placed at the south entrance to San Vincenzo's territory, it was the first image of the great monastery to greet many pilgrims and visitors. As we shall see, a church of similar proportions, found in excavations made in 1990-91 at Colle Sant' Angelo, served the ninth-century community at Colli a Volturno.

Colle Sant' Angelo

In 1990, in search of a Dark Age homestead, we followed up a suggestion by a local informant at Colle Sant' Angelo, a spectacular pinnacle with a commanding view of virtually the entire upper Volturno valley. On the west side of the rocky pinnacle is a terrace about 80 m long and up to 20 m wide. Its name was one factor in the choice of this outlandish place to dig: Colle Sant' Angelo is the name by which Colli a Volturno is described in its tenth-century foundation charter. Was this the forerunner of the *castello*? When an electricity pylon was installed here the engineers unearthed a moulding from a Samnite sanctuary and two simple graves. A dwelling here might have dominated not only the surrounding territory, but also the principal route up and down the valley.

The 1990-91 excavations showed that the terrace was occupied by a shrine established in the sixth century. The simple small rectangular shrine, dated by a bronze *nummus* of the Emperor Justin II, was incorporated within a larger church two hundred years afterwards. Samnite mouldings from a sanctuary were used to add a touch of elaboration to the step into the Carolingian-period chancel. Fragments of wall plaster as well as ninth-century glass hanging lamps made in San Vincenzo's workshops show that attempts were made to emulate the monastery's elegance. Around it was disposed a small irregular cemetery. In size and form it brings to mind the little early medieval chapel of Naturno in the upper Adige valley. Like the abbey, though, its moment of grandiosity was short-lived. It appears to have been burnt, perhaps by the Arabs when they passed up the valley. Although rebuilt, the final structure was simpler; perhaps the relics held here since the sixth century had been plundered. Finally, the building was systematically demolished; its stone was removed, presumably for the new church at Colli a Volturno.

The short but vivid history of Colle Sant' Angelo is tantalising. Its discovery raises many questions which, as yet, cannot be answered. Was the church one of the many shrines sponsored by San Vincenzo to the cult of St Michael the Archangel, associated with the pilgrimage to Monte Sant' Angelo on the Gargano peninsula? (Another, for example, was founded by San Vincenzo in Isernia.) Was it constructed by a pre-eminent Lombard family of these parts, ancestors of one of those many families who negotiated with the monastery when Colli a Volturno was made? Is it indicative of the mid-slope occupation of the Volturno valley since the desertion of the valley bottom in the sixth century?

Irrespective of its association with the cult of St Michael the Archangel, the excavated remains provide some genuine measure of a ninth-century forerunner of a church serving one of San Vincenzo's communities. Like the chapel beside the Ponte Latrone, it was tiny because the resources of the community were underdeveloped. Its purpose, we may surmise from its architecture, paintings and glassware, was to promote the new liturgy.

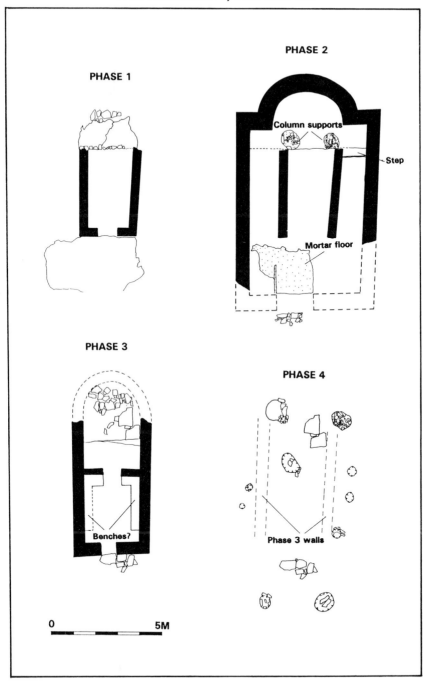

Fig. 9.7. Phase plan of the remains at Colle Sant'Angelo.

Its model may be found in the many small chapels erected by lords on their lands since later Merovingian times in Austrasia and Neustria, and from the later Lombard period in Italy. These chapels confronted the anti-Christian ethos of the wilderness which had recolonised the classical landscape since late antiquity. The domain of dwarfs and evil spirits, so perilous to man, was being reconquered by Christian culture.

Castelli

The chronicler ascribes a real change in the level of population to the later tenth century. Nature was tamed when the forests were cleared and appropriated by the Christian world represented by new villages. *Incastellamento*, the creation of new villages (*castelli*), was a conscious strategy executed by a succession of San Vincenzo's abbots. Prince Pandulfo I confirmed the monastery's right to *ius incastellandi* in a diploma of 27 July 967. Pandulfo was acknowledging what the monastery was actively doing. Abbot Rambaldus (920-44) launched the process with the creation of Santa Maria in Oliveto in 939 explicitly to cultivate a largely abandoned zone at the southern end of the *terra*. Ten families were party to this accord. As the village overlooked the corridor between Venafro and Isernia – a main road into ancient and medieval Samnium – Santa Maria would also have served as San Vincenzo's first line of defence. Six years later a charter was issued to Castel San Vincenzo *castro / castello Samnie* (Fig. 9.8). The lease was granted to four men for 29 years. They had to clear as much land around the castello as they could. Their rent was to be one quarter of their crops. (The monastery lay within the bounds of their territory.)

Leases were next concluded in 962 with tenants at Cerasuolo (*ad Causa*), to the west of San Vincenzo, and *Olivella*, in the southern part of the *terra*. *Ad Causa* is known today as Cerasuolo Vecchio, a hilltop village which dominated the skyline until the late eighteenth century when its inhabitants moved down to an adjacent valley, the present site of Cerasuolo. The tenth-century village was situated close to the ninth-century church of San Pietro *ad Itrias* at a point where the old Roman road between Venafro and Sora met a track leading up to the high mountain pastures on Monte Mare. Four families are mentioned in the charter. *Olivella*, by contrast, was almost certainly the low hill of Colle Castellano near modern Montaquila. Three families were signatories to the lease. Our investigations of this hill are described below.

In 972 leases were concluded with the villagers of *Vadu Traspadini* (later *Vadu Porcinum*), with Colli (*ad San Angelum*) and Fornelli (*Bantra*). *Vadu Porcinum* today is a wooded hill known as Porcina, beside the river Volturno. Thick vegetation conceals abandoned dwellings of later medieval times. In 972 sixteen families lived here. A combined lease for Colli and Fornelli in 972 mentions 22 men in fourteen family groups. In 988 a new lease for Colli was made for 40 men. In 975 a lease was drawn up for

Fig. 9.8. View of Castel San Vincenzo. (Photo: Ray Manley)

Alfedena, the old pre-Roman and Roman centre in the mountains to the north of San Vincenzo. The charter indicates that some men were already living here, but the monastery was concerned to encourage more settlers. In 982 a lease was drawn up with four men at Scapoli, a few kilometres west of San Vincenzo. These men were offered favourable settling-in terms: three years without rent. Three years later the monastery reached an accord with six men at Vacchereccia, a low hill close to Rocchetta Vecchia (which will be described more fully below). Cerro (*Cerrum*) was founded in 989. Fifteen men were signatories to the charter, and agreed to build and inhabit the *castello*. Its territory, extending towards the Sangro river, had been given to the count of Isernia 25 years earlier. The switch of ownership may have reflected the monastery's concern about this block of land. Half a century later in the 1040s Cerro was snatched by the Borrelli, Lombard counts from the Sangro valley (see p. 39). Charters were also issued for a place called *Ficus* in 995; and for Licinoso and Colle Stefano during the early eleventh century. *Ficus* was situated on a craggy spur known today as Il Seggio, a high vantage point commanding the deep, sinuous Vandra valley. The remains of later medieval dwellings stood on this remote spot, situated among the hill pasture. Eight men signed the

189

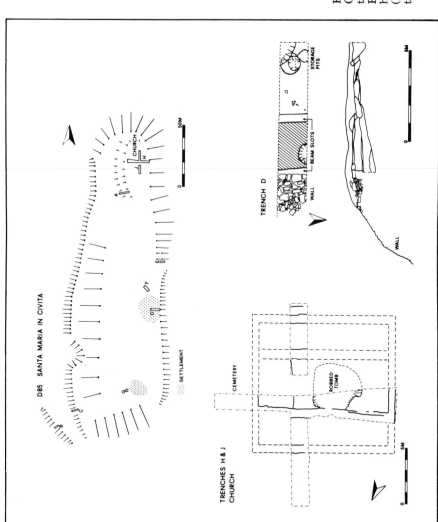

Fig. 9.9. Santa Maria in Civita (D85) – a ninth-century hilltop village in the Biferno valley. Plan of the hilltop (top), the church (left), and a cutting through the fortifications (right).

D85   SANTA MARIA IN CIVITA

CHURCH

SETTLEMENT

50M

TRENCH D

WALL   BEAM SLOTS   STORAGE PITS

WALL

5M

TRENCHES H & J
CHURCH

CEMETERY

ROBBED TOMB

5M

lease. Colle Stefano is a similar, high saddle-backed hill, overlooking the Volturno.

Incastellamento in the *terra* of San Vincenzo led to the creation of regularly spaced villages across its hilly terrain. In principle it was a project that was every bit as ambitious as making a new monastery. It involved the intention to bring together communities, and through partnerships to embark upon programmes of economic development. As we shall see, the illustration of *Olivella* reveals the scale of this investment. Over the course of 50 years approximately a hundred families were encouraged to clear woodland, to farm and in some cases to fortify their settlements. By the turn of the millennium between five hundred and a thousand peasants lived in the territory. In return for administering these communities, the monastery demanded a rental of about one quarter of their produce. Recent research has shown that the monastery carried out much the same programme of work on its long-held estates in the Abruzzo. Here it operated through a dependent church called Santa Maria di Musano, which owned land in the territory of Asti, between the rivers Piomba and Vomana. Andrea Staffa has shown that after 944 San Vincenzo created villages on exactly the same pattern as the chronicler describes for this time in the Volturno valley. On this basis it is likely that the monastery also introduced the idea to its estates in the rich, lower-lying lands around Capua too.

The history of San Vincenzo's policy of *incastellamento*, nevertheless, is somewhat sketchy. From the beginning of the San Vincenzo project in 1980 we appreciated that only archaeological evidence would enable us to integrate the related worlds of the monastery and its villages. The distinguished French historian Georges Duby noted long ago that only 'by examining the abundant objects dug up by archaeologists, which for the first time reveal the atmosphere of the interior of a peasant's hut, the plan of a village, the organization of an estate, or the tools to be found in a craftsman's workshop, it is possible to uncover economic reality and to lay bare, with the help of some quantitative data, the mechanics of growth and decline'. But as these places were not identified in the field survey, how were we to find them?

Our search began with a model of a *castello* in mind: Santa Maria in Civita, discovered in 1978 in the Biferno Valley, some hundred kilometres from San Vincenzo (Fig. 9.9). Santa Maria in Civita is a fortified hilltop site near the modern hilltop village of Guardialfiera, situated where the inland hills meet the Adriatic coastal plain. Besides its impressive stone enclosure wall, the settlement contained traces of a cluster of well-built timber houses and an aisled church (demolished in the tenth or eleventh centuries) with its own cemetery. Significant quantities of well-thrown pots and a little glassware, as well as evidence of storage for agricultural produce were discovered in the excavations.

Remains of other early medieval settlements are few in Italy. Dwellings

Fig. 9.10 View of Vacchereccia from Rocchetta Vecchia, the village which succeeded it. Vacchereccia is the wooded saddle-backed hill to the right of Rocchetta castle. (Photo: Ray Manley)

have been found only at Piadena, a village in the Po valley near Brescia, and at Montarrenti and Poggibonsi, hilltops near Siena. At Piadena traces were found of square structures not dissimilar from the small structures created within the ruins of post-Roman Brescia as well as the later tenth-century tenements recently excavated in Ferrara. At Montarrenti the floors had been cut into the rock; but barely anything else survived. At Poggibonsi the remains of sunken huts with associated post-holes have been found. In these cases the houses were versions of the thatched farm-buildings once common in Molise. These buildings are roughly 5-6 m long by about 4 m wide; often they have low drystone walls and a thatched roof, the pitch of which is supported by a line of irregular uprights. After such a building is demolished, virtually nothing remains to help the archaeologist other than a few post-holes and a beaten surface stained by the presence of a hearth. Only by chance, therefore, are such ephemeral dwellings discovered in excavations.

Our first solution to finding such sites was to test-pit carefully chosen hills. Our second, less systematic solution was to quiz local farmers about likely sites. Before undertaking any fieldwork we selected the sites carefully, first identifying the *castelli* described in the tenth-century charters. Places like Castel San Vincenzo, Cerro and Colli are still occupied, making it virtually impossible to carry out systematic investigations. Pipe trenches in Castel San Vincenzo have brought to light tenth- to eleventh-century potsherds, while in Colli part of an eleventh-century tower still survives in the heart of the modern village. Cerasuolo Vecchio, Colle Stefano, *Ficus*, *Olivella*, Porcina and Vacchereccia are today overgrown hills.

Two sites were selected for initial investigation. The choice was guided by several factors. With different climatic, ecological and economic zones dividing the northern half of the territory from the southern, it seemed wise to select a site from each zone. Since we were hoping to find evidence from the enigmatic sixth to ninth centuries, we needed sites located close to successful Roman settlements. By the same token, we also needed sites with access to good ground where subsistence farming might have been readily practised. After some debate Vacchereccia and *Olivella* (Colle Castellano) were selected. Vacchereccia was attractive because the hill was only 4 km from San Vincenzo. *Olivella*, on the other hand, lies 20 km away towards the southern end of the *terra*. When we started to work we found the contrast between the sites even greater than we had imagined.

Vacchereccia (*Baccaricia*)

The investigations at Vacchereccia proved challenging. Vacchereccia is today a thickly wooded hill. The remains of a modest Roman villa were found in the ploughed fields at the foot of its south side; on its wooded summit are the remains of a small late medieval village. In between, within the thick woodland, we identified twelve terraces, some of which were associated with eighteenth- or nineteenth-century farms.

We first excavated a line of pits up the steep south face of the hill. These pits revealed only twelfth- to fifteenth-century sherds from the first terrace occupied by the late medieval village; no early medieval potsherds were found on the summit. Sherds of early medieval date, however, were discovered in test pits further down the slope, on terraces four and five. Having found these, we next excavated a small trench on the summit (terrace one) to confirm our initial observations (Fig. 9.11). This trench was situated behind the late medieval dwellings and contained a good range of the pottery once used by these farmers. Once again early medieval pottery was absent. We then test-pitted terraces four and five more thoroughly and pin-pointed a conspicuous concentration of early medieval material. Before proceeding further we had to clear away the thick undergrowth and small trees. Then we laid out a trial trench. This bisected a deep deposit which had been partially destroyed by two later phases of terracing. Overlying this deposit were the vestiges of an occupation layer. We enlarged the excavation in order to get a closer look at this crucial layer, but unfortunately no more of it had survived.

From these layers came two fourth-century bronze coins, a sixth- to seventh-century penannular brooch, a great variety of potsherds, a fragment of a ninth-century glass vessel made at San Vincenzo, many tile fragments and a small collection of animal bones. Although unprepossessing, this modest haul was revealing. Evidently a homestead had existed on the middle slope of this hill since the sixth or seventh century. The layer probably dated back to the tenth or eleventh century. Slight though the archaeological evidence is, it suggests that a homestead was built here after villas like that at San Vincenzo had been deserted. The wide terrace (five) immediately below the putative early medieval debris offered sufficient scope for the subsistence needs of a family. The location also commanded a panoramic view down the Volturno valley, useful from a defensive standpoint. The material poverty cannot be ignored in the light of San Vincenzo's stupendous affluence by the standards of these times. Did the homestead belong to a cultural periphery, albeit only 4 km from the monastery, where man was closer to nature with all its anti-Christian overtones?

The majority of the finds post-date the ninth century, belonging to the period of *incastellamento*. Hereabouts, it would seem, lay the residence of one of the six men mentioned in the charter of 985. Leo, David, Maio, Alberico, Aczo and Garipaldo, the six named men of *Baccaricia*, acquired rights to use a large block of land embracing the southern part of the Rocchetta plain. The terms of the lease were generous. It is no surprise to find that these families could afford glazed pottery and glassware like that used in the monastery. Their simple dwellings were graced with floors paved with rough hewn tiles scavenged from classical sites of all periods.

194

Fig. 9.11. Trial trench through the mid-slope of Vacchereccia. (Photo: author)

195

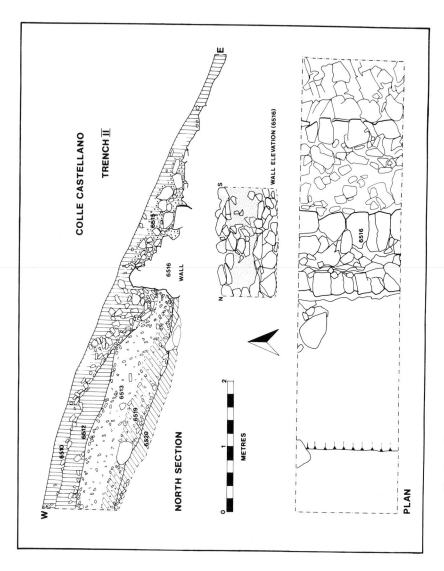

COLLE CASTELLANO

TRENCH II

W ... E

6510
6512
6513
6519
6520

6515

6516
WALL

NORTH SECTION

WALL ELEVATION (6516)

N ... S

6516

PLAN

0 1 2
METRES

Fig. 9.12. Section through the tenth-century wall of Colle Castellano (*Olivella*).

The mid-slope location was deserted in the twelfth century, when the villagers sought out a better-defended hilltop.

Colle Castellano (*Olivella*)

Colle Castellano is a prominent hill surrounded by rich agricultural land towards the southern end of the *terra* of San Vincenzo. Distinctive early medieval pottery littered the upper slopes of the hill. Even so, several local informants were convinced that the tenth-century *castello* lay not at Colle Castellano but on the hillside due west of modern Montaquila, which is known today as Olivella. A search of this hillside proved fruitless. We approached Colle Castellano more cautiously than Vacchereccia. Traces of a circuit of walls survive around the crest of the hill. At one point there are the remains of a building. Traces of a second high wall survive on the west side up against which is the stump of an enigmatic, apsed building. The archaeology of Colle Castellano was conspicuously promising by comparison with Vacchereccia.

Three small excavations confirmed the calibre of the archaeological remains. Trench one was cut through a platform along the eastern length of the enclosure wall. This showed that the platform was modern, though it had been built over a deep midden of tenth-century material. Trench two was designed to cut a profile through the midden and the enclosure wall which retained it (Fig. 9.12). The rich black midden had accumulated against the massive 1.5 m wide wall (the same width as the ninth-century nave wall of San Vincenzo Maggiore) in a comparatively short period. Large amounts of pottery and animal bone as well as iron-smelting slag made up the bulk of the finds. Quite clearly the villagers' dwellings had not been built up against the wall.

Test pits on the crown of the hill were unhelpful: the bare rock was covered only by thick leaf litter. The middens fell away on two sides suggesting that the dwellings had been cut into terraces close to the rocky summit. A third trench confirmed this. A cutting through a west-facing terrace once again revealed the fortification wall; but this time it sealed the substantial foundations of a powerfully-built small tower. The tower was constructed upon a terrace which contained a lens of ninth-century material. This fortuitous discovery appears to indicate the following sequence. In the ninth century a small habitation was made upon a raised terrace on the west-facing slope of the hill. This was soon superseded by a tower, occcupying approximately the same area. With the decision to make a *castello* here, the tower was demolished and an enclosure wall was constructed. This was accompanied by the settling of numerous households, presumably occupying post-built structures, gathered around the knoll of the hill. It is a powerful image of the origins and development of *incastellamento*; of the monastery's investment in the colonisation of nature.

The large quantity of tenth- to eleventh-century finds shows that *Olivella* mostly shared its source of pottery throughout its brief history with San Vincenzo and Vacchereccia. As at Vacchereccia, tenth- to eleventh-century glazed wares made in Campania were commonplace. The assemblage included crudely made *testi* – dishes for cooking over open fires – utensils which are notably absent in the monastery where the monks were served by a kitchen with its oven. Also as at Vacchereccia, a miscellany of broken tiles was found in the midden. The villagers, rather surprisingly, were scavenging deserted classical sites for these, presumably because the monastery's tileworks were restricted to supplying its own needs. The animal bones show a managed stock economy: pigs were raised and killed in a regular cycle, as were the cattle. The mortuary pattern of the sheep and goats is less regular than that for cattle and pigs: culling often occurred when they were at their prime for producing wool and milk.

Olivella was apparently deserted by *c.* 1100 in favour of Montaquila, a more readily fortified promontory protruding into the Volturno valley 4 km to the north. But was Colle Castellano occupied between the fifth and eighth centuries? A Roman site lies at the foot of the hill, as at Vacchereccia. No trace of later Roman material has been found among the sherds revealed in the ploughsoil. It is difficult to imagine that this conspicuously rich ecological niche was abandoned entirely until the ninth century. On the contrary, we might surmise that some small and elusive part of the settlement was founded in the sixth or seventh centuries when many of the classical sites were finally abandoned. But the evidence has eluded us.

Overpopulated islands?

Georges Duby has conjured up a picture of monastic territories in the ninth century as overpopulated islands surrounded by an ocean of wilderness. Duby belongs to that distinguished group of historians who ascribe the origins of regional economies to monasteries, challenging Pirenne's thesis about monastic self-sufficiency in this era. The evidence from San Vincenzo is perplexing. The monastery undoubtedly became a centre of urban proportions by the ninth century, but its *terra* remained underdeveloped until the process of *incastellamento* began in the tenth century.

The results of the field survey, as well as the accompanying excavations, compel us to study the history of *la longue durée*. Only with a wide-angle lens, through space and time, does the history of settlement in the upper Volturno valley begin to make sense. In classical times the region flourished through its relations with the rich coastal plain of Campania. But by the sixth century the valley was too marginal to matter, as the Ostrogoths, Byzantines, Romans and Lombards divided the Italian peninsula between them. The demise of the Roman state ruined the villa economy, and its diminished community must have sought refuge on wooded hills

198

such as Vacchereccia and the slopes around Colle Sant' Angelo, much as they were doing at Montarrenti and Poggibonsi in Tuscany. With this shift of settlement from the plains to woodland niches we are witnessing the change to a domestic mode of production. This is the world of self-sufficiency which Henri Pirenne had in mind (see p. 10). It was a change, according to the historian, Massimo Montanari, from the predominantly cereal-based diet of the classical age to a meat-based diet. The size of the population remains a tantalizing mystery. It is inconceivable, though, that the numbers in the territory exceeded a few hundred.

These people lodged in simple dwellings, but during the sixth and seventh centuries retained the spirit of the past. Some of their dead were buried in the old villa. They even acquired the jewellery much in fashion in the plains around Naples and further south in Byzantine Apulia. These were simple prestige goods, obtained through gift-exchange and other non-commercial activities. Some objects were used to furnish the bodies of their dead; others, such as the brooch from Vacchereccia, were kept in domestic circumstances. This jewellery is a modest last witness to the last echo of the classical symbiosis connecting the mountains and plains.

Few peasants occupied this frontier zone when Paldo, Tato and Taso founded San Vincenzo. Barely more peasants can have lived in the *terra* even in the ninth century. Only the many hundreds at the monastery, it seems, bore any resemblance to an over-populated island. The evidence from Colle Castellano and Vacchereccia reveals the persistence of a predominant domestic mode of production in the upper Volturno valley well into the ninth century. The monastery doubtless engaged local peasants to work for it. Some will have participated in the construction of buildings (such as the refectory of the craftsmen, made with pisé walls). Many may have lived in the *vicus*. Doubtless the local peasantry rendered some surplus produce to the monastery, to be stored in buildings of a local vernacular form in the *vicus* (see p. 116). Yet the small population in the valley means that the renders were inadequate to the monastery's needs. The poverty of the ninth-century archaeology in the valley – not least the minute investment in the *plebes* at Colle Sant' Angelo – reveals that San Vincenzo's economic strategy involved other places. The evidence reveals the historical debate between Pirenne and his critics to be oversimplified. But with the changed status of San Vincenzo in the tenth century, and as the market for agricultural goods re-opened with Campania, the wild territory was rationally reorganized. The affluent disposal of simple commodities in the middens at Colle Castellano and Vacchereccia bears witness to the new circumstances in the region. The powerful fortification around Colle Castellano, a mighty investment, illustrates the implications of the commercial revolution. With the revolution came seigneurial competition. The monastery, traditionally dependent upon state support, was now extremely vulnerable to the onset of feudalism. The mountains and plains were once more connected; just as San Vincenzo and Capua were joined by an umbilical cord. But with this new political climate this symbiosis was not to favour San Vincenzo.

Two worlds co-existed within the *terra* during the later first millennium. After the 780s the Benedictines enjoyed an urban affluence. In the monastery's shadow were peasants only ephemerally affected by its extraordinary history. The contrast led us to one indisputable conclusion: the creation of a monastic city at San Vincenzo in the ninth century owed little or nothing to the agrarian resources of its estates in the upper Volturno valley. The reason for its affluence must be sought elsewhere.

10

San Vincenzo and its European
Context

Everyone who visits the excavations at San Vincenzo asks why it was there in the first place. Molise is quintessentially what Carlo Levi, the painter, called 'the other Italy'. To answer this question we must reformulate our picture of Italy. Indeed, much as we hoped at the outset of the project, the archaeology compels us likewise to reconsider the history of the early Middle Ages. John, the twelfth-century chronicler, has offered us one perspective of how it was; the excavated remains provide another. By combining the evidence of the two sources we arrive at a version of Italian and European history that takes into account both the physical remains and the way the monks wished their contemporaries to see them.

A centre for a millennium

Up to the fourth century BC San Vincenzo lay in a remote mountain zone with poor connections with the plains of Campania. As the Greek and Roman civilizations stimulated social and economic growth the circumstances in Samnium changed: the peoples of this region, the Pentri, were incorporated within a larger Samnite (Iron Age) polity. Later, this Samnite polity was itself incorporated within the much grander aegis of Republican Rome.

The integration of mountain valleys and coastal plains brought social and economic opportunity to these remote parts. The mountain regions produced wool, cheeses, beef and mutton, while the lowlands produced not only wines and olives, but miscellaneous manufactured commodities as well. Trade was mutually advantageous. The place of exchange had to be located at the interface of the two eco-systems. The Rocchetta plain was just such an interface. Here, as at the nineteenth-century fair described by the Hon. Keppel Craven, farmers and traders from the two zones might meet.

The Samnite and Republican *vicus* flourished here. Under Roman control a small town took shape. The investment, despite the absence of epigraphic evidence, was far from negligible. A deep, rock-cut ditch defined its south side, and traces of monumental buildings, a piazza, and minor

Fig. 10.1. Fragment of a large Roman imperial marble vase with Bacchic imagery found in the garden of the guests' palace. (Photo: James Barclay Brown)

structures have been discovered in the excavations. By the age of the Emperor Augustus, the settlement covered as much as 10 hectares. It was a little larger than Saepinum, modern-day Molise's most renowned classical town.

The Roman Empire expanded still further. This necessitated reshaping the management of its lands. Villa owners and tenant farmers were encouraged to specialize in cash cropping for the vast (international) market now at their disposal. New colonies were created to handle the produce, and new forms of land management evolved. In particular, the villa estate superseded the villages and loose-knit communities of earlier times. Unsurprisingly, the effect of these far-reaching changes was soon felt at San Vincenzo. Some of its population, so it seems, was enticed to the new towns of Isernia and Venafro or else to cottages dotted about the upper

202

Volturno valley. Meanwhile, the old *vicus* fell into ruin, although its heritage was sustained to some small degree by the villa that succeeded it. Inscriptions associated with this large farm show that at first its owners were people of substance. Their estate would probably have included a cross-section of land from the mountains to the valley.

But the heyday of the Roman Empire was short-lived. The polity was too huge to be managed efficiently and too poorly integrated to survive indefinitely. As in all economic systems, those on the periphery were destined to suffer first. Upland villas like San Vincenzo could not realistically prosper 30 km from the nearest market. Steadily increasing taxes enervated such places. The result, as we noted in Chapter 3, was the steady attrition of the rural community. As in most parts of Italy, numerous cottages were deserted as Molise had its first experience of large-scale peasant emigration.

The fifth century was an historical watershed. The great traditions of the classical world were waning. Christianity had now become a state religion; holy men executed God's will on earth. Individuals such as St Benedict played a powerful if indirect part in the spiritual life of the state. The land was Christianized, with an inner world dominated by the new culture and an outer world in which natural sprits prevailed. It was also a time when connections between the plains and mountains were briefly reinforced by a revival of commerce in the Mediterranean fostered by enterprising new leadership in Byzantium. Yet we must remember that the bases on which this history rested had altered considerably since Augustan times. Rural populations had declined dramatically. Ancient towns such as Boiano, Isernia, Larino and Venafro – key places in ancient Samnium – were falling into ruin.

The new villa built around AD 400 beside the Ponte della Zingara must have assumed much of the status of its first-century precursor. As many neighbouring places disappeared, it prospered from control of a rich niche. The later story of Contantine's presence at San Vincenzo, recounted by the chronicler, doubtless owes much to tenth-/eleventh-century fascination with the first great Byzantine emperor. Nevertheless, the foundation story was not wholly mythic. The tower as well as the arrangement of space bear the hallmark of an aristocratic élite taking firm control of this place. The aristocrat might even have been the bishop of Samnium. At some stage after 450 a cemetery and accompanying church were constructed here. Up to seventy people, including many families, made up its population at its height. To judge from the numerous small bronze coins (*nummi*) found in the excavations, as well as the great range of glassware and pottery, San Vincenzo continued to sustain its long-held connections with Venafro and various Campanian cities beyond. The material affluence belongs to an Indian summer in the empire, before an irreparable rift in inter-regional relations.

The rupture occured in the early sixth century. Historians debate

Fig. 10.2. Recording a late Roman grave from the fifth-century funerary church. (Photo: author)

whether it was a consequence of the Gothic intervention in Italy, or the abortive Byzantine attempt to reconquer these lands. The reality was that the barbarians sought to define themselves as different and thus opposed to the polyethnic late Roman state. The inevitable outcome on rural society and its economy was as dramatic as Edward Gibbon described. Mountain regions once again became remote; only the coastal plains, connected by the seaways to Constantinople, managed to pursue the rhythm of classical culture, albeit on a reduced scale. If the tower at San Vincenzo had been home to a bishop, as some believe, then the emigration of his community left him without any purpose. Some, of course, stayed on, seeking refuge in what had been the outer world, on hilltops such as Vacchereccia.

For a short time the graveyard at San Vincenzo continued to be used intermittently. The tower forming the centre of the villa was also used as a burial ground. Perhaps it was a mausoleum of sorts, commemorating a remarkable past. The dead were sparsely furnished with ornaments such as openwork silver ear-rings and the gilded fibulae then in fashion in the Byzantine south. These were prestige goods, acquired through primitive exchange networks like those of prehistory.

Late in the sixth century the Lombards under Duke Zotto conquered a vacuum. Recent excavations in the towns surrounding San Vincenzo – places such as Larino, Saepinum and Venafro – reveal that these were now largely deserted. Burials took place in the theatre at Larino and the forum area of Seapinum. But some trappings of late antiquity outlived the two centuries of oblivion. The indomitable spirit of the Benedictines was, if anything, reinforced by the tide of change; they were the new opportunists. All over western Europe, enterprising lords were astute enough to forge mutually advantageous accords with these holy men. Gisulf, Duke of Benevento at the end of the seventh century, like his Lombard counterparts further north, recognized the need for partnership with the Church. He granted Paldo, Tato and Taso a largely deserted block of land on the northern frontier of his duchy. San Vincenzo was a buffer between the potentially hostile Spoletan Lombards to the north and the heartlands of Beneventan Lombardy. On its east flank lay the main Apennine road, the Via Numicia, which ran like a thread down the centre of the peninsula linking the Lombard territories. Situated on San Vincenzo's west flank, Monte Cassino was soon to become another buffer, separating the Beneventans from the duchy of Rome.

San Vincenzo's founders, for their part, took possession of a derelict Roman villa and lands which, as we saw in Chapter 9, were sparsely populated. This was a retreat fully consistent with the prevailing isolationist doctrine of the Benedictines. But the emphasis of the doctrine shifted in the mid-eighth century. Far from the birthplace of Benedictine rule at Monte Cassino, Anglo-Saxon monks such as Boniface and Willibrord advocated a new missionary zeal. The outcome was a revised code compiled by their spiritual successor, Bishop Chrodegang of Metz. This code eschewed the spirit of isolationism in favour of an active propagation of the Church's place in society. The Frankish kings Charles Martel and Pepin the Short, with their ambitious territorial plans, appreciated the political advantage of involving a reforming Church in their plans for territorial expansion. South of the Alps, the Lombard kings, Aistulf (749-56) and Desiderius (757-74) were engaged in a parallel policy. In the patchwork quilt of Italian duchies and kingdoms, peer-polity interaction was a powerful feature. Lombard culture, which owed much to the cross-fertilisation between Byzantine and Germanic traditions, was in the ascendent. Both kings, engaged in an ambitious search for alliances in their bid to unify the peninsula under their dominance, proved a menace to the papacy and thereby earned the enmity of the Franks. As it happens, both kings visited San Vincenzo.

San Vincenzo's abbots cannot have been ignorant of the importance of these royal visits. By the 780s, as Duke Arichis II built Santa Sophia, a cathedral of Byzantine proportions in his capital at Benevento, the close connection between ideology, resources and political control must have been apparent to many of the community at San Vincenzo. The construction of a modest ambulatory beyond the apse of San Vincenzo Minore, where its relics might be viewed, was intended to cultivate pilgrims and visitors. Despite its short history, San Vincenzo was seeking to promote its own image as an up-and-coming ecclesiastical centre. A critical factor was that its ranks included the celebrated philosopher Ambrosius Autpert, who, we are told, was a Frank by connection if not by birth.

Investment follows credibility. In the eighth century investment took the form of gifts of land and valuables. Such gifts were used to garner a status that might lead to further steady growth. The partnership was particularly effective in the later Merovingian kingdoms. In promoting monasteries, the Franks engineered the meshing of public and secular values at centres of civilization. Their policy simply advanced the speed of investment made by Lombard dukes and kings. When Charlemagne invaded Italy, ostensibly to proffer support to the papacy as well as to challenge the Lombard hegemony, San Vincenzo, like many monasteries, was compelled to examine its allegiances. Few would have mistaken the Frankish king's intention to emulate the Lombard kings in attempting to conquer the peninsula. By 787, when Charlemagne's army made a swift foray into the duchy of Benevento, the monastery pledged itself to the Carolingians.

The Carolingian connection

The Carolingian renaissance was consciously cultivated by Charlemagne and his court. Charlemagne's personality, however much we attempt to deconstruct the power of the individual in history, is central to the extra-

Fig. 10.3. Recording the tile floor in the ninth-century assembly room. (Photo: author)

ordinary ambitions of later eighth- and early ninth-century Europe. In the opinion of Walter Ullmann, 'we are confronted by a conscious effort to shape the character of a particular society in consonance with the axioms of a particular doctrine, with Christian norms'. On the one hand Charlemagne learned from Christian writers such as Ambrose, Augustine and Tertullian how a Christian king should govern, and what a Christian society should be like. He readily appreciated what a cohesive force the Church could be in his new Holy Roman Empire. The Church, in short, became a crucial instrument of power in the Carolingian Empire.

From *c.* 771 until his death in 814, Charlemagne created an empire that was not exceeded in scale until Napoleon's brief imperial reign. But unlike the Emperor Augustus or, indeed, Napoleon, Charlemagne managed his polity from his palaces with the help of only a handful of administrators and a warband raised each spring. The immediate successes of the warband are succinctly listed in the Frankish Annals. More enduring, however, was the administration that followed the conquest and inculcated the spirit of a common future. In many respects this was achieved by a monastic conquest promoting a focused ideology. The Church reinforced Charlemagne's authority, the writings of Christianity being suffused with allusions to empire, to the glory that was Rome, and to the Old Testament. Charlemagne was portrayed as the new Constantine or the new David. His people were the *populus Dei*, the people of God. After this, as the Council of Frankfurt of 794 illustrates, followed the instruments of economic policy.

Charlemagne therefore nurtured the Benedictine reform started by Boniface, the missionary, and Bishop Chrodegang of Metz. Benedictinism, the Carolingians evidently concluded, was more benign and effective than the austere, almost irrationally severe rule of St Colambanus, the seventh-century Irish missionary. Benedict of Aniane (750 – c. 821), with Carolingian support, fashioned Benedict of Nursia's rule to be consistent with the changing social values of Charlemagne's world. The Frankish royal family poured investment into its monasteries as if they were part of the defence of the realm. Charlemagne even founded a monastery at Jerusalem. As Carolingian law codes became more exacting, so immunities were granted to monasteries. As the concept of property ownership, in the form of charters, gained increasing currency, so Charlemagne encouraged the donation of estates to the Church. As lay lords vied for position in government, so Charlemagne raised his abbots and bishops to political prominence.

Charlemagne invested in public works and simultaneously encouraged investment on two other fronts – trade and technology. Long-distance trade expanded rapidly at the end of the eighth century: Carolingian merchants and their agents ventured to Denmark, for example, in search of Baltic and, somewhat improbably, oriental goods brought northwards via western Russia, including silver, spices and perhaps dyes. These were used to good effect within the ranked exchange networks of Christian Europe. Such gifts served as means of consolidating power. At the same time, the concept of commodities began to change. The Carolingian court revolutionized social learning and the process of cultural transmission in Latin Christendom. Agrarian surplus was actively encouraged. Equally, treatises were prepared to propagate technological development. All the archaeological evidence shows that classical technology was reintroduced on an increased scale throughout the empire. Agricultural technology was improved; the reintroduction of ancient building technologies facilitated the advent of a new architecture; and Roman metal, glass, pottery and soapstone technologies were revived. The impact of trade and technology was at first regionalized. The Rhineland, then the Seine and Po valleys, began to change. The investment was far from uniform throughout the empire. Some Italian territories, such as Tuscany, had to wait more than a century to share in the revolution.

Not surprisingly, the monks at San Vincenzo were bitterly divided in their attitude to Charlemagne. Some were loyal to the Beneventans, now threatened by the Franks; some favoured the promise of Carolingian patronage. Pope Hadrian I, at Charlemagne's instigation, intervened in this dispute, summoning Abbot Poto to Rome. We should not lose sight of the complicated politics of the age. The Pope needed Carolingian support to confront Lombard aggression. Charlemagne looked to Hadrian to support his vaunting ambition. Abbot Poto was a Lombard who could vouch for the steady support of the Beneventans. Moreover, the Benevantans under Duke Arichis had prospered from a modest expansion of their fortunes. The new ducal palace at Salerno, the new cathedral of Santa Sophia, and, indeed, the revival of urban life in Benevento itself were tangible images of economic revival on the fringe of the Byzantine world. Neither Charlemagne nor Abbot Poto could have ignored Arichis' growing authority in Italian affairs. Accordingly, Abbot Poto resisted Pope Hadrian's pressure, and left Rome determined to keep the monastery firmly within the Beneventan political orbit. But Poto died on the short journey. Was he the victim of his successor, Abbot Paul, a Frank? Four years later Charlemagne granted the monastery many privileges, enabling it to accumulate large tracts of territory. It was a well-tried formula.

To these years we must surely ascribe the addition of the fine annular crypt to San Vincenzo Minore, and the construction of a refectory fit to accommodate more than a hundred monks. The scale of these alterations should not be exaggerated. Yet they reveal Abbot Paul's commitment to transform San Vincenzo. The chronicler, Paul the Deacon, then at Monte Cassino, described San Vincenzo as a large community, mindful of its growing importance. But this was a mere prelude to the great monastery of the early ninth century.

Interestingly, the twelfth-century chronicle records munificent Beneventan gifts to San Vincenzo from the very beginning of the ninth century. With its royal privileges, it attracted numerous donations from the Beneventan aristocracy. It also acquired the means – the labour and materials – to make the transformation to a monastic city modelled upon later Merovingian and Carolingian centres north of the Alps.

The size and complexity of the new monastic city should not distract us from the powerful concept inherent in its design. The architect created a conspicuous sense of hierarchy and logic in his plan. The new abbey church, raised up like a temple on a podium, was at the nexus of this plan. Pilgrims and travellers venturing southwards to the great shrine of Monte Sant' Angelo on the Gargano peninsula and its counterpart at Olevano sul Tusciano, near Salerno, as well as Byzantine ports in the heel of Italy, could not fail to be impressed by the gigantic venture. The overarching logic was to control all encounters with the public. As in all parts of the new monastery, a succession of spaces led from one to another within San Vincenzo Maggiore. Confronting the basilica itself, the traveller was directly addressed by a large bronze inscription of the façade, and informed that Abbot Joshua was responsible for its construction. There was an unmistakable cult of the individual. The inscription, clearly imitating monumental imperial inscriptions, effectively cast Joshua in the role of emperor. It is no surprise, then, to find a portrait of Joshua (and his successor, Talaricus), placed directly in front of the relics of St Vincent in the great annular crypt of the church. In the new hierarchy, the abbot took

Fig. 10.4. Excavating in the north aisle of San Vincenzo Maggiore. (Photo: Sarah Cocke)

on a semi-divine status, or at very least the part of a hero in the later Roman sense, extolled by the grandeur of his surroundings. A subsidiary nexus in this plan was reserved for receiving distinguished guests. Long corridors connected these two axial points in the monastery. The reception rooms for distinguished guests served to transform wealthier visitors into clients. As in late antiquity, clients were induced to make lavish donations to the monastery. The logic of the new plan was a series of interconnecting modules, each with buildings arranged in a hierarchy defined by building materials, the use of *spolia* and decoration.

The symbols of a new age were apparent everywhere. New instruments, along with images of the past, were fused to new rules of social engagement. The archaeology tantalisingly reveals only what survived demolition and decay, notably the ubiquitous use of spoils from ancient sites, and literacy on display. The presence of craftsmen engaged in endorsing the spirit of revival is equally apparent. Architects, builders, tile-makers, mosaicists, painters, glaziers, glass-workers and smiths shared the same sense of purpose. We may imagine that an army of scribes, leather-makers, coopers and other craftsmen also contributed to the creation of the new environment. Added to this, it seems likely that the sounds and rhythm of the monastery would have been attuned to a Carolingian ethos. Beneventan chant was replaced by the ubiquitous gregorian chant. And time itself was more rigorously measured, as the evidence of bell-making in the ninth-century levels indicates.

The instruments of this great enterprise all existed in Italy. Indeed, to some degree the Lombards had already incorporated ancient imagery in their arts. The Carolingians simply fused all these commonly held ideas together and, with the support of the papacy, forged a European policy of revival.

But unlike the great monastic domaines of France and Germany, San Vincenzo could not draw upon the resources of its estate in the upper Volturno valley to support this new project. Here the archaeology sheds light on a long-standing historical debate between those who ascribe a prevalent mode of self-sufficiency to this age, and those who interpret monasteries as the motors of regional economic transformation. In Chapter 9 we showed that San Vincenzo's *terra* was poorly developed at this time. The peasantry practised a domestic mode of production, occupying ecological niches in an outer world first colonised in the aftermath of the collapse of the Roman state in these parts. Not until the mid- to later ninth century, with the foundation of small chapels in the *terra*, did the monastery interest itself in its immediate context. Meanwhile, in the coastal plains of Campania and Molise, new fortified villages were being created on the monastery's property, which produced surpluses that were consumed either directly or indirectly by the monastery. The contrast in strategies permits us to use San Vincenzo as a metaphor of change in ninth-century Italy. Clearly, its transformation, so brilliantly achieved by Joshua, owed much to the modest but significant revival of inter-regional connections.

Its craftsmen, labour and servants, like its treasure (later taken by the Saracens) were acquired as gifts. The critical questions are why such gifts should have been made, and by whom? Buried in the chronicler's text are some immediate answers to these questions. The majority of gifts were made by members of the minor aristocracy of Benevento. Lands, and the labour attached to them, from the heartlands of the principate were donated to San Vincenzo. Here is an interesting paradox: Abbot Joshua, a Frank, created a major monastery espousing the concepts of the Carolingian reform movement in Beneventan territory.

The reasons for such an investment lie in the larger political context. For a time in the 780s the Duchy of Benevento looked set to become part of the Frankish polity. But by the 790s its dukes, now kings, bridled at this Carolingian hegemony and only intermittently, so it is said, paid their tributes. Charlemagne grudgingly accepted this. The principate benefited from its location between Frankish territory and Byzantine southern Italy. It was also a gateway to the Mediterranean. Close to one of the principality's northern gates stood San Vincenzo. The archaeology of Joshua's monastic city reflects not only the richness of Lombardic culture induced by the peer-polity interaction of the preceding century, but also powerful

211

Fig. 10.5. Gold solidus of Prince Sicardus (833-9) found on Colle della Torre in the 1950s (now lost).

references to ancient and early medieval Rome. Notably, old St Peter's clearly served as a model for many elements of San Vincenzo Maggiore. Its decorations, though, belong to a Lombard idiom. The glassmaker, limited evidence suggests, belonged to a tradition practised at this time in the Veneto. As for the pottery, much of this belongs to a Beneventan tradition, although one type with a collar-like rim is strikingly similar to pots made in the Paris basin at this time. The scripts on the gravestones, tiles and graffiti are, for the most part, Beneventan. In sum, while San Vincenzo had become a powerful expression of the Carolingian Renaissance – a pan-European revolution, any visitor would have regarded it as Beneventan.

It is not hard to follow Charlemagne's reasoning. Having made himself Holy Roman Emperor in 800, he was sensitive to Byzantine hostility. A Byzantine revival was in progress by the the early ninth century. The Emperor Nicephorus I was retaking lands lost to the Slavs in western Greece and the Balkans. The Adriatic, in effect, was once again under

Byzantine control. The geopolitical configurations would not have been overlooked by the Carolingians. The new centres of San Vincenzo and Monte Cassino were possibly designed to retain the Beneventans within Latin Christendom to prevent them seceding to the Greek Church. In this capacity they served as a valuable buffer state. But more was at stake.

Professors Armando Citarella and H.M. Willard have recently drawn attention to Beneventan commercial links with the Aghlabid Arabs of North Africa soon after *c*. 800. The Aghlabids were concurrently revitalizing the Maghreb, having conquered a region in abject decline in the later seventh century. With the Aghlabid revival the city of Kairouan was founded, with its monumental architecture, and the port of Sousse served as an emporium, sharing in the Abbasid expansion of Arab commercial power. For these traders it was only a short crossing to the Principate of Benevento. The Arabs brought prestige goods to Gaeta, Naples and Salerno. Paolo Delogu, commenting upon this unlikely trade, noted that 'the coastal cities of Campania, exposed to serious consequences for their economies as well as for their very survival, if they lost their commercial contacts with Sicily and Africa, were amenable to letting themselves be Islamicized rather than oppose the Saracens, and they accepted within their walls, Muslim merchants and armed bands'. Several chroniclers register the presence of silver, gold, spices and oriental treasures. Such objects almost never occur in excavations either in North Africa or, for that matter, at San Vincenzo. Excavations at San Vincenzo have produced a few sherds of Arabic polychrome bowls, and a few exotic items such as the jade sword-chape (see p. 136). African gold may also have been brought across by the Aghlabids. Cereals, and doubtless slaves, were exported from Italy. At the same time Arab traders, paradoxically, took growing numbers of Christian pilgrims to the Holy Land. The strains of these relations are revealed in a letter of November 813 from Pope Leo III to Charlemagne, in which an accord between Gregory, the imperial governor of Sicily, and Arab envoys is discussed in the light of similar accords over the previous 85 years which, apparently, had been violated. Other accords with Byzantine and Italian merchants – known collectively to the Arabs as Rum – were registered at Kairouan between 812-17. A ninth-century document from Kairouan amplifies these bilateral arrangements: 'Concerning the ships of Christians captured both in proximity to our ports or on high sea, one must distinguish between two different cases. If they are merchantmen known to trade with the Moslems their capture is not legal, except if it takes place within the waters of their country and they are sailing toward non-Islamic ports. In the second case, if they are not ships publicly recognized to specialize in the commerce with Moslems, then their capture is legal.' By these means, Monte Cassino's treasury must have amassed the array of oriental exotica which attracted ninth-century admiration. We may surmise that San Vincenzo's treasury, later plundered by the Arabs, contained comparable riches.

Charlemagne, a master of politics, must have appreciated the significance of this commerce. Equally, having founded a monastery in Jerusalem, he must have been familiar with the part played by Arab merchantmen in carrying pilgrims to the Holy Land. Close to home, Frisian traders at this time sailed to pagan Denmark from Carolingian ports, and were the middlemen in acquiring similar types of precious goods that reached the Baltic Sea by the long riverine route through western Russia. Being a zealot in the Christian cause, however, Charlemagne did not care to deal directly with the heathen. A better solution was to contrive the growth in commerce. Pagan Denmark, therefore, was supplied with Carolingian manufactured goods, including swords, tablewares and jewellery as well as sweet Rhenish wine. South of the Alps, Venice had a similar relationship with the Carolingians. After 812 it enjoyed a sort of suzerainty, but was able to determine its own mercantile policy. After *c.* 820 it even minted Carolingian deniers, conforming to the weight-standards of Louis the Pious' monetary reforms, even though it was technically a separate state. Christian Beneventum, on the other hand, posed a challenge. It was too far away to control readily. This much had become evident since the later eighth century. The solution was more appropriate to the world of the Mezzogiorno: its aristocracy might be manipulated by the force of the new ideology focussed upon the reforming monasteries. The monasteries could not only acquire oriental treasure as gifts from Beneventan aristocrats directly engaged in the commerce, but more significantly they could ensure the regular payment of such goods demanded as tribute by the Carolingians. Little, of course, is said of this, any more than the motives for dealing with the Danes or the Venetians have been made clear by the contemporary historians of the Carolingian court. A coin hoard found in the bed of the river Reno, near Bologna, over a century ago offers a modest illustration of Charlemagne's motives. The hoard, buried perhaps by a luckless merchant, contained over a hundred gold coins, of which 39 were examined, and found to be 23 Byzantine solidi, 5 Beneventan solidi and 11 Abbasid dinars. How much more gold was being carted northwards, indirectly bringing wealth not only to San Vincenzo and Monte Cassino but also to Rome, now spectacularly revived after nearly two centuries of dereliction? It is unlikely that this will ever be known.

The intersection of such patronage undoubtedly contributed to San Vincenzo's astronomic growth. Its international status was founded on its geography. Whereas previously it had been isolated, now its location on a major trans-European highway was essential to the political harmony and economic evolution of Italy. Federico Marazzi has shown that its economic policy followed this logic. Whereas its properties in the eighth century lay mostly in the uplands, close to the Via Numicia, those acquired in the ninth century took an altogether different form. In competition with Monte Cassino, San Vincenzo sought estates on the coastal littoral, including many around river estuaries and lagoons. These were the site of landing-places, small-scale periodic fairs where marine commodities as well as manufactured goods might be exchanged for upland produce. The abbey of Farfa engaged in the same territorial strategy in the neighbouring Dukedom of Spoleto, and northern Lombard monasteries such as Santa Giulia at Brescia were active in exploiting the revitalized riverine commerce passing along the Po.

In an important essay devoted to fairs and markets, Aldo Settia has convincingly illustrated that northern Italy was not a closed economy by the later eighth century. He shows that whereas only two rural markets are described in eighth-century documents, nineteen are mentioned in the ninth century, and tenth-century sources record fifty-eight. Monasteries established the two mid-eighth-century markets, whereas as the economy grew monasteries were only responsible for half the nineteen documented ninth-century markets. Sketchy though the sources are, it is evident that commercial activity was being promoted by certain monasteries. We can only speculate whether San Vincenzo, like the abbey of Novalesa, had its own *homines monasterii* – merchants – who were actively working *pro eius utilitate negociandum*.

The ranked spheres of exchange should not be exaggerated. Markets articulated by the circulation of Carolingian coins did not exist. Indeed, the numismatic evidence suggests the contrary: there was only limited recourse to monetarism. The incipient markets of Austrasia and Neustria were probably models for the underdeveloped territories of Italy. Only by the later ninth century had the Italian regions begun to catch up. Critical investment was needed in communications. The huge effort involved in transporting cartloads of heavy *spolia* over poor roads to San Vincenzo may well have required imperial intervention. As for the revival of Italy's towns, recent archaeological evidence indicates an age of investment, but ranked according to the political significance of the centre in question. Much of Naples, for example, remained unoccupied well into the tenth century; it was hardly a thriving emporium of North Sea proportions. The ninth-century rubbish deposits found in the excavations of the Cripta Balbi, Rome, reveal the plundering of the ancient levels for marbles, as great emphasis was placed upon renovating Rome's churches. Certainly, the city was coming to life once again. On the other hand, Andrea Staffa's brilliant reconstruction of the archaeology of Pescara, ancient *Aternum*, an Adriatic port placed on the frontier separating Spoleto and Benevento, reveals a low level of inter-regional trade by comparison with, say, the sixth or seventh centuries.

Directly or indirectly under Carolingian hegemony, the old polities of eighth-century Italy were being harnessed towards more effective interaction connecting central Europe to the Mediterranean. It was a mirror-image of Carolingian relations with its other marches in the south Baltic and Bohemia. The catalyst of change – as the huge investment in

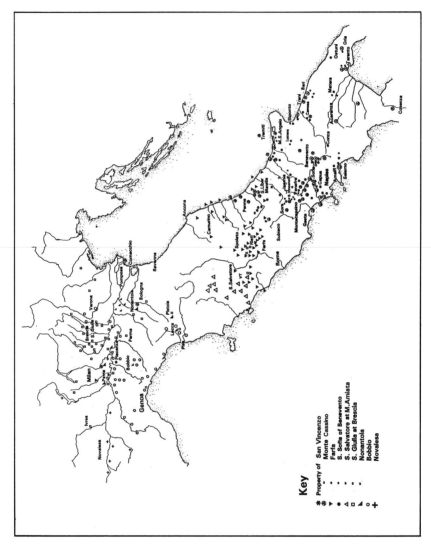

Key

Property of
San Vincenzo
Monte Cassino
Farfa
S. Sofia of Benevento
S. Salvatore at M.Amiata
S. Giulia at Brescia
Nonantola
Bobbio
Novalesa

Fig. 10.6. The distribution of monastic estates in ninth-century Italy.

the refurbishment of churches in Rome in the later eighth century illustrates – was a commonly held ideology.

Like Rome, San Vincenzo's status rested upon the unswerving support of its patrons. After Charlemagne's death, bit by bit royal power was reduced, as Walter Ullmann put it, to 'stunted sovereignty'. By 830 Frankish churchmen had turned Louis the Pious into their puppet, although their moment of power was short-lived. The grandsons of Charlemagne partitioned his empire after a civil war. The fall-out affected Benevento where a by-product of the civil war was the looting of Monte Cassino's treasury in 842. Commerce with the Baltic faltered and unleashed the Vikings, who now obtained primitive valuables by raiding. Similarly, we may suspect, trade with North Africa faltered in the 820s, giving rise to a century of Arab piracy. The Carolingian Empire, in short, was little more than the remarkable concept of one man who held it together. His vision revived dormant technologies and injected medieval Europe with a social and economic vitality that had been sorely lacking. But his vision did not long survive his death.

San Vincenzo was an inevitable victim of Carolingian collapse. Abbot Epyphanius, nonetheless, was able to complete Joshua's vaunting vision. By the 830s San Vincenzo's dependence upon its Beneventan context had become increasingly important as the Carolingian connection faltered. It became imperative to persuade the monastery's benefactors to sustain their largesse. One family, as the brilliant cycle of paintings in the crypt shows, certainly did. Others doubtless were seduced by the monumental new eastwork of San Vincenzo Maggiore. It is perhaps appropriate that Epyphanius, of all San Vincenzo's abbots, should be best known to us. Unlike Joshua, whose project belonged to the zenith of European expansion, Epyphanius experienced the destabilising downswing. By 842, when he died, the original reason for the monastic city had become suspect.

The rhythms of change

San Vincenzo was a product of an extraordinary moment of history. Like Roman campaign fortresses, it was borne of a particular time and space. The monastery was in decline well before the Arab attack in 881. The flow of gifts had long since diminished, although the monastery's workshops were active on the eve of 10 October 881. After Epyphanius the excavations offer no evidence of new building or paintings. San Vincenzo survived on its earlier reputation, profiting from its old investments. The events of 881 abruptly changed all this.

The archaeology confirms the chronicler's sad description of his tenth-century forebears. Like many monasteries throughout western Europe, it found new patronage hard to acquire. New states were building upon Charlemagne' achievement, but without recourse to ecclesiastical support. As new polities took shape in Italy (not least with the expansion of

Fig. 10.7. A Danish cartoonist's impression of the monks' refectory.

Byzantine control in southern Italy), so once again were the mountains connected to the plains, and Byzantium and the Arab emirates began to search out commercial opportunities in Italy.

These factors all stimulated investment in rural development, as Charlemagne had encouraged it in the Rhineland, Hesse and Lombardy where new feudal manors had been created. The process of *incastellamento* in the later tenth century was a conscious extension of the Carolingian concept. Farfa and Monte Cassino set the pace of village founding in central Italy. San Vincenzo energetically emulated them, systematically managing the spatial arrangement of its landscapes with a logic as striking as that invested in the ninth-century monastery. Each monastery must have thought that the marketing of surplus goods taken as rents could finance fresh monastic rebuilding. Farfa encouraged a market at its gates; Monte Cassino fostered the new town of San Germano on the Via Casalina; San Vincenzo sent its surplus to Capua, where the new monastery had taken shape in the aftermath of 881.

Notwithstanding its investment in Capua, in common with Monte Cassino and Farfa, San Vincenzo restored its ruinous buildings in the eleventh century. Refurbishing San Vincenzo Maggiore, we should remind ourselves, was no mean achievement. The great Romanesque abbey, richly decorated by an artist as talented as any known at Monte Cassino, enabled the monastery to recapture some of its earlier status. Its revival was tempered by the presence of a new menace. In the eighth century monasteries were sacrosanct; but the rise of secular power had bred secular

218

Fig. 10.8. The tombstone of a monk, Ermecausus. (Photo: John Mitchell)

competitors. First the Borelli, minor counts from the Sangro valley, sacked the monastery in 1042; then the Normans threatened its southern villages. The archaeology plainly bears witness to this. The powerful defences at *Olivella*, and the shift to Vaccereccia's hilltop show the increasing level of insecurity. Worse was to follow: the frontier running along the crest of the Mainarde was moved. The bounds of the Norman kingdom were fixed to the north of Rieti, nearly 200 km to the north.

When John began his chronicle in the early twelfth century, in the age of the Crusades, San Vincenzo's lands had been reduced to a rump around the abbey. The abbey itself was rebuilt yet again, this time as a powerful fortress. Here, memorials and oblivion went hand in hand as a new history was shaped. John's exquisitely illuminated elegy for an epic past was a

219

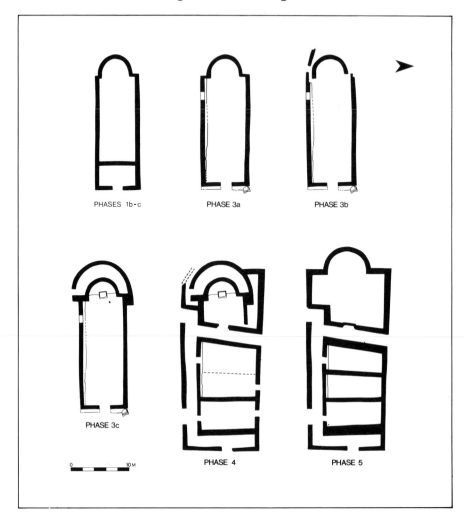

PHASES 1b-c

PHASE 3a

PHASE 3b

PHASE 3c

0   10 M

PHASE 4

PHASE 5

Fig. 10.9. Rhythms of change: the south church between the fifth and ninth centuries: phase 1 (fifth/sixth centuries); phase 3 (San Vincenzo Minore) (eighth century); phases 4 and 5 (ninth century).

particular gesture. The binary opposite of this great work was the systematic obliteration of almost every trace of the old monastery. Old tombstones and even the bronze inscription that graced the façade of San Vincenzo Maggiore were rudely treated as no more than ornamental motifs. The chronicle, however, was designed to be placed before another audience – a literate one. Here, Joshua's achievement was enlarged by the association with the Carolingian court. The formula was familiar to monkish authors throughout Christendom. As Europe really took shape with a significant shift from rural to urban power, the Church sought to stake out its importance by reference to its history of personalities and properties. In San Vincenzo's case the formula failed.

San Vincenzo passed into obscurity soon after John compiled his book. Yet the abbey continued to occupy a spot well-suited to limited inter-regional marketing and skilful farming. Its presence must have deterred the building of any other substantial centre on the Rocchetta plain. San Vincenzo's history since John wrote his chronicle has created a self-made remoteness; it has become trapped in a first millennium time warp. Only the sheep fair, visited by Keppel Craven, shows how suitable this place is for more ambitious inter-regional activities.

*

San Vincenzo is an archaeological site of special importance. The palimpsest of remains embodies a long history spanning almost all of the first millennium AD. Much of this history tells of a succession of classical

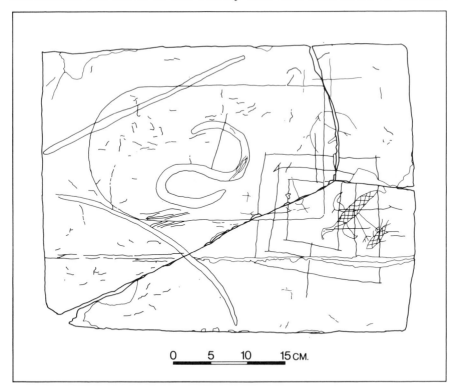

Fig. 10.10. Tile inscribed with game-boards and other graffiti, from the north-east corner of the east portico of the garden.

settlements, located on the fringe of the mountains, typical of many parts of the Mediterranean. The monastic history is more complicated. It reflects the episodic if inexorable rise of a community in the aftermath of the collapse of the Roman state. The archaeology of this valley 200 km from Rome leaves us in no doubt of the cataclysmic impact of the Roman collapse, yet illustrates how, at a later date, far-flung personalized connections enabled San Vincenzo to become an international centre.

San Vincenzo was briefly a powerful exponent of Carolingian ideology. Its archaeology attests to this aberration in its history. But lying, as it did, at the farthest point of the Carolingian Empire, almost 2,000 km from Aachen, its patronage was bound to dissolve as swiftly as it had appeared. Like the great Roman fortresses fossilized in the pre-Sahara, this Carolingian renaissance monument was left stranded by the rhythm of relations between the core and its peripheries – between a court and its far-flung marches. This bred aspirations which no ordinary Beneventan monastery could have expected. San Vincenzo's glorious history was to some extent its undoing. The chronicler made much of it. Perhaps the discovery of a unique expression of a brief but important moment of European history will make San Vincenzo famous once more. If so our project will have achieved another of its aims. Perhaps, too, these remains will serve to convey some notion of the changing fortunes of history, reminding us of the importance of the Mezzogiorno and the people of the 'other Italy' in the making of the first millennium.

Further Reading

This book has drawn upon the numerous scientific studies of the archaeology, art history and history of San Vincenzo. A vast bibliography now exists for the site and its history. In this section I list mainly those studies in English.

Richard Hodges, *San Vincenzo al Volturno 1. The excavations 1980-1986, part I* (British School at Rome, London, 1993), and *San Vincenzo al Volturno 2. The excavations 1980-1986, part II* (British School at Rome, London, 1995); and Richard Hodges and John Mitchell, *The Basilica of Abbot Joshua at San Vincenzo al Volturno* (Miscellenea Vulturnense 2, Monte Cassino, 1996).

Interested readers should also see the reports on the studies of Vaccureccia (*Papers of the British School at Rome* 52 (1984), 148-94), the bridge-chapel at the Ponte Latrone (*Papers of the British School at Rome* 58 (1990), 273-97, and the local vernacular architecture (*Papers of the British School at Rome* 62 (1994), 311-21).

Chris Wickham's study of the history of the *terra* has appeared in three versions. The English version can be found in Richard Hodges and John Mitchell (eds.), *San Vincenzo al Volturno: the archaeology, art and territory of an early medieval monastery* (British Archaeological Reports International Series 252 (1985), [hereafter Hodges & Mitchell], 227-58.

John Patterson's studies of the classical history can also be found in Hodges & Mitchell, 185-200; 213-26.

John Mitchell's many studies of the art history include a seminal essay on the painting in Hodges & Mitchell, 125-76; essays on the inscriptions and issues of literacy, for example 'Literacy displayed: the use of inscriptions at the monastery of San Vincenzo al Volturno in the early ninth century', in R. McKitterick (ed.), *The Uses of Literacy in Early Medieval Europe* (Cambridge University Press, Cambridge, 1990), 186-225; and 'The display of script and the use of painting in Longobard Italy', in *Testo e immagine nell'alto medioevo* (*Settimane di Studio del centro italiano di studi sull'alto medioevo* 41), 887-954; an essay on the metalwork: 'Fashion in metal: a set of sword-belt mounts and bridle furniture from San Vincenzo al Volturno', in D. Buckton and T.A. Heslop (eds.), *Studies in Medieval Art and Architecture presented to Peter Lasko* (Alan Sutton/Trustees of the British Museum, Far Thrupp, 1994), 127-56; and an essay on the use of ivory in the monastery: 'A carved ivory head from San Vincenzo al Volturno', *Journal of the British Archaeological Association* 45 (1992), 66-76.

On the glass see Judith Stevenson, 'Glass lamps from San Vincenzo al Volturno, Molise', *Papers of the British School at Rome* 56 (1988), 198-209.

On the pottery see Richard Hodges and Helen Patterson, 'San Vincenzo al Volturno and the origins of the medieval pottery industry in Italy', in *La Ceramica medievale nel mediterraneo occidentale* (Insegna del Giglio, Florence, 1986), 13-26.

Readers are also advised to see Federico Marazzi's essay on the history of San Vincenzo's estates in F. Marazzi (ed.) *San Vincenzo al Volturno: Cultura, istituzioni, economia* (Miscellenea Vulturnense 3, Monte Cassino, 1996), where essays by Paolo Delogu on the history of studies of San Vincenzo, by Antonio Sennis on lordship in the region, and by Flavia de Rubeis on the scriptorium, can also be found.

Note should also be taken of Angelo Pantoni, *Le chiese e gli edifici del monastero di San Vincenzo al Volturno* (Miscellenea Cassinese, 40, Monte Cassino, 1980).

The following provide a basic introduction to the wider Italian and European context of San Vincenzo al Volturno: Chris Wickham, *Early Medieval Italy* (Macmillan, London, 1981); Carlo Bertelli (ed.), *La pittura in Italia: l'altomedioevo* (Electa, Milan, 1994); Walter Horn and Ernest Born, *The Plan of St. Gall: a study of the architecture and economy of, and life in, a paradigmatic monastery* (University of California Press, Berkeley, 1979); Carol Heitz, *L'architecture religieuse carolingienne: les formes et leurs fonctions* (Picard, Paris, 1980); and Richard Hodges and David Whitehouse, *Mohammed, Charlemagne and the Origins of Europe* (Duckworth, London and Cornell, Ithaca N.Y., 1983).

Index

194, 198, 212; (tile and brick-
making) 94-6, 100-1, 169, 174,
175, 210; (consoles) 141
timber buildings, 63, 116, 135, 167,
173, 176, 191, 193, 197
tombstones, 54, 151, 158, 174, 212,
220; (of Tamfrid) 158-9; (of
Teudelas) 158, 160
Torcello, 98
Toto (Abbot), 33
tourism, 2, 7, 15, 22
towns and urbanism, 9, 62-3, 209,
215, 221
trade, 7-8, 10-11, 59, 62-3, 139, 176,
181, 199, 201-5, 208-9, 213, 214-
15, 218, 221
transhumance, 49, 179
Trigno valley, 26
Tripoli (Syria), 35
Tuscany, 21, 199, 208
Tyrrhenian, 1

Uffizi, Florence, 22
Ullmann, Walter, 207, 217

Vacchereccia (*Baccaricia*), 161, 189,
193-7, 198, 199, 205, 219
Valencia (Spain), 93

van Heemskerck, Martin, 121-2
Vatican, 23, 34
vaults, vaulting, 4, 121, 122, 127, 139,
140, 154, 185
Venafro, 1, 35, 39, 47, 61, 146, 176,
177, 181, 182, 188, 202, 203, 205
Veneto, 212
Venice, 10, 214
Via Casilina, 40, 218
Via Numicia, 25, 27, 33, 81, 174, 182,
205, 214
Vikings, 37, 144, 145, 217
Volturno, river, 1, 2, 3, 19, 35, 45, 49,
64, 74, 101, 121, 161, 173, 184,
185, 188; (valley) 16, 37, 146, 161,
176, 177, 179, 181, 182, 184, 186,
191, 194, 198, 199, 200, 202-3,
211, 222

Waitz, G., 23
Walcharius of Sens, 79
Wessex, 10
Wheeler, Sir Mortimer, 16
Whithorn (Scotland), 11, 63-4
Willard, H.M., 170, 213
Willibrord, 205
Winchester, 98